The GOSPEL *in* BLACK & WHITE

Theological Resources for Racial Reconciliation

Edited by
Dennis L. Okholm

InterVarsity Press
Downers Grove, Illinois

InterVarsity Press
P. O. Box 1400, Downers Grove, IL 60515
World Wide Web: www.ivpress.com
E-mail: mail@ivpress.com

InterVarsity Press® is the book-publishing division of InterVarsity Christian Fellowship/USA®, a student movement active on campus at hundreds of universities, colleges and schools of nursing in the United States of America, and a member movement of the International Fellowship of Evangelical Students. For information about local and regional activities, write Public Relations Dept., InterVarsity Christian Fellowship/USA, 6400 Schroeder Rd., P.O. Box 7895, Madison, WI 53707-7895.

ISBN 0-8308-1887-1

Printed in the United States of America ♾

Library of Congress Cataloging-in-Publication Data

The Gospel in Black and White : theological resources for racial
  reconciliation / ed., Dennis Okholm.
    p. cm.
   Includes bibliographical references (p.   ).
   ISBN 0-8308-1887-1 (alk. paper)
   1. Race relations—Religious aspects—Christianity.
  2. Reconciliation—Religious aspects—Christianity. 3. United States—Race
  relations.   I. Okholm, Dennis L.
  BT734.G66 1997
  261.8'348—dc21

                                      96-29817
                                          CIP

21	20	19	18	17	16	15	14	13	12	11	10	9	8	7	6	5	4	3	2	1
15	14	13	12	11	10	09	08	07	06	05	04	03	02	01	00	99	98	97		

93107

Introduction

Dennis L. Okholm

As I write this, another season of America's favorite pastime has just begun. Despite the fact that the Chicago White Sox could not give away tickets during the opening week, baseball is still a defining aspect of life in the United States. This is the reason that Jackie Robinson's achievement fifty years ago is so significant—an achievement marked by a presidential speech at Shea Stadium. The shame is that it was only fifty years ago that the American game tolerated a black man's crossing the line—though he still could not drink, sit or sleep in the same location as did whites.

The irony is that fifty years from now we may have to repeat the observance on a golf course, to commemorate the first black man's victory in the Masters tournament at a golf club that has admitted only two blacks into its membership. As Eugene Rivers writes in this volume, the rhetoric means nothing, whether it comes from the mouth of a president or a Promise Keeper, if there are not more fundamental changes in society.

Christians are no exception to this contradiction. I teach at a college that is known for the involvement of its first president in the Underground Railroad, yet no African-American has ever been a president, vice president or dean since the college began in 1860. The percentage of people of color who populate its student body and faculty is embarrassingly small too.

The underlying assumption in this book is that the achievements in racial reconciliation we celebrate are not widespread realities even in the church because we have not addressed the issues at more fundamental levels. The chapters in this book probe beneath the surface to the level of Christian theological assumptions and methods. The lesson to be learned is that theological ideas have consequences: for instance, hermeneutics can undergird nineteenth-century slavery or twentieth-century Aryan superiority. In either case people's lives are affected—and sometimes terminated. Citing Marx and Hitler as examples, J. Gresham Machen once observed, "What is today a matter of academic speculation, tomorrow moves armies and brings down empires."[1] As a corollary to this, Glenn Usry and Craig Keener rightly assert, "A Harlem Renaissance or a Spike Lee can have some positive influence in the larger society's perspective, but changing our status must include transforming our own perspectives."[2]

Eugene Rivers constantly reminded the participants of the conference at which these essays were originally presented[3] that we must first study to get at the root of racism and reconciliation. Perhaps evangelicals want the "feel good" that Rivers rejects at the beginning of his chapter, but unless we get at the conceptual roots, any reconciliation will be short-lived in practice. A mere esprit de corps is not enough. In fact, Gary Deddo argues that the call for reconciliation is weakened if it is not adequately grounded in the indicative of God's grace and its living center, Jesus Christ.

Ronald Potter and Michael Cartwright powerfully demonstrate how theological concepts underlie race relations when they illustrate how evangelical apologetics and dispensational theology have fueled white racism. The burden of this book is that such fundamental considerations are a prerequisite to overcoming racism in evangelicalism. And lest we forget that this intellectual chore is merely a human work, Deddo reminds us of another important underlying conceptual principle: "Burnout in the service of racial reconciliation is a theological problem"—namely, a kind of Pelagianism.

These chapters were written by theologians and practitioners on both sides of the color line. Of course there are more than two sides in matters of race. Yet one must focus the discussion by being specific about race; attempting to deal with issues that concern Asians, Hispanics and Native Americans, as well as Africans and Europeans, in such a small volume can become a shotgun approach that hits the target broadly but not deeply. Furthermore, dealing theologically with reconciliation in black and white may in some way be paradigmatic for other hues of racial and ethnic reconciliation.

What is remarkable about all of these chapters is that, no matter how academic they get, each is laced with a personal narrative. Potter remembers his intellectual encounter with Cornelius VanTil that left a sour taste in his study of evangelical apologetics. Julius Scott's recommendations for a hermeneutic and methodology in thinking about race relations in New Testament terms come home as he recalls his racist Southern ancestors. Cheryl Sanders's ministry at Third Street Church of God and Pamela Baker Powell's at Messiah Church vividly recount the experiences of two women in ecclesiastical leadership, one black and the other white. In fact, when these chapters were in their original form as addresses, they struck a chord with the audience as no other theology conference at Wheaton College had. More than any other issue, perhaps, this is one in which we must marry head and heart, academy and church, systematician and pastor.

So, here are academics and clerics telling their stories, as their stories become part of the larger Christian story. And Deddo reminds us, "The history of humanity is essentially the history of its relationship to God." That history is not yet finished. It takes time and sanctification, until all of the debris from the walls that Jesus has destroyed by his death and resurrection is finally swept away.

Potter's essay sets the stage for all that follows. Borrowing from Gunnar Myrdal's analysis earlier this century, he reminds us of the "continuing American dilemma," in which a nation "conceived in justice and liberty" was also a nation conceived in the sin of slavery. The realities of racial injustice and discrimination contradict the biblical and democratic principles of freedom and equality. The effects are with us today. For instance, Louis Farrakhan has been successful selling Islam as the "black man's religion" in part because European-Americans made Christianity the "white man's religion." Evidence is as close at hand as a mid-1970s church film entitled *The Gospel Road* with its blue-eyed, blond-haired Jesus, or as fresh in our memories as the old Bible we grew up with, interspersed as it was with pictures of white people from the Middle East and Northeast Africa.

Later in this volume Scott demonstrates for us a hermeneutic and method that lay theological foundations for ethical principles whereby we must approach racial reconciliation if we are to be faithful Christians. Moving from the indicative to the imperative, Scott makes the case that God's nature is prescriptive for us. We cannot make requirements for church membership that God does not make for salvation. That is to say, theology proper, soteriology, and ecclesiology are inextricably linked in the question of racial reconciliation. As a systematician, Deddo demonstrates this for us, arguing that what is true of the God who exists in triune relationship must be reflected in our relations and behavior. Since covenantal relations essentially constitute our human existence and since the shape of our covenant relations with one another has been given its norm in and with the reality of our relation to God in Christ and in the personal hypostatic union between God and humanity, Deddo leads us to the undeniable conclusion: racism is idolatry.

The temptation is to avoid the idolatry of racism by contextualizing all theology. But, as Willie James Jennings argues, confining ourselves to contextualization can be equally idolatrous. Theology as a reflex of cultural or racial identity can never really transform that identity. Vincent Bacote's chapter concurs implicitly; he argues that the sociological origins of any theology must include the context of race, but to avoid becoming idolatrous and blind in the process, Christian theology is bound to another defining context: the teleology of the church universal.

What makes the essays in this collection specifically Christian reflections on racial reconciliation is that they do not begin with societal agenda or political visions. They begin with the triune God revealed in Christ and then, because this God is relational and incarnational, they end with a societal agenda and political vision. As Michael Cartwright's chapter makes clear, the way we read Scripture demands this procedure if, unlike his illustrations from the Second Great Awakening and his childhood experience in the Royal Ambassadors, we are going to have a Bible with which we must wrestle and read over against ourselves.

There is perhaps no other way to be the kind of non-Constantinian church to which Cartwright's essay calls us. As Sanders points out, this has been the failure of liberation theology, for it is inadequate to engage the surrounding culture. A church that begins with good trinitarian theology and an adequate soteriology must be not only an inclusive community, as Scott already reminded us, but also an exilic community, as Sanders argues. Only in this way will the church have the sense of identity it needs to challenge racism at its fundamental levels in a manner that goes beyond hugs and rhetoric. What Jesus did to break down the barriers between Jew and Gentile (Eph 2) should also shake us at the foundations. Craig Keener drives this home in his contention that racial and economic justice cannot be dismissed as peripheral to the gospel while simultaneously maintaining the importance of a fully biblical soteriology.

As people in the church live together in the reconciliation effected by Christ, an apologetic beachhead will be established whereby the church can forcefully attack walls of segregation and prejudice in the wider society. Certainly Powell's moving recitation of her experience as a white pastor of a small black church is a witness to this apologetic. But only when we take seriously at a conceptual level the New Testament theology as it is inaugurated by our Lord in passages such as John 13, 15 and 17, will the world know that we are Christ's disciples by the foot-washing, life-giving love we demonstrate for one another.

I thank Rodney Clapp for his support as editor and for his involvement with InterVarsity Press in the annual theology conference at Wheaton, where the ideas expressed in these chapters were first aired and then refined. For involvement in the same event kudos also go to Dwight McKissic and Cornerstone Baptist Church (of which he is the pastor) in Arlington, Texas. James Hoffmeier, professor and chair of the Bible, Theology, Archaeology, and Religion Department at Wheaton College, hovered helpfully behind the scenes from the inception of this confluence that brought together voices of different colors (i.e., it was Jim's idea).

Finally, this book is dedicated to two people who, appropriate for this collection of essays, are on both sides of the color line and both sides of eternity. At the conference's opening session Dr. Morris Inch reflected on his evolutionary involvement and personal development in racial reconciliation over the past few decades, including years spent chairing the Bible Department at Wheaton, when he encouraged his colleagues to wrestle with the application of Scripture to society. During these same decades, the late William Bentley institutionalized such wrestling by founding the National Black Evangelical Association, calling on black and white Christians to think conceptually and practically about racial reconciliation, a call that this book hopefully but only partially fulfills. To these two Christian brothers this volume is dedicated.

ONE

The Responsibility of Evangelical Intellectuals in the Age of White Supremacy

Eugene Rivers

It is important that I begin in such a way that you have some sense of who I am. I was educated in Philadelphia and got drafted into a street gang. Eventually I ended up at Harvard. For the past few years I've been a fellow at the Center for the Study of Values in Public Life at Harvard Divinity School. I am also a founding member of a national grassroots movement called the Ten Point Coalition, which is a movement of black churches and others that are focusing on the issue of black-on-black violence in the inner city from the Christian perspective. And so I speak to the family, the people of God. I am saved, sanctified, filled with the Holy Ghost and a mighty burning fire, on my way to heaven and enjoying the ride.

The Apologetic Challenge for the Family

Before we get deep, I want to establish my credentials as a member of the family, because in a loving, functional family, once you are clear that you are dealing with kin, you can listen to the hard sayings. There's an old adage, "I don't care how much you know until I know how much you care." So I speak as your brother, as a member of our family, the people of God. God calls us to deal with some hard stuff, and we are going to deal with it in a loving way.

Now when I say "loving" that doesn't mean that I am going to say it the way you would say it. Some of us are very parochial in our outlook on love, which means that if I don't say it the way you said it, I didn't say it right. Well, since you love me, you'll permit me to say it the way God told me to say it. So I want to lay the theological and familial context for what we're going to do.

I speak with the mind of an intellectual but with the heart of a pastor. That's important because there are also certain truths that are just too heavy to deal with outside of the context of faith, and your mind and back will break down under the weight of the truth that you've been confronted with.

I also believe that criticism, like love, should begin at home and spread abroad. So I'm going to have something to say about the black side of the family. I want to get that out and clean house—talk about the sin in my camp.

God has called us to a challenge, and the integrity of our witness before the world hangs in the balance: "But in your hearts set apart Christ as Lord. Always be prepared to give an answer to everyone who asks you to give the reason for the hope that you have" (1 Pet 3:15). This is an apologetic challenge. It has epistemological and political implications that are unavoidable. Reconciliation—the language and the rhetoric of reconciliation—divorced from a commitment to truth and justice is a sham. I don't care how many football stadiums you all go to, and hug and cry and shout, if it is not bathed in the practice of telling the truth to my brothers and sisters and the practice of a spiritual discipline—of justice—then we're shuckin' and jivin'. So when we talk about reconciliation, I love to hug you, I love to cry, I love to beat my chest and howl at the moon. But in the absence of the truth, in the absence of justice, in the absence of compassion and forgiveness, we're living a lie. It's a lot of "feels good." It's a lot of "sounds good." It's a good photo op. It's great public relations. I can use it for fundraising purposes, especially when I get that one with the black and white boys hugging each other. Send that out and call it reconciliation. I can make a lot of money. But minus justice, minus the truth, we're living a lie.

Now why is that important? People lie every day. Christians lie every day. We tell stories about things that aren't true. We say reconciliation, but we don't live it. We talk reconciliation with our lips, but we don't walk reconciliation with our hips. There is something very important at stake here. Louis Farrakhan is the major force he is today because of the hypocrisy of the church. That boy is up to a lot of mischief because he recognizes that the black church is talking a big Jesus with no cross: I want to live large, preach big and drive fine, but I'm not going to the cross.

Consequently Farrakhan exploits our indifference to the poor. And on the white side, he says, "Look here now, Mr. Khadafi, those white Christian boys in America say they love their black Christian brothers. They'll send a missionary to Bwana-Bwanaland, Tanzania, Mozambique and South Africa, but you can't find them in the south side of Chicago. Mr. Khadafi, they say they love their black brothers, but you gave me a five-million-dollar, interest-free loan, and I went out of the country to get it. They live in the same country, and all they can do is get in a football stadium and howl at the moon." I'm telling you, God is using Farrakhan as judgment on the church. He's a false prophet that God has permitted to expose our hypocrisy—the hypocrisy of the white church and the hypocrisy of the black church. And despite black preachers' best efforts, Farrakhan brought one million men to Washington, D.C., and six hundred thousand or more of them were Christians. God's talking to us.

Institutionalized Spiritual Forces and Shape-Shifters

It is important to begin with Scripture because what we are talking about is major surgery. We've got to cut out some cancer, and we've got to know what the tools are to exorcise this demonic cancer. So we begin with a familiar passage concerning the nature of our struggles: "For our struggle is not against flesh and blood, but against the rulers, against the authorities, against the powers of this dark world and against the spiritual forces of evil in the heavenly realms" (Eph 6:12). Ultimately what we are addressing is a spiritual problem that is mediated through mechanisms of domination that have institutionalized themselves and reproduced themselves at every level of this society.

Now, let's apply this to the area of knowledge. As philosophers like Pierre Bourdieu have demonstrated, your theory of knowledge, or what you presume to know and, on the basis of your epistemological presumption, to defy, is itself an expression of political power. That is true in the hermeneutical realm: the power to name and impose names on others is itself an act of politics.

In advanced, postindustrial society perhaps the most distinctive feature of the institutional processes by which various political and social inequalities and injustices are reproduced is the fact that it's flexible and dynamic. At one level the reasons are fairly obvious. The ideological face of political and cultural domination must continually adapt to ever-changing internal and external challenges to the system.

The mechanism by which people are oppressed will change like the Shape-shifter in *Star Trek: Deep Space Nine,* and so oppression is a dynamic practice, not static. The ideological defense of inequality is therefore continually undergoing dynamic transformation. In other words, the language, the rhetoric and the mechanisms for how the rich get richer and the poor get screwed are continually being refined, so that what was a "nigger" sixty years ago may now be a "minority" or "special-interest group." The reality is that we didn't just adjust the language. Sixty years ago I was a nigger. Now I have to clean that up because people got upset about that and burned some cities down; so now I'm called a minority, and when we get hip to that, we'll change that and I'll be part of a special-interest group. My point is that there is an elaborate and dynamic process by which political domination and cultural domination continually transform themselves to keep ahead of the game. And so the poor are continually under ideological and cultural assault.

Capitalism in this regard is to be applauded for its genius. In this society poor folks are getting screwed. In this society they downsize them, while they upsize the salaries of the people who are downsizing. Folks who get rich on the top don't know what to do with their money, while poor white people are on the streets. And then they redo the game in such a way that the poor folk feel it's their fault that the rich can't put them out on the street. And then when all else fails, you can always say that some old black welfare mother is the one who's taking everybody's money. The process by which the structures of domination are reproduced involves this mechanism, which is very flexible.

This process neither involves nor requires back-room conspiracies. There is not a group of people who don't look like me who sit in a room and do this. It is part of the logic and structure and process of social reproduction that these mechanisms exist. So it's not a conspiracy. You don't need one! The system is so refined that it's automatic. You teach a people to hate themselves for 385 years, calling them everything but a child of God, and you don't have to pull the trigger. If you program that child for so long to see himself a certain way, he'll self-destruct. This isn't rocket science. Let me grab your daughter and tell her for 350 years she's the ugliest thing since dirt. She's going to hate herself and anybody that looks like her. I don't have to pull the trigger. I just let the gun come in the neighborhood. She'll pick it up and do a job for me. Then I'll lock up the one who was standing next to her.

The Ideology of White Supremacy

The process of social reproduction is essential to this system, and the conceptual foundation for economic inequality is the ideology of white supremacy. Or, if you wish, white racism is the central conceptual hermeneutic or the psychocultural and psychosexual mediating lens through which social reality is itself framed in this society. White supremacy is the central mechanism through which all of what takes place in this society is framed. Thus Timothy McVeigh can murder hundreds of people and not give any indication of remorse, but it will not have the same impact and sting and power as an O. J. Simpson does. There is something deeper going on.

Let's tighten up the term "white supremacy" so that there's no conceptual ambiguity—so that it doesn't appear as though I'm simply engaging in rhetorical excess.

If one draws upon history, depth psychology, sociology and comparative cultural anthropology and pays close attention to the great works of literature, there are a number of things that we may assert about "white supremacy" or "white racism."

Western civilization itself is saturated, not merely with racism, but with the elementary gesture out of which racism is constructed, binary opposition: the splitting of the world into the dominated and the dominant. In that sense racism antecedes the notion of race. Indeed, it generates the races. Before there was an elaborate anthropological system devised by the West that established a biological and anthropological hierarchy with the white West on the top and the black on the bottom, there was racism. There was the presumption that the West (and this is unique) was a white civilization. It was the apex of the food chain. It was the thing to which all aspired. Racism supersedes the psychology of prejudice. Indeed, it creates that psychology for its purpose.

In other words, when we talk about racism we're not simply talking about attitudinal bad faith ("you don't like me because I'm black, therefore you're racist"); racism as the presupposition of the superiority of that which is Western and white is preattitudinal at the conscious level. It is so deep that we almost preconsciously articulate this presupposition. Angel food cake is white; devil's food cake is chocolate. Good guys wear white cowboy hats; bad boys wear the black hats. There are black lies and there are white lies. There is black magic and there is white magic. There is an entire constellation of symbols and images that permeate every dimension of our thinking. Racism evolves historically and may be expected to appear in different phases in different epics and locales. White supremacy is the dominant ideology that undergirds all of Western civilization. In North America it's white on the top and black on the bottom. In South America, or what some call Latin America, it's white on the top and black on the bottom.

There is some confusion about blacks, whites and Hispanics. For example, most of you don't know that Cuba is a black country. Eighty percent of the people in Cuba are black. But we have been looking at Fidel Castro so long we cannot even imagine that. Most people don't know that the major reason that the Cubans in Miami hate Fidel isn't because of the communism per se; it's because Castro improved the quality of life for black people, and black people in Cuba now have access to the homes and institutions that the white people whom he had run out had stolen before. So here again, our naiveté is revealed because we do not have an adequate understanding of the nature of the beast.

This is deeply theological. Daniel 9 and 10 suggest that the prayers of the people can be hindered. In the same way, I submit to you that the prince of America is the demonic ideology of white supremacy, and that is what blocks America's prayers. The thing that keeps America from being what it wants to be—the thing that keeps America from realizing its promise—is the fact that it was born in sin and shaped in iniquity and has not repented. And every other form of oppression and domination is mediated through the lens of white supremacy.

Why is it that this country could so irrationally do what it did in the Civil War? This country was torn apart over the issue of our sin and slavery. We went to war murdering each other, and Lincoln observed that it was God's judgment on America. Yet we haven't dealt with this because we in America have not made the decision whether we're going to be white or Christian.

How is it that the Gauls and Franks and Goths and Lithuanians ended up white? Then, not content to define yourself as white (and pure and resembling God), you have to make me black. I was Kukuu, I was Ashanti, I was Ibo, I was Yoruba, but when you're finished with me I'm black and a nigger.

This is the major thing that divides this country, yet to the whites I say that your whiteness is a political and social construction. Literally you are not white. And I am not literally black, yet I organize everything on the basis of my blackness because you won't permit me to do anything else. America is descending into a state of psychological apartheid. And we'd better wake up.

The O. J. Simpson verdict blew all the whites away. The fact that a black man got away with what white boys do every day brought to the surface the racism. Ted Kennedy drove a girl at Chappaquiddick into the water, and the first thing he did was call his lawyer. He didn't even call the hospital; he called the lawyer and let that girl drown. Then he was reelected senator! He even considered running for president! His nephew William Kennedy Smith was suspected of raping a young woman in the Kennedy compound at Palm Beach, but nobody marched outside of Hyannisport in protest. Claus von Bulow was suspected of killing his wife. There was no drama over Ted Kennedy, William Kennedy Smith or Claus von Bulow like there was over O. J. Simpson. Some old ignorant Negro with bad taste got out there with somebody he shouldn't have been with, and then there's a big drama. My point is this: it highlights the depth and the power of the white supremacy that says it's okay to play God and dominate others. But this is a sin bordering on violating the Holy Ghost. How many white people got as upset about the Kennedys or von Bulow as they did about O. J. Simpson?

And then I want to suggest something else for you to consider. How much drama would there have been had Nicole Brown Simpson been black? Had she been black, how many white women would have marched outside that boy's house? It would have been another case of old ignorant black people cutting each other up, doing what they're doing to get some money. That's what people would have said. It was like Richard Pryor. "Old ignorant Richard Pryor set himself on fire, but you know how them black people are." That would have been the attitude. But most of us don't want to deal with this business.

What is my point? My point is that there is a psychology that is at its base demonic, and we in the church must repent of this thing and see the deception and duplicity on both sides.

What the Church Must Do

First, we in the black church have lied to you white people. Most of us don't want to offend you, so we don't tell you what we really think. We smile and are congenial, hoping we might get some money out of you. We all get around white people and pray, smile and grin, knowing that those folks are not thinking about us. But we do our best because we try to make it in this world. Yet we are being unfair to white people. White folk might not be saved all the time, but they're not stupid. And they are concerned about this society just as we are. But we get into this game where I'm going to smile and grin and go along to get along, so I don't really tell you what I think.

And we are wrong. So I'm coming down on the black side first. We are wrong because we've not been honest and told the truth. And for that reason, Louis Farrakhan is on *60 Minutes* with Mike Wallace going off because we in the church have not had the courage of our convictions. We in the church have not been willing to really do what we should do. Consequently God has used a false prophet to judge us.

Let's go back to racism. Racism cannot be legislated out of existence. And in this sense the conservatives are right. Racism cannot be legislated out of existence since what is put into law always serves to legitimate the system that generates racism and is defended by it. It is illogical to presume that a system that is itself created and conceived in the iniquity of racism would then have in its structure the capacity to cancel out the thing which gave it birth. That makes no sense. This then brings us to the unique position that we as Christians are in today. We now have the opportunity, because the society has fallen down in every corner, to play a unique role in terms of bringing about authentic reconciliation that is rooted in a commitment to the gospel truth, justice and compassion.

So what do we mean when we're talking about racism? There are different forms of racism. There is dominative racism. That is the racism of brutality and violence. That is the racism that most of us would abhor. That is the racism of burning down black churches in the South. That is the racism of beating up Rodney King. That is the racism of indiscriminately locking up young black males who are guilty of driving while black.

Then there is aversive racism. That is the racism of respectability. That is the racism of bourgeois respectability where I am cold and rational and aloof and I construct a psychocultural force field that makes me inaccessible to you. We call this refinement, but that's a lie. And it's the mechanism by which I establish the black otherness.

Finally, there is metaracism. That is the racism of technology where you have in place a social system that now operates on the force of a logic that has been put in place. So even though I'm not engaging in dominative racism, even though I have no direct contact with you in the aversive sense, I have constructed an institutional mechanism that now plays out the logic of social reproduction so racism takes on a life all its own, completely removed from dominative and aversive forms of racism and contact.

What does that mean then for black people? Today more than ten million black people face a crisis of catastrophic proportions. Life in the major postindustrial centers of the United States is generally poor, nasty, brutish and short. Life now is often a choice between suffering and abject misery.

The prospects for black males are perhaps a bit more exciting. There is of course death due to homicide or drug-related HIV infection. Then there is incarceration, which provides an opportunity to refine the skills required for a career in criminality.

In all this horror there is a certain depraved consistency, for the persistent poverty of black and brown urban poor serves a variety of ideological functions. Conservative policy elites (whether Republican or Democratic) perceive correctly that poor blacks are a politically disposable population. And this is the thing that is dangerous. We now have a context in which poor black people who live in the domestic Soweto of this country are being increasingly isolated, and the process of segregation is twofold. Not only are black people being segregated from the larger society, but also black middle-class and professional people are now resegregating more black people and isolating them too.

In that context we have a volatile situation. In that context the black church must be challenged because the blood of innocent women and children is dripping from the hands of the black male leadership of the black church, which has failed to respond adequately, which has failed to tell the truth and speak honestly regarding the spiritual condition of America, which has refused to articulate with integrity to the larger society the truths that are so painful yet must be executed if America is to be healed. God has given America a unique opportunity to heal itself. More important, God has given us, the church, the opportunity to provide leadership. There is no other quarter in this society that has the institutional, moral or spiritual capacity to bring this country back together again. The secular mechanisms do not work. The Republicans aren't going to do it. The Democrats cannot do it. The secular civil society can't do it. The only hope that this country has is for the church to become in fact the body of Christ. That means that we must enter into a dialogue as family that is committed to truth.

We must begin a serious conversation. The black community must stop lying, smiling, profiling and putting on fronts for the white folks. We play the race card when it's convenient. Anytime I want to duck my sin I call the white boy racist because he doesn't understand my contradiction. We need to get out of that. We need to be dealing with integrity and honesty. We need to be calling our own black church leadership to account for our indifference. How do you explain the fact that there are sixty-five thousand black churches in America who represent twenty-three million black people, and we've got more problems now than we had forty years ago? Why is there an inverse relationship between the proliferation of black churches and the growth of crime? Why aren't the black church and its leadership dealing with that issue? Why aren't we providing more leadership for our young people?

The white Christian community must now engage in a process of historiographic reexamination. Your understanding of who you are is rooted in white supremacy. Your historiography presumes that you are the center of the universe. When you talk about evangelicalism, remarkably you eliminate twenty-three million black people who are more conservative than you are. How could you talk about evangelicals and ignore the most conservative Bible-believing people in the world? That is white supremacy. That is arrogance. That is a lie.

Part of the problem in the white evangelical community is intellectual. Its historiographic lens is too limited. So I suggest five books that serious evangelical intellectuals should read if they are intent on developing a new vision.

First is *White Racism* by Joel Kovel.[1] Blacks need to read it, too.

Second is *The Languages of Paradise: Race, Religion and Philology in the Nineteenth Century* by Maurice Olender.[2] This book illustrates how white supremacy plays itself out in nineteenth-century philology. The study of languages was based on a fascinating question that goes back a couple of centuries. Philology was inaugurated by the church in Europe because a theological question emerged: What language did they speak in Eden? If the language was not European that meant that Adam and Eve weren't white. If they didn't speak French or German or English, we may then have to doctor history so we can end up with Europe at the center of church history. So philology itself was born in sin and shaped in iniquity in that Europeans were so fanatically preoccupied with establishing themselves as superior that they had to create a discipline to figure out how they could ideologically backtrack to Eden to make sure that Adam was white and spoke English, French or German, and then move forward. (Biblical scholars must get involved in the business of deconstructing the white supremacy that permeates our historiographical understanding of who we are and provides an ideological basis for why we say that everybody else is inferior to us.)

So when we talk about evangelicalism, one of the ways that white supremacy finds its most dramatic expression is how we in the evangelical community constructed a vision of the Garden of Eden that avoided the possibility that Adam and Eve might have come from Africa. We put that thing in Turkey. We look all over the world for a place to locate Adam and

Eve to make sure they didn't come up too dark. And we don't care what Leakey says or what all of the anthropological and archaeological findings say; Adam and Eve will be someplace where they aren't black. And that is central to our understanding and self-identity. Eve must be white. Adam must be white. What does it say about us that they might be black? If they are our first parents, then I might not be white.

Third, *The Wages of Whiteness: Race and the Making of the American Working Class* by David R. Roediger[3] is a major study that, remarkably, has never been reviewed in one evangelical periodical of which I am aware.

Fourth, in *The Invention of the White Race,*[4] Theodore Allen does a historiographic reconstruction of how ethnic groups who came here as Irish and German and Swedish, and who understood themselves as such, in the course of the evolution of the labor process went from being Danes and Swedes and Irish to being white people. And then they forged an identity for themselves through their collective ideological repudiation of black people. The one thing that unified them was that they all hated black people. What drove the Irish, who hated the British, who didn't like the French Canadians, who didn't think much of the Italians, who didn't understand the Swedes and didn't trust Germans, to come together and create this ideological fiction called white people? Most of us don't know that history.

Finally there is *The Rise and Fall of the White Republic* by Alexander Saxton.[5]

I am suggesting these titles because I'm challenging you as Christians to expand the parameters of your thinking. God might free you from your whiteness so you might be able to live a more saved life, freed from oppression to your own demonic conceptions of what counts for beauty and human nature. God is calling us to a new level of understanding. God is asking us to pray and to intercede so that we can pull down the stronghold of the prince of America and be free to become the people of God. God is calling us to get off our ego hype, because what really makes this thing demonic and indicates it is straight from hell itself is the fact that it feeds on idolatry and pride. We manufacture a pack of lies and myths by which we can put everything under our control. The white man plays out the God-complex as a control freak who has been socialized to believe that he must dominate and be the lord of the world, supervising the planet. And then all of our relationships are sick. And we look sick to all the world. Yet we call ourselves Christians.

God is calling us to a new level of understanding. God is calling us to philosophically reconstruct our identity rooted in the gospel. God is calling us to renounce the idolatry of white supremacy; blacks must renounce it as well as whites. But if you, my white brothers and sisters, who created whiteness, who created the white race, who created the anthropological ranking system, who created the visions of beauty that many of us adhere to, who created these distorted notions of humanity—if you fail to renounce this sinful idolatry, you bring shame on the church, and the world will continue to reject us as credible expressions of the gospel of Jesus Christ because we chose idolatry over the Suffering Servant who gave his life for us and shed his blood that we could be free from sin.

PART I
Thinking About God in Black & White

TWO

Race, Theological Discourse & the Continuing American Dilemma

Ronald C. Potter

In recent years racial reconciliation has been uppermost on the agenda of many conservative Protestants. The National Association of Evangelicals/National Black Evangelical Association (NAE/NBEA) consultations, Promise Keepers mass rallies, Southern Baptist public confessions and interracial Pentecostal worship services are all indicative of this new spirit of racial healing.

The particular issues that this chapter will address with respect to racial reconciliation are explicitly theological in tone. More pointedly, this paper will explore the character of black and white evangelical theological discourse, providing us with a narrative of whence we have come and suggesting how we might go on. We will attempt this exploration against the backdrop of what has been referred to as the continuing American dilemma.

The American Dilemma

In 1944 a little-known Swedish social scientist named Gunnar Myrdal published the most comprehensive study on race relations in the United States in this century.[1] It has still not been eclipsed. Focusing especially on the myriad problems confronting African-Americans, Myrdal examined the contours of what he called "the American dilemma." The American dilemma, according to Myrdal, is the conflict and contradiction between such biblical and democratic principles as justice, freedom and equality and the realities of racial injustice, discrimination and inequality.

Myrdal's assessment of America's racial crisis at the end of World War II echoed W. E. B. Du Bois's evaluation at the dawn of the century. In prophetic candor Du Bois stated that "the problem of the twentieth century is the problem of the color line."

To be sure, the genesis of this socioeconomic dilemma commenced with the founding of the republic. Noted African-American C. Eric Lincoln poignantly described this nation's origins:

Two centuries ago, despite the moving rhetoric of the revolutionary impulse, and despite the fact that thousands of black patriots fought and died for the cause of American freedom, the American Commonwealth, which was conceived in liberty for some, was born in slavery for others. The stage was therefore set for this strange dilemma which today mocks our cultural pretensions, enervates our national purpose, and challenges the moral commitments implicit in our claim to be "one nation under God." As a nation, we were conceived in the most patent of political contradictions. We asserted that all men are created equal, with certain inalienable rights, as we casually stripped vast numbers of Africans of every vestige of their rights, both human and political. We were holding men in abject slavery, and we were remarkably oblivious to the moral and rational incompatibility of what we were saying with what we were doing.[2]

This is a grave predicament for our national and ecclesial life together. Contrary to Dinesh D'Souza's thesis in *The End of Racism,* the American dilemma grossly deformed the birth of a nation and continues to affect most areas of contemporary American life.

The contours of this dilemma have changed significantly over the past fifty years. New macroeconomic realities coupled with an unprecedented ethical and spiritual crisis within African-American communities have rendered implausible the thesis that white racism is the sole impediment to black social progress. Notwithstanding its changing contours, however, the American dilemma remains this nation's foremost ethical, political and ecclesial problem.

The Nature and Context of Theological Discourse

If this is the context in which we must discuss the theological discourse of black and white evangelicals, it would help us to be clear about what we mean by "theological discourse" before we go further.

Princeton sociologist Robert Wuthnow carefully examined the nature of discourse in *Communities of Discourse*. Wuthnow argues that "discourse subsumes the written as well as the verbal, the formal as well as the informal, the gestural or ritual as well as the conceptual."[3] Such a definition precludes the possibility of limiting discourse to highly theoretical speech-acts. It might therefore be more helpful to speak in terms of discourse—modes that range from the most rudimentary to the most sophisticated. So, what are the implications for theological discourse?

Theological discourse entails a metanarrative or, better, what Richard Lints calls a "theological vision."[4] This is something akin to what many of us would refer to as a worldviewish theology, which Arthur Holmes distinguishes from academic theology.[5] Discourse along the line of worldviewish theology or a comprehensive theological vision may or may not be as intricate as some modes of academic theology, but, like Wuthnow's understanding of what counts for discourse, it is expansive in its scope. In this sense, then, theological discourse can be understood as that project which makes explicit our typically implicit Christian convictions about God, the world and ourselves.

Given all of this, the nature of theological discourse must also take into account contextualization. Evangelicals have sometimes been slow to understand the reality of the contextualization of all thought. Once again Wuthnow states:

> Great works of art and literature, philosophy and social criticism, like great sermons, always relate, in an enigmatic fashion, to their social environment. They draw resources, insights, and inspiration from that environment. They reflect it, speak to it, and make themselves relevant to it. And yet, they also remain autonomous enough from their social environment to engage in a broader, even universal, and timeless appeal.[6]

All modes of discourse, while they find their matrix within a particular social and cultural context, do have the ability to rise above that particular context—to speak to it, to be relevant to it, and yet to transcend it. In the case of theological discourse this point was made by Professor James H. Cone, the major architect of what we now refer to (in the United States, at least) as contemporary black theology, in his groundbreaking work *God of the Oppressed* (1975), as well as by recent evangelical authors like Lints and Stanley Grenz.[7]

The Unfinished Agenda of White Neo-evangelical Theological Discourse
With these definitions in mind, we will first focus on the American dilemma and white evangelical theological discourse since 1946. I call this particular time frame the "unfinished agenda of neo-evangelicalism."

In the late 1940s, Carl Henry called for an evangelical public theology.[8] In *The Uneasy Conscience of Fundamentalism* (1947) Henry challenged conservative Protestants to take seriously the project of engaging their social environment. Henry argued that from the 1920s through the 1940s fundamentalism sponsored no program of attack on acknowledged social evils, and the movement ignored serious intellectual reflection on how an evangelical ecumenism might impinge on the cultural crisis. Henry charged that such a truncated understanding of Christian faith was impotent in challenging

> the injustices of totalitarianism, the secularisms of modern education, the evils of racial hatred, the wrongs of current labor-management relations, [and] the inadequate basis of international dealings. . . . An assault on global evils is not only consistent with, but rather is demanded by a proper world-life view. . . . If Protestant orthodoxy holds itself aloof from the present world predicament, it is doomed to a much reduced role.[9]

For Henry this theological vision, this worldviewish theology, has tremendous import for enabling us to engage our public environment. Henry believed passionately that "we must offer a new evangelical world mind, whose political, economic, sociological and educational affirmations reflect the Christian world view."[10]

In 1948, four years after the monumental study done by Myrdal, Henry penned a series of articles in *Christian Life* entitled "The Vigor of the New Evangelicalism." Disheartened by fundamentalism's nonengagement with the intellectual, cultural and social climate of the time, Henry set out to sketch the contours of the renewed evangelicalism for which he had called. The pivotal question that Henry raised in that series of articles was this: "Is evangelicalism's only message today the proclamation of individual rescue from a foredoomed generation? Or has this evangel implications also for the most pressing social problems of our day?"[11]

But what makes this particular era in neo-evangelical history problematic has to do with the race equivalent of what Mark Noll has called "the scandal of the evangelical mind."[12] The scandal that Noll described is the evangelical evasion of the world of critical thought. The scandal we are describing is the white evangelical evasion of the American dilemma. This manifests itself in what many of us within the African-American church refer to as sins of omission and sins of commission.

In terms of the former, the great fathers of the neo-evangelical movement—Carl Henry, E. J. Carnell, Paul Jewett, Bernard Ramm, to name just a few—could have addressed more directly the racial climate of the time. There is no excuse for white neo-evangelical thinkers to have failed to engage the premier scholarly study on race relations of their own generation, the two-volume work by Myrdal, *The American Dilemma*. While they engaged the intellectual and cultural climate of their time, they failed miserably in addressing in any meaningful fashion the racial crisis as their contemporary Myrdal depicted it.

Such were sins of omission. But there also were sins of commission. For example, with a bit of irony, one of the brilliant lights of the neo-evangelical movement, E. J. Carnell, was caught up in the failure to address meaningfully the American dilemma in such a way that the absence of engagement manifested itself in questionable attitudes. When he was asked why he had not spent more time on what we have called the American dilemma, Carnell answered, "Too much stress on racial injustice will divert the sinner's attention from the need to repent of his totally self-centered life. Albert Schweitzer has outstripped us all by identifying himself with the misfortunes of the Negro, but this in no way justifies self-righteousness."[13] And then he said something telling, which I think is at the crux of the problem:

> I find it easy to be patient with Billy Graham. Though I have been
> preaching for many years, I have never devoted an entire sermon to the
> sins of the white man, and the chief reason for this failure is my failure
> to find a final way to measure and defeat racial pride in my own life. It
> is not easy to preach against oneself. Ministers expose the sins of the laity
> with great passion and eloquence, but they seldom expose the sins of
> ministers.

And then, the sin of commission. Carnell concluded on this dubious note:

> The tragedy is that our desire to actuate the law of love is not matched
> by wisdom and virtue needed to succeed. If we pass real estate zoning
> laws, we do an injustice to the Negro. But if we let the Negro buy a house
> in a fashionable suburb, we do an injustice to vested property interest.
> With rare exceptions, real estate values are certain to plunge.[14]

The high view that many evangelical thinkers had of such persons should have plunged when they read such statements.

So, where do we find ourselves today? How has recent white evangelical theological discourse meaningfully addressed the continuing American dilemma? Contemporary works in evangelical theology abound. Such mature scholars as David Wells, Donald Bloesch and Clark Pinnock, along with such superb younger thinkers as Lints, Grenz and Alister McGrath, have produced first-rate theological treatises. In my judgment, however, there exists little if any theological reflection on the continuing American dilemma among these representative thinkers. One interesting exception to this pattern of "benign neglect" is the posthumous book of Paul Jewett, *Who We Are: Our Dignity As Human—A Neo-evangelical Theology,* which engages substantively the issue of racism as a theological problem.[15]

The continued evasion of the American dilemma by second-generation neo-evangelical theologians in particular renders their discourse vulnerable to needless criticism. More than twenty years ago, Cone leveled this criticism at the white theological establishment:

> Twentieth-century white theologians are still secure in their assumption that important theological issues emerge, primarily if not exclusively, out of the white experience. Despite the sit-ins and pray-ins, the civil rights movement and black power, Martin Luther King and Stokely Carmichael, white theologians still continue their business as usual.[16]

This same critique could be leveled at numerous well-meaning and conscientious sons and daughters of the postfundamentalist theological giants.

Contours of Black Evangelical Theological Discourse

Before we probe the discursive practices of black evangelicals with respect to the continuing American dilemma, we need to recall what constitutes the nature of discourse in general. According to Wuthnow, discourse is both formal and informal. It is activistic as well as theoretical and conceptual. Within black Christian discursive practices, theological reflection can be found in sermons, tracts, pamphlets, addresses and popular books, as well as written formal theological treatises.

Contemporary black evangelical thought and discourse, like most other forms of black Christian theological reflection, is primarily theologically informed social criticism. This particular mode of social criticism is predicated upon a biblical anthropology and is constitutive of what religious ethicist Peter Paris refers to as the "black Christian tradition."[17]

Black evangelical discourse as social criticism is first of all a critique of white evangelical ideational structures and social practices. To the extent that these ideational structures and social practices become incongruent with the moral principles within the black Christian tradition, they are judged ethically deficient. In this respect white racism becomes a gross distortion of genuine biblical anthropology. Almost thirty years ago, black evangelicalism's quintessential public intellectual, William E. Pannell, really understood what was at stake. He wrote: "The issue here is plainly philosophical and theological and it really boils down to our understanding of man."[18]

Contemporary black evangelical thought and discourse were shaped primarily by engagement with the black power and black theology movements of the late 1960s and early 1970s. The late public intellectual William Hiram Bentley in many ways was correct when he said that prior to the 1960s one could not differentiate meaningfully the organic structure of black evangelical thought (or "Negro evangelical thought") from that of its white counterpart. But during the middle to late 1960s we experienced an awakening—what I call the Black Awakening—of Negro evangelicals. During the years 1968 through 1970 at the then-NNEA conventions, this new form of black consciousness began to permeate black evangelical thinking. In 1968 Bentley read an important paper entitled "Our Engagement with Black Power,"[19] in which he set into motion a meaningful way for black evangelicals to engage the ethos of the Black Power movement of that time. In 1969, in Atlanta, black evangelicals began to awaken even more. And then in 1970, when Professor Columbus Salley, coauthor of *Your God Is Too White*, addressed the NNEA convention in New York City, the lid was blown off many previously Negro evangelicals. The emergence of such noted persons as Salley and William E. Pannell (now at Fuller Theological Seminary) and the late evangelist Tom Skinner marked the rise of bright and shining lights during the late 1960s and early 1970s. These were prophets of God, used in this process of black evangelical reawakening.

How, then, did black evangelicals engage the theological ethos of that time? Within the construct of what is now the NBEA, at least since 1974, black evangelicals have begun to take seriously the nature of a distinctively black, or African-American, mode of theological discourse. They have engaged themselves with what many of us refer to as the so-called black conceptual (not cultural) revolution of the 1970s. Lerone Bennett Jr., historian and editor of *Ebony*, defined that conceptual revolution:

The overriding need of the moment, is for us [African-Americans] to think with our own mind and to see with our own eyes. We cannot see now because our eyes are clouded by the concepts of white supremacy. We cannot think now because we have no intellectual instruments save those which were designed expressly to keep us from seeing. It is necessary, therefore, for us to develop a new frame of reference which transcends the limits of white concepts. It is necessary for us to develop and maintain a total intellectual offensive against the false universality of white concepts.

We must create a new rationality, a new way of seeing, a new way of reasoning, a new way of thinking. Our thinking, and the scholarship which undergirds that thinking presently, is Europe-centered, white-centered. We see now through a glass whitely, and there can be no more desperate and dangerous task than the task which confronts us now, the task of trying to see with our own eyes and to think with our own minds.[20]

This conceptual revolution was personified in the various black theology movements of the late 1960s and early 1970s. Black evangelicals engaged themselves in that particular ethos by attempting to struggle with a distinctively black evangelical black theology. Black evangelicals during this time span did not want to throw out the baby with the bath water. But they understood the import of what Bennett was saying and tried to apply that to their own particular setting; therefore, within the context of such groups as the NBEA, from 1974 to the present there has been the ongoing struggle to develop what Bentley referred to as a black evangelical black theology.

From Theological Discourse to Racial Reconciliation

How can progressive white and black evangelical theological discourse provide a meaningful framework for genuine, biblical racial reconciliation? I suggest that we first proceed by together grappling with the following worldview questions.[21]

Where are we? Or, to put it differently, what is the nature of the reality in which we find ourselves? And by "reality" we are referring not just to a cosmic reality but to a social reality as well, one upon which we reflect theologically.

Who are we? Or, to phrase that question differently, what is the nature, purpose and task of human life? Related questions would be: Who are we as the people of God? Is our primary self-understanding predicated upon our ethnicity, race, gender and social class or upon who we are as the community of God?

What is wrong? Or, to put that differently, how do we understand and account for evil, brokenness, alienation, oppression, injustice and the like? It is on this question that white and black evangelicals will find themselves often at opposite ends of the pole. Here we need to talk about the development of a biblically informed social hermeneutic—that is, a viable conceptual framework that would enable us to interpret correctly our social circumstances. Such a construct would have import for the previous two worldview questions.

What, then, is the remedy? Or, how do we find a path through our brokenness and alienation to healing, mending, repairing and transformation? I believe that the answer to this question will require us to revision both a theology of the cross and a doctrine of the church.

Paul's letter to the Ephesians has tremendous import for this revisioned theology of the cross as well as a revisioned ecclesiology. Theological reflection on Ephesians 2:11-22 as it relates to our contemporary setting is instructive here.

The most salient concept in this passage is the centrality of the cross of Christ. It is through the cross that Gentiles are now able to become full citizens of the commonwealth of Israel. It is through the cross that God ends the hostility between Jew and Gentile by reconciling both groups to himself, thereby creating "one new humanity" (Eph 2:15 NRSV).

The centrality of death is paramount in this biblical passage! It is only through Christ's death on the cross that human alienation, estrangement and hostility are put to death (Eph 2:16). Before a renewed humanity can come into being, both groups must place themselves at the foot of the cross and literally die to whatever they have been in the past. Cone states in this regard:

> That's what repentance means; that's what conversion means—becoming a new [person]. And to become new means to die, and that's what baptism is the sign of. . . . The symbol involved here is that you die and become a new [person]. Of course, a lot of people are baptized who don't become new people. But the symbol is not destroyed by those who misuse it. The significance here is that you do actually, literally die. You cannot be what you were in the past.[22]

Within our context, what must we die to? First, white evangelicals must die to the myth of American origins and must honestly face the reality that our republic was born in sin. The near genocide committed against Native Americans, coupled with the enslavement of millions of Africans, constitutes our nation's "original sin." White evangelicals in particular will never be fully healed until they honestly admit this truth, understand the full moral gravity of this truth, truly repent from this past and work toward a "new birth of freedom."

African-Americans must die at the foot of the cross as well. They must die not only to a false notion of self that has been perpetrated by white supremacy but also to their own hubris that inhibits genuine forgiveness. When white Christians, out of the genuineness of their hearts and out of a renewed sense of commitment, say, "Brothers and sisters, we have sinned and are ready to repent," it becomes the responsibility of African-Americans within the framework of a biblical Christian ethic to die to that particular pride that would inhibit forgiveness.

Once black and white evangelicals have genuinely placed themselves at the foot of the cross, they must begin to see themselves as they really are: one new humanity, the people of God. In this regard there are no we-versus-them categories. We see ourselves literally as family members. This obviously means that racial reconciliation is not something optional or peripheral to the gospel. The gospel is reconciliation. The passage from Ephesians makes that abundantly clear. It is only as we intentionally ponder this truth, remind ourselves of this truth and finally submit to this truth that our ecclesial "life together" will begin to be authentic.

THREE

Wandering in the Wilderness

Christian Identity & Theology
Between Context & Race

Willie James Jennings

T he Christian church in the West has not been able to mount an adequate theological response to the questions of race and culture or the problem of racism. The lack of an adequate response exposes our continuing failure to grasp this common problem that has defined our Christian lives. When it comes to issues of race and culture and the problem of racism, we Christians are very much like the children of Israel, wandering in the wilderness. This is especially the case in relation to our theological reflection on race and racism. Christian theology today wanders in the wilderness of race. In this state of wandering, our theologies have not been able to follow the path laid before us by the delivering God, and thus in a sense they redouble our wandering as people who cannot trust our God or each other. In what follows I seek to outline the characteristics of our theological wanderings and to tentatively and humbly suggest a way out.

Our Wanderings: The Person as Problem in Theology

We can seize the first characteristic of our wandering by looking directly at the dominant way in which theology is being written and taught, which fundamentally has to do with what we understand theology to be.

What is theology? That question found at the beginning of most texts on theology has in recent years been joined to another seemingly basic prolegomenal question: Who does theology? This question is now an essential part of answering the primary question of theology's nature. That these two questions are being linked signals some of the tremendous changes that have taken place in theology in the last thirty years. At the risk of making too great a generalization, it would be fair to say that in theology today the emphasis now falls on the "who." In other words, the person who does theology has now become the focus of much theology. As Shirley Guthrie notes in his classic textbook *Christian Doctrine*, "[people's] understanding of the truth *is distorted* because they see or hear from the perspective of their particular race, sex, economic class, religious and national heritage."[1]

Guthrie is pointing to the importance in contemporary theology of recognizing the limitations of one's social location, one's context. He points to the now unassailable axiom that we all engage in theological reflection out of some social and cultural context. Yet Guthrie also recognizes the dubious nature of this axiom. Not only is our theological reflection bound to some social and cultural context, but also our context is the locus of our downfalls, our limitations, our theological distortions—all rendered such by our culturally soiled hands. Therefore the person who does theology must be addressed as part of the task of doing theology, and this can best be done with the recognition that all theology is contextual.

The wide recognition that all theology is contextual represents a stunning transformation of how one thinks about theology. For example, in *Narratives of a Vulnerable God*, Reformed theologian William Placher begins with a kind of confession of his cultural-contextual identity before he proceeds to theological reflection.[2] He states he is a white, socially privileged male who is a Presbyterian, who trained at Yale University in the new Yale school of theology and who now teaches in a socially elite school.

Placher is by no means the first theologian in North America to admit a cultural-contextual reality to theological reflection. It was Paul Tillich in his still significant text *Theology of Culture* who pressed the constructive aspect of culture as the womb of theological reflection. In this collection of essays Tillich notes the organic connection between religious reflection, the production of theologies, and cultural existence.

The form of religion is culture. This is especially obvious in the language used by religion. Every language, including that of the Bible, is the result of innumerable acts of cultural creativity. All functions of man's spiritual life are based on man's power to speak vocally or silently. . . . There is no sacred language which has fallen from a supranatural heaven and been put between covers of a book. But there is human language, based on man's encounter with reality, changing through the millennia, used for the needs of daily life, for expression and communication, for literature and poetry, and used also for the expression and communication of our ultimate concern.[2]

Tillich's theology of culture had a demystifying intention and certainly had a great impact on a generation of theological scholarship. Tillich sought to show Christianity's unbreakable and necessary connection to culture. He did this not in order to disestablish Christianity or its intellectual expression (theology). Rather he sought to show how religious faith (i.e., Christian faith) voices the basic ontological structure of human religious consciousness, not some direct divine consciousness. While many scholars no longer find Tillich's theological program attractive, his proposal for conceiving theology as bound up with cultural existence resonated with the North American theological community. Tillich's thought may or may not be considered the first significant reflection on theology and culture or culture as theology, but it would be fair to say that a Tillichlike program continues in the methodological placement of cultural context as central to theological reflection.

We can see this in the recent work of a Canadian theologian, Douglas John Hall. In *Thinking the Faith: Christian Theology in a North American Context*, Hall raises the notion of context beyond a prolegomenic level to a programmatic level.

> *Doing* theology, as distinct from imbibing the results of the theological exertions of others, involves entering at depth into the historical experiences of one's own people. . . . This prerequisite of all authentic theology entails for us—a people at the nerve center of the affluent nations of the Northern hemisphere—the acquisition of a critical self-awareness which may well produce in us acute forms of mental discomfort. To do theology anywhere in the First World today means to suffer.[3]

For Hall, as for many others, the notion of context has broadened to include not only history, society and economics but also gender and race. And in each case the axiom is reasserted: no theology can be done today without recognition of context. My purpose in noting this transformation in the doing of theology is not to deny it as genuine intellectual and theological advancement. By noting the importance of considering context in theology we mark this awareness as the dominant theological response to the question of race and the problem of racism for Christianity in the West.[4]

While my task is not to give a historical accounting of the history of the problem of racism for theology, it is correct to say that the problem of racism for Christianity in the West has been rightly delineated along two important lines. On the one hand there has been the narrowness of the theological enterprise in the West, that is, the hegemony of white male intellectual expression. Only white males were theologically educated, and only they spoke and wrote so-called authentic theology that was recognized as legitimate and that formed the dominant conversations of the church. On the other hand there has been the involvement of the theological enterprise (such as the writing and teaching of theology in church and school) in forming or supporting structures of slavery, racial oppression, violence and death in societies. To these problems we will return later; however, at this point our concern is to return to the sheer power of the idea of context over theologians as they seek to address the questions of race and culture and the problem of racism.

Our Wanderings: The Contextual Lens Through Which We Envision Theology

To say "all theology is contextual" opens a multiplicity of meanings, meanings that cannot be overlooked.

Generally in its strongest form this maxim implies a relativism in the very substance of theology. This would mean that there is no universal, constantly applicable theology, no doctrine that has been the same throughout history and that now binds us together. Such a vision of contextual theology means that doctrines have appeared and reappeared in history often under the same name, using the same terminology, but, because our understanding arises out of different social and cultural contexts, the content or substance of doctrines is very different. In its strongest forms, then, the assertion that all theology is contextual means that the actual substance of theology is diverse, changing over cultural space and time.

In its weaker form this saying may imply that we all look at and understand the common teachings of the church from different cultural perspectives. Some will emphasize or gravitate to one dominant theological motif as the key to understanding the whole, while others will emphasize another theological motif as central. Such a vision of contextual theology means that there are common theological texts and ideas but a diversity of interpretations. In this weaker form the assertion that all theology is contextual means that our understanding of the common substance of theology is diverse.

In whatever form one understands the importance of context for theology, we have before us a powerfully appealing way to begin to address issues of race and culture for theology. The power of this appeal is rooted in the authentic desire to liberate theology from the problems we noted earlier: the narrowness of the Western theological enterprise and its compliance with racial oppression and violence. This desire has been best articulated in theologies of liberation. While envisioning theology through a contextual lens presents some real advancement and honors an authentically Christian desire to liberate theology from the problems of race and racism, it also unfortunately hinders the power of Christian theology to directly address these problems.

Let me be clear: theologies of liberation with their desire to liberate theology from the problems of race and racism do not hinder the power of Christian theology to address the problem of racism. I call attention to the envisioning of theology through a contextual lens as problematic, because this intellectual procedure continues modernity's policing and marginalizing of theology. This intellectual procedure builds upon the very problems of race and racism in the modern enlightened West within which Christian theology has been articulated and formulated. Though we cannot here examine all the salient features of this connection, two features need to be highlighted.

First, the discovery of context is in one sense the other side of the demystification of theology. With the various European enlightenments, theology comes to be understood not as the words of God spoken by God but as the words of humans (literally). Sometimes called the turn to the subject and formally called the anthropocentric turn in theology, this reconsideration of theology broke the essential connection of human pronouncement to divine decree while it left intact the centrality of reason as the marker of divinity. What is often overlooked in this accounting is the manner in which theology is repositioned. These enlightened proto-Europeans recognized that human beings, not God, do theology, and with this recognition they also realized that certain essential qualities of people can be learned by how they have positioned theology in their social discourse.

In *The Invention of the Americas: Eclipse of "the Other" and the Myth of Modernity*,[5] Enrique Dussel comments on the famous statement of Immanuel Kant concerning the nature of enlightenment in Kant's *Foundations of the Metaphysics of Morals*.[6] Dussel reminds us that in the essay "What Is Enlightenment?" Kant rendered a powerful description of humanity, a humanity that had reached maturity (i.e., enlightenment). This is a humanity bold enough and courageous enough to think for itself, having stripped away external authority inasmuch as that authority continued to promote a Godlike status, a theological posture. Yet Dussel notes that this powerful description opened up the possibility of envisioning human beings who are immature and in need of tutelage, even to the point of slavery, in order to reach maturity.

The primary way to gauge that human maturity is to ascertain the freedom a people enjoyed from the "self-incurred tutelage—chiefly in matters of religion."[7] Theology then becomes fundamentally an object for critique in order to control the reach of its authority. Whether with the formation of critique found in the rise of modern science, or with the formation of critique found in the distancing of philosophy from theology and its metaphysics, or with the formation of critique in the rise of ethics, in each case theology is again and again shown to be merely the word of morally fallible and often intellectually weak human beings. Of course some human beings are more fallible and intellectually weaker than others. The point is that theology—whether understood as church dogma, ecclesial pronouncement or ecclesial interpretation of texts, history and human nature—is shown as it is demystified by the Enlightenment to be simply linguistic code for the operations of human consciousness and imagination. As Ludwig Feuerbach convincingly demonstrated to the philosophers and theologians who followed him, we discover theology's real importance once we understand it to situate us in the realties of human beings and their desires:

> Man is the God of Christianity, Anthropology the mystery of Christian Theology. The history of Christianity has had for its grand result the unveiling of this mystery—the realization and recognition of theology as anthropology.[8]

Theology then becomes compelling not by its claim to a divine authority or a witness to such authority but in its accurate description and prescription of the world we envision or desire. The world Feuerbach envisioned was wholly without the presence or the influence of those cultural others he theorizes as theologically primitive. They are present as those who have not yet arrived at civilization, and thus their difference, contextually speaking, is quite obvious. We see this difference in their primitive way of under-standing theology, that is, theology without critique. In his *Lectures on the Essence of Religion* Feuerbach notes that primitive peoples show theological reflection at its most primordial level: the worship of nature based on fear of nature.

The more primitive peoples of Africa, northern Asia, and America are afraid "of rivers, especially in places where they form dangerous whirlpools or rapids. When they navigate such places, they implore mercy or forgiveness, or beat their breasts and throw propitiatory sacrifices to the angry gods. Certain Negro kings who have chosen the ocean as their fetish are so much afraid of it that they do not dare look upon it, much less travel it, because they believe that the sight of this terrible god would kill them on the spot."[9]

Feuerbach here draws from the work of nineteenth-century anthropologists and philosophers of religion in discerning the presence of fear as a basic element in human religious consciousness and theological imagination. And in this discernment Feuerbach resists the idea (held then by some anthropologists and philosophers) that these primitive cultures exhibit what he understands as the culturally advanced characteristics of *Geistsreligionen*, that is, monotheistic religions.[10] To attribute monotheistic characteristics to the primitive nature religions of these cultural others would be to ignore the developmental differences between cultures that are exposed exactly in their theologies. To be fair to Feuerbach, he sees a clear continuity in the religions of all cultures. All religions have fear as an essential aspect in the production of their theologies.

The only difference between Christians and uncivilized peoples or so-called heathen, is that Christians do not transform the phenomena that arouse their religious fear into special gods, but rather into *special attributes* of their God. They do not pray to evil gods; but they pray to their God when they think He is angry, or when they fear that He may become angry with them and strike them with harm and disaster. Just as evil spirits are virtually the sole objects of the worship of primitive peoples, so the angry God is the chief object of worship among Christian peoples; here too, in other words, the chief ground of religion is fear.[11]

With Feuerbach, however, we find that judgments of civilization—its presence or absence, its strength or weakness, its maturity or immaturity—come with the recognition of theology's origins in humanity and humanity's cultures. It is a very short walk from Enlightenment's critique of theology to colonialism's discovery of other cultures that are primitive and in need of the guidance of "advanced races."[12] But this brings us to the second feature of this connection.

Second, the discovery of context is, in another sense, the other side of the rise of a social vision of theology. Here we refer to the development of the social sciences as alternative ways of viewing reality. First, sciences of the social set aside theology; then, over time, they policed a theological vision of social life. Sociology, anthropology and psychology were substituted for theology by being presented as the advancement of the power of science to understand humanity in its multiple environments. These disciplines then situated theology within a so-called larger view of the ways various peoples construct reality. For example, consider Émile Durkheim and his path-breaking vision of the social construction of reality. Ultimately for Durkheim, sociology would replace theology as a more compelling way to discern the ways people conceive God. For Durkheim religion is a social fact and therefore cannot be denied by an authentic science of the social, nor can a social science replace religion as a way of religious life. Thus the existence of religion is not the point of conflict with science; instead Durkheim finds what he considers to be the real point of conflict:

> There is no conflict [between religion and science] except upon one limited point. Of the two functions which religion originally fulfilled, there is one and only one which tends to escape it more and more: that is its speculative function. That which science refuses to grant religion is not its right to exist, but its right to dogmatize upon the nature of things and the special competence which it claims for itself for knowing man and the world. *As a matter of fact, [religion] . . . does not know itself. It does not even know what it is made of, nor to what need it answers. It is itself a subject for science,* so far is it from being able to make the law for science. . . . It is evident that . . . [religion] . . . cannot play the same role in the future that it has played in the past.[13]

Religion for Durkheim is the product of human beings bound in concrete human societies and cultures, and therefore its existence cannot be denied. In a sense the power of belief is all that matters and constitutes the power of the object of belief, God. But theology that is tied to concrete human societies and cultures cannot fully explain the operations or even the existence of a human community or culture, because it is always an intellectual reflex of that culture. Durkheim represents a powerful policing of theology and its reach, a policing that lives in the other sciences of the social. And of course the primary religious objects theorized upon with these sciences were the so-called primitive cultures, those peoples located beyond the veil of civilization. On their cultures the tools of scientific discernment were sharpened, enabling these developing sciences to claim the humility of truth and the accuracy of scientific fact.

My point is that an intellectual procedure now widely adopted as appropriate to forming a response to the questions of race and culture and the problem of racism continues to reinforce the framework within which those problems live and breathe. Within the framework provided by the procedure of contextualization, theology can be only a reflex of identity and can never really transform identity. Given this problem, however one wishes to speak of theology—as doctrine, creed, theological assertions or lived experience—is unimportant because the power of theological reflection to change the way we see ourselves continues to be resisted, thwarted and policed.

This resistance to theology stands at the center of the legacies of racial construction and the ideology of racism in the modern West. Yet we must understand that this resistance marks our wandering in the wilderness. We as church are lost in a place where we cannot find our true covenant selves. Worse, in this crucial matter we have no theologian—no Moses, no Aaron, no Joshua—to lead us forward.

Pressing the contextual lens in a real sense continues to promote theology as disembodied knowledge that makes up the stuff of an academic discipline. We must remember that in order to become a part of the formation of the modern university theology became organized and arranged so as to present itself as knowledge in a way similar to scientific knowledge. This made theology appropriate for scientific study. This meant that we in our particular contexts bring shape, form and actual body to this knowledge. Theology is dead information that we bring to life by bringing ourselves to its study.

Along with this, pressing the contextual lens means that theology continues not to be understood as part of a vital set of activities that Christians engage in which themselves constitute the content of theology and which form real concrete identity. Theological reflection (an inherent part of reading and reflecting on scripture, praying and worshiping, and testifying to God's goodness) is central to forming Christians. This means that without its embeddedness in a set of practices theology becomes at worst ideas that we can define any way we find suitable to our cultural needs. Instead, theology understood as practices and activities stands in a complex and critical relationship with cultural and social contexts, much more complex and critical than we have been willing to acknowledge or allow.

By pressing forward the contextual lens as the starting point of theology, we have also separated the truth of theological belief from who we believe ourselves to be. There exists a great wall between what we believe about God and what that belief means for our self-understanding. Bound up in the history of white racism and colonialism is the power of white identity.

Merged with Christian existence, this form of identity remains untouched by our Christian commitment, confession and even death. It is reborn in each new generation of white Western Christians, ready to hold to both Christian existence and an unarticulated but clearly understood white existence. For such a Christian it is no trivial matter to realize that all theological reflection arises from one's culture or social location, because such a recognition serves only to reinforce the historic power of white identity as that power which has led to the formation of every other form of racial identity. Attempting to capture the constructing nature of this white identity has been central to my own work. But my goal is to point not to the need for theology's transformation but to the need for our own transformation. Yet another characteristic of our wandering must be noted, and that is the continuing failure of Christians to honestly face the question of race and culture and the problem of racism.

Our Wanderings: The Docetism That Haunts Us

In days to come
    the mountain of the LORD's house
shall be established as the highest of the mountains,
    and shall be raised above the hills;
all the nations shall stream to it.
    Many peoples shall come and say,
"Come, let us go up to the mountain of the LORD,
    to the house of the God of Jacob;
that he may teach us his ways
    and that we may walk in his paths."
For out of Zion shall go forth instruction,
    and the word of the LORD from Jerusalem. (Is 2:2-3 NRSV)

There is an unrelenting docetism that haunts the way Christians in the West deal with race, culture and the problem of racism. Early Christian docetism was an attempt to maintain a vision of the divine life unhindered by the realities of human flesh. Certainly there was a soteriological motive behind docetic Christologies: Christ must be unhindered by the obstacles of human existence. Essentially docetism marks the body of Jesus as not being human in the ways we are human; rather, with Christ there is an appearing to be human so that the saving operations can be effected for us.

Our docetism in matters of race surfaces in our articulation of a social redemption that is beyond the actual realities and operations of our humanity. Our docetic tendency is not merely our inability to deal with human "differences." Our docetism in matters of race comes to light in our desire to see racial harmony and peace without the actual transformation of identity rooted in the real conversion of our forms of social existence and community. We docetists say, "I don't see anyone as black or white, just my sister or brother in Christ. There is no such thing as race; we are all one in Christ." Or we say, "We just need to learn how to forgive, respect and live together and go on to the future." Or we say, "Where I was raised there were no black people; therefore race was and is not an issue for me."

These kinds of statements commonly found in the mouths of Christians exhibit the worst kind of theological deception. Here we claim a commitment to a changed perspective without the requirement of any significant display of that commitment. Such ways of speaking and thinking exhibit the total denial of any christological mediation that would shape the way we live and that would demand a way of life that indicates the seriousness of Christian transformation. Here we exhibit the foolishness of Western individualism as it deceives us into thinking that a changed heart means a changed world.

Our theological docetism enables racist life and racist segregation to continue in our churches. And the stronger our commitment to this kind of docetism is, the greater is our wandering in the wilderness. As long as this kind of response to racism carries the day in our churches, it will enforce in the academy the power of a contextual lens as the strongest response to this docetism. Yet the docetism and the problems of contextual thinking are bound together.

Our Way Forward: Theology and Discipleship

As Jesus passed along the Sea of Galilee, he saw Simon and his brother Andrew casting a net into the sea—for they were fishermen. And Jesus said to them, "Follow me and I will make you fish for people." And immediately they left their nets and followed him. As he went a little farther, he saw James son of Zebedee and his brother John, who were in their boat mending the nets. Immediately he called them; and they left their father Zebedee in the boat with the hired men, and followed him. (Mk 1:16-20 NRSV)

In a real sense the way beyond theological docetism and the problems with a contextual procedure that distorts Christian theology will be found only when we respond to God's call to raise up a new generation of Christians who (with their theologians) are prepared to move, at whatever the cost, out of the wilderness—prepared to move appropriately from the legacies of their parents in order that the promise of the new covenant for new identity may be reconceived and Christian hope revived.

At the center of this endeavor must be a renewed vision of theology as the framework within which new identity, Christian identity, is formed. And here we desperately await a new generation, because we need people who can dream dreams and have visions of what we do not have the courage or even the desire to envision. That is, we need a church made up of people who refuse to live out racial politics, who refuse to participate in the racial realities of this nation, who refuse the power and privileges of whiteness, who reject the stereotypes of blackness, who claim a new way of life born at the cross and the resurrection, who will not be known even by family, tribe, friends or nation after the flesh, but who would know themselves only through the power of resurrection and the call of the cross of Christ.

FOUR

Theological Method in Black & White

Does Race Matter at All?

Vincent Bacote

Is there such a thing as black or white theology? When the task of theological reflection is undertaken by people of different ethnic backgrounds, do those backgrounds make a difference? Should they make a difference? Should there be different theological methods reflective of race and ethnic background? To these questions I answer both yes and no. I intend to explain this answer by reflecting on the sociocultural origin of theological reflection and subsequently the ecclesiological ends and scope of theology.

Theology in Context

I begin by asking, What is theology? Generally theology is God-talk, or dialogue and reflection on God's revelation to us (this includes both special and general revelation). Theology is done "from above" when it addresses questions concerning God and his relationship to us. Theology is done "from below" when its questions concern the contextual situation of the church and of life. When theological reflection takes place, it occurs in a particular context, and the resultant theology will reflect aspects of its origin, especially when it is done from below.

In a similar vein Stanley Grenz, in his recent one-volume systematic theology, *Theology for the Community of God*, says,

> Theologians do not merely amplify, refine, defend, and deliver to the next generation a timeless, fixed orthodoxy. Rather, by speaking from within the community of faith, they seek to describe the act of faith, the God toward whom faith is directed, and the implications of our faith commitment in, for, and to a specific historical and cultural context.[1]

Grenz's point is important because white evangelicals often convey the perspective that there is a seamless theological tradition stretching back to the first century or at least to the Reformation. Within this perspective lies a perception that theology is primarily or exclusively a product of reflection on Scripture and the tradition, with a minimal dependence upon or reflection of sociocultural context. In view of the Reformation tenets of *sola Scriptura* and *sola fide*, this is not surprising. At the same time, is it not true that these tenets are practiced within a context and that this context will have some effect? This is not to say that sociocultural context is determinative in a totalizing or reductionistic sense, but that theological reflection can be shaped by context.

An example of this impact of sociocultural context is examined by Robert M. Kingdon in an essay on John Calvin's ideas about the diaconate.[2] Kingdon asks whether Calvin developed his understanding of diaconal function from a theological or a social origin. What is Calvin's understanding of the diaconate? In Calvin's *Institutes of the Christian Religion* we read:

> The care of the poor was entrusted to the deacons. However, two kinds are mentioned in the letter to the Romans (12:8). . . . Since it is certain that Paul is speaking of the public office of the church, there must have been two distinct grades. Unless my judgment deceives me, in the first clause he designates the deacons who distribute the alms. But the second refers to those who had devoted themselves to the care of the poor and sick. Of this sort were the widows whom Paul mentions to Timothy (I Timothy 5:9-10). Women could fill no other public office than to devote themselves to the care of the poor. If we accept this (as it must be accepted), there will be two kinds of deacons: one to serve the church in administering the affairs of the poor; the other, in caring for the poor themselves.[3]

Kingdon argues that Calvin's structure of the diaconate is derived not only from biblical exegesis but also from observing the administrative structure of the General Hospital in Geneva, which was created before he arrived in 1535. This hospital addressed the needs of the poor, and the charitable obligations of the community were carried out by two different groups of functionaries. First, there was a group of procurators who gathered alms and handled the administrative affairs of the poor. Second, there were a hospitaller and staff who took care of the poor and sick.

Thus Calvin found a double diaconate in operation when he arrived.[4] Kingdon argues that this institutional structure influenced Calvin's concept of the diaconate, and he arrives at this conclusion not only because of the obvious parallels between Calvin's teaching and this institutional structure but also because of some aspects of Calvin's language. In particular, Kingdon points out the fact that Calvin occasionally used the labels *hospitallers* and *procurators* for the two types of deacons he believed were required by Scripture. Calvin used these terms in some of his biblical commentary, particularly in his sermons on 1 Timothy, which he believed contained significant proof texts for his understanding of the diaconate.

From the perspective of chronology, Kingdon also argues that in the development of the *Institutes* between 1536 and 1539, years of critical importance in Calvin's career, his teaching on the diaconate developed significantly. The concept of the double diaconate appeared for the first time in the 1539 edition, after Calvin had the opportunity to observe the General Hospital's social welfare structure.

Why did Calvin develop this view of the diaconate? Kingdon suggests the probability that Calvin was impressed by the function of the General Hospital and that he sought a scriptural warrant for the way it handled social welfare, which he found in Romans 12:8. While conceding that other explanations are possible, Kingdon argues that Calvin's observation of the Genevan example seems to be the greatest factor in shaping his diaconal concept. It is important to note Kingdon's comments on the fact that in the mentality of the Reformation period, the most compelling argument for the diaconal concept was one based on "explicit and precise appeals to Holy Scripture."[5] With this in mind, we should recognize that even if the organization of the Geneva hospital suggested the concept of the double diaconate to Calvin, he would not have said so.

My purpose in using this extended example is to point out that John Calvin did not develop his theology in a vacuum; rather, he developed his theology in a sociocultural context, and this context had an influence on his thought. He was not a great theological mind abstracted from culture and society. My concern is to emphasize that the origins of evangelical theologies—indeed all theologies—are at least partly influenced by sociocultural factors. Moreover it is important to notice that scripturally and traditionally derived principles are inevitably contextualized through practical theology in a particular environment, where those principles spring to life. While *sola Scriptura* is the ultimate interpretive and formative principle, it has not been practiced, and theology has not emerged, without reflecting the marks of its particular context. I hasten to reiterate that this does not mean that evangelical theology is culturally relative and therefore only sufficient for its context of origin, but that we need to acknowledge that context is a significant factor which at least partly informs our theological method.

Theology in the Black Context

With context in mind I come to the question of why there is a corpus of literature known as black theology. Why did this explicitly contextual theology come about? In the general introduction to *Black Theology: A Documentary History*, James H. Cone says that black theology arose from asking the following questions:

What does it mean to be Black in a world that defines Whites as human and Blacks as less than human? Is Blackness an unfortunate accident of birth that African Americans should be afraid of? . . . Or is Blackness a gift of creation to be affirmed with joy and thankfulness? . . . What does it mean to be a Christian, a follower of Jesus, in a world that portrays Jesus as a White man and Christianity as a European religion? Is Christianity a religion of love and hope that empowers oppressed Blacks to fight against racism, as Martin Luther King, Jr. proclaims in his sermons? Or is Malcolm X right when he calls Christianity "a perfect slave religion," "skillfully designed to make us look down on black and up at white"?[6]

Black theology sought to address the condition of African-Americans in an oppressive society. In *The Failure of White Theology*, Patrick Bascio adds:

There has always been a notable absence of the black agenda when leaders of the American Christian denominations meet to discuss religion, so the black church became the focal-point of developing amongst blacks a self-consciousness proper to the black psyche, one that reflected African religious concern for social and political expressions. The assumption that white religious expression should fulfill the needs of the black community was based on classical theology's failure to understand the critical role of culture in religious expression. . . . Black theology is, in part, the response of black men of religious feeling and commitment to what they perceive to be the failure of the theology of the dominant culture in American society to understand and relate to their spiritual needs. Further, black theology is a protest against the continued reality of racism amongst white Christians in our society.[7]

Both of these authors make the point that black theology is a contextual theology that developed because of an apparent vacuum in theology, because of a burning desire to have questions central to the lives of African-Americans answered theologically. This theology emerged because of racism and the failure of classical or white theology to address issues at the core of African-American existence. Classical theology is understood as white because of its extensive European heritage and because of a real or a perceived identification of essential Christianity with Europe, particularly Western Europe. Evangelical theology has been understood as white because of this European heritage and because, throughout the history of evangelical theology, it has either upheld or failed to challenge the status quo on matters of race, justice and freedom.

What should we say then about the legitimacy of a theological method that is white or black? I argue that race, ethnicity and culture significantly influence theological reflection. As I have already illustrated, it is undeniable that our sociocultural context influences our theological reflection, regardless of our method. More specifically in reference to black theology, I argue for its essential validity because the questions raised are vital to all theological discourse. While one can debate the manner in which black theology has developed and question many of the directions it has taken in its short history, the essential questions raised by black theologians (or by any other marginalized group) are issues of theological anthropology, ethics, politics and soteriology—fundamental theological questions.

The unique aspects of these questions that are highlighted by Cone and others have received minimal reflection from classical theologians (though some might object that Augustine, Luther, Calvin and Wesley did write extensively on these matters), but they must be addressed if theology is to be relevant to the complete life experience of African-Americans. That these questions are legitimate and consequently produce black theology is a fact that theologians should acknowledge. They need not align themselves with any particular political framework to agree with this. A theology emerging from a particular context is not problematic; it is natural. What we must do is acknowledge this and understand in a carefully nuanced manner that context plays a role in all theological reflection, a role that is greatest when theology is done from below.

I am troubled by the direction that some prominent black theology has taken, but I fully acknowledge that even the more radical perspectives raise legitimate questions. I also understand why the responses to these questions have come primarily from the liberal camp; it is because the theologically conservative voices have been silent on race issues or have perpetuated the status quo. Theologically conservative voices have also failed to acknowledge the effect of society and culture on their own tradition of theological discourse. This myopia, characteristic of the majority culture, needs correction. When we consider the origins of theological reflection, it is important for us to remember that context is a significant though not necessarily determinative element. This is what I mean when I answer yes to the questions raised at the outset of this chapter.

Theology in the Ecclesiastical Context
What do I mean when I answer no? I answer no to the question of whether theology is black and white, and whether this should be the case, because I understand the ultimate end of theological reflection to be universal in its ecclesiological effects. One unfortunate aspect of labeling theology as black or white is that it can be perceived as a theology relevant only for the group identified by the label. The impression can and has been made that white theology is insufficient because of the theological vacuum on the questions of race and justice. By characterizing such theology as inadequate, it is then set up to be dismissed and replaced by another, more relevant theology arising from the context. In the same way, white Christians can understand black theology as relevant only for people who identify with some notion of blackness. In either case the label-specific theology is ghettoized. The result of this situation is that potential enrichment for the entire body of Christ is thwarted by virtue of labeling, by virtue of perceptions that inadequate theologies need to be discarded and replaced by something new. Is it not a better path to examine how the entire church, with a true spirit of catholicity, can benefit from the theological reflection of those whose experience is different, of those whose vision can shed much needed light on our blind spots?

Do we not produce a truncated ecclesiology when we on the one hand discard the rich tradition of classical theology with the benefits of its emphasis on spiritual life and on our relationship with God and on the other hand fail to do the hard work of theological reflection on the questions that arise from the sociocultural situations of those who have questions about self-identity, liberation and injustice? The church ignores either extreme to its own peril. It is a detriment to the body of Christ if all voices are not heard. The church is in an unnecessarily weakened position in both theory and praxis when all voices are not heard. Having said this, it is important to note that not everything that is said is of equal weight. We must practice discernment if we are to determine what will be perceived as more or less significant. Irrespective of our race, we are impoverished if we do not understand that we need theological contributions from all quarters.

Further, the witness of the church will remain suspect as long as there is unwillingness or perceived inability to recognize that theology, regardless of its origin, has universal benefits for the church. If the church chooses a path of division, a path where there are black and white camps that hardly acknowledge one another or relate with cool indifference, then Jesus' prayer for unity (Jn 17) becomes the object of rebellion. Admittedly there is a long history of division and schism in the church, but this is no legitimate rationale for ceasing to strive for unity and true catholicity.

How might this be practiced? How, as evangelicals, do we address issues such as liberation? Will we dismiss it as a theologized Marxism or divinized radical politics, or will we see liberation not as the purpose or final end but rather as a stage in the exodus as we move toward the covenant and its renewal of a whole people? Critiques of liberation theologies are valid, but does that mean that the questions can be dismissed? I submit that a better course is to accept the questions as valid and then to produce excellent theological reflection that offers a reasoned alternative to the prevalent forms of liberation theology.

How do we attain the larger vision in which theology is universally applicable? It is imperative that theologies, regardless of their origin, retain enough of their character in order to remain relevant to their original context, and yet also be able to transcend their context in order to be generally applicable to the universal church. It is important to retain the significance of our particular context, but it is equally important that our particularity not obliterate the universal character of our faith. Likewise it is important to vigorously hold to our universal faith, but to do this in a fashion that does not subsume the richness and relevance of our particularity. Our particular contexts and our universal faith must be held in constant tension, with our transcendent and transcultural Lord at the center. This is not an easy task, but I do not see it as an impossible one. In relation to black and white theology, this means that each does not dismiss the other as hopelessly irrelevant from the outset. Rather their first step should be an attempt to understand the other on its own terms and subsequently to ask how one's own theology can be challenged, enhanced or modified by the other and then how the result of this process contributes to the larger theological picture. This process of enhancing one's own theology provides the greatest challenge.

What criteria do we use to determine whether our theology will indeed be enhanced by the other? Do we use a spiritual criterion, where the ultimate question is whether one's own theology is enhanced because of greater access to God by virtue of this dialogue? Do we use a more pragmatic criterion, such as a greater affirmation of one's humanity by gaining a deeper and more practical understanding and application of the *imago Dei* or of *koinonia*? Or do we ask how our theological systems might be strengthened by this process? The aspects of the other theology that will enhance one's own theology will be determined precisely by the weaknesses of the latter. It is likely that our spirituality, as well as our practical and dogmatic theology, will be edified by the process. It is important to note that this is not a one-time effort of which I speak. Given the changing nature of our life situations, this is a lifetime task. It is a necessary task that requires our greatest effort.

If this task is taken seriously, steps could be taken toward recognizing the general applicability of theologies, whether their origins and aims are primarily local or universal. The performance of this task requires a mindset of humility, in which no one assumes that all questions have been raised and answered, particularly when doing theology "from below." It calls us to put aside defensiveness and distrust. It ultimately requires the greatest degree of applied Christian love in which others are considered more important than self and deeds exceed words.

Some might retort that I am a naive theological Pollyanna who has not yet encountered the retrenched attitudes and practices of those in power, those who have no desire to have their theology enhanced by those with less power. While history certainly affirms this response, I reply that it is the defeatist and pragmatist Christianity that gives up the struggle for true catholicity. If there must be division and mutual frustration, then I have no desire to be a part of such a faith. Yet my faith is in a God who can destroy barriers and turn the most stony hearts into hearts of flesh. The path will be paved with much difficulty, but the witness of the church will be more effective if we work at developing a theology that broadens our horizons and enhances our intimacy both with God and with our fellow citizens of the heavenly kingdom, regardless of their skin color or ethnicity.

Conclusion

Do black or white theologies exist? Indeed they do, for sociocultural context will inevitably affect theological reflection at certain points, and the resultant theologies will bear marks that are characteristic of their origin. Do race, ethnicity and culture matter? Yes. These factors can serve as the basis for significant perspectives and unique questions when one approaches the theological task. Should race-based theologies exist intentionally? Perhaps, but only in a nuanced fashion. Such theologies should be self-critical and able to minimize or eliminate the potential for ghettoization.

It is important to be able to recognize the limitations and weaknesses of one's particular theological reflection and also to be aware that one's theological reflection is only part of a larger theological task—that it cannot stand alone. Without such self-criticism, without any nuance, we run the risk of producing an anemic church. We are at risk if we balkanize ourselves through injudicious labeling. It is legitimate and necessary to address the questions arising from our various contexts, but we must keep ourselves mindful of the larger vision of our faith. As we combat various issues in our own local communities of faith, we do well if we look beyond our own context and draw upon the resources of those in the body of Christ whose context is different. We do well if we are mindful to seek ways in which our own local theologies can enrich the universal church. May we undertake the task with humility and with a desire to learn.

FIVE

Persons in Racial Reconciliation

The Contributions of a Trinitarian Theological Anthropology

Gary W. Deddo

I want to highlight four aspects of a trinitarian theological anthropology that I believe have great promise for securely grounding any approach to racial reconciliation in the deepest verities of a historically orthodox Christian faith and for providing the most hopeful impetus for its embodiment in the life of the church as a witness to the world.[1] Then in eight theses I will draw out some important implications.

Humanity as Being in Personal Relationships
The basic insights of a trinitarian theological anthropology arise out of a consideration of the person and work of Jesus Christ. For Jesus Christ reveals to us both who God is and who humankind is.[2] In Christ we discover that the answer to the question about God corresponds to the question about human being. In Christ God is revealed to be the triune God, the God who exists from all eternity by virtue of the triune relations among Father, Son and Spirit. In Christ humanity is revealed also to exist by virtue of its relations, first with God and then with others and the rest of creation. In Christ we discover that there is a correspondence among all three of these relationships. Our love for one another is to reflect God's love for us in

Christ, and God's love for us in Christ has its source and ground in the Father's eternal love for the Son in the Spirit. Thus Jesus tells us: "As the Father has loved me, so have I loved you" (Jn 15:9); and then, "As I have loved you, so you must love one another" (Jn 13:34).[3]

In Christ it is revealed that these relationships are not accidental or external to who we are. Relationship is essential and internal to divine and human existence. God would not be God were God not triune. If humanity did not exist in relationship, originally and continually with God, there would be no humanity. Humanity has its existence in and through personal relations.[4]

The essential question about the constitution of humanity then must be about its relationship to God. Humanity is such that it cannot be discerned without an essential reference to its relationship to God. It is in Christ that true humanity is fully revealed to exist in a threefold relationship to God. First, we are the creatures who belong to God by virtue of our being created and preserved by God through the eternal Word. Second, we are sinners reconciled to God through the atoning work of God in Christ. Third, we were created, preserved and reconciled according to an eternal and determinative purpose: to become the glorified children of God, perfected by the Holy Spirit of God for all time, to live within the eternal communion of God—Father, Son and Holy Spirit.[5]

Humanity exists from God, through God, with God and for God. The history of humanity is essentially the history of its relationship to God. No description of humanity without such an essential acknowledgment of this purpose and relationship can be adequate. Alternative descriptions may correspond in some way to what humanity is, but if these descriptions are regarded as anywhere near comprehensive, the result will be a distorted, dehumanizing reductionism. In Christ we see that, as utterly different as human creatures are, all humanity is God's humanity. In Christ there is an eternal place in the heart of God for humanity. Humanity was created for union and communion with God.

In a derivative way, on the horizontal plane, human being is revealed to exist in relationship as well.[6] Within the created sphere the most profound level of relationship involves interhuman relations, especially those of parent and child, men and women, as near and far neighbors.[7] We live in these relationships in order to represent and extend to others the same kind of relationship we have with God through Christ and in the Spirit. Our interhuman relationships provide the context in which we embody in word and deed the truth of our communion with God. Such quality of relationship is also to be extended in its own proper way toward all dimensions of created existence. However, this often neglected dimension of relationship is beyond the scope of this chapter.

Being in Personal Covenantal Relations

It is not enough to merely say abstractly that human being is constituted by being in relationship. In Christ such relationships have a particular quality. We exist by virtue of being in personal relationship. In biblical terms this means that humanity exists by virtue of being in a covenantal relationship of holy love. All our belonging to God as creatures, reconciled sinners and redeemed children are manifestations of God's freely bestowed love upon us that demands and enables us to respond with a creaturely reflection of that freely given love. By God's covenant love we are made to be God's own covenant partners in the world.[8]

Existing in such personal covenantal relations means then that human existence is not static, inert or mechanical. Such relations involve a willing, acting, discerning, deciding and communicating that first of all are directed toward loving God and then toward loving others.

Being and becoming in relation. Two crucial aspects of our being in personal covenantal relationships need to be pointed out. First, in and through such dynamic relationships we do not remain the same. We are affected by these relationships. Human existence in relationship with God is a becoming.[9] In such relationship we become personalized. God is the personalizing Person.[10] Human existence is a history of relationship, of interaction, of communion and communication whereby we become more than what we were. In right relationship with God humanity is becoming truly personal, truly human. In Christ we see that union and communion with God are no threat to humanity but its foundation and fulfillment. For true humanity is perfected in and through covenantal holy communion with its creator, reconciler and redeemer.

But this relationship with God does not take place in a vacuum. It takes place in the context of relationship with others and within the nonpersonal environment. Within the matrix of these intersecting relationships we are called to order our lives under the commanding grace of God so that in our relationship with others the truth concerning God's relationship to all humanity comes to light.

Consequently all attempts to resist, disregard, deny, denigrate or obliterate our being as the covenant partners we are can only contribute to our dehumanization.[11] The gracious, reconciling work of God in Christ is designed to overcome every such possibility. Humanity is preserved and then rescued from its own dissolution by the atoning work of God himself in the incarnate, crucified and risen Son of God. It is within this reality that we are called to live out our lives in covenant relations with others.

Extending relations. There is a second aspect to our living in personal covenantal relationship. We live within the matrix of our human relationships for the express purpose of extending such covenant fellowship first to other persons and then, in ways proper to each, to all other dimensions of created existence. All relationships are to bear witness to and thereby reflect God's own personalizing covenant love extended to us in Christ and by the Spirit. The love of Father, Son and Spirit did not remain internal to God, but through creation, reconciliation and redemption God has sent forth his love to include us within the life of the triune fellowship. Covenantal love contains within it a centripetal force. We are sent out on a mission to include others, even the enemy, within God's covenantal fellowship.[12] Those who contain their love for themselves and their own kind do not bear witness to the extensive love of God in Christ. The extension of our love to those who are different, even to enemies, is the test of the genuineness of our love.

The ultimate source for our being in personal covenantal relation. We have not yet reached the ultimate mystery of our humanity. In Christ it is revealed that the ultimate ground for our existing in personal covenantal relationship is not merely the example or the command of Christ. It lies rather in the being of Christ and our being created, reconciled and redeemed through him. That is, the mystery of our humanity lies in the eternal triune relations of Father, Son and Spirit.

Jesus does not only emulate and command the kind of love we ought to have for one another. His own existence is constituted by his relation of holy love with the Father in the Spirit. He is who he is by virtue of his union and communion with the Father in the Spirit from all eternity. In Christ it is revealed in time and space and in flesh and blood that the eternal being of God is personal being—that God is a triune communion of love between Father and Son in the Spirit. Personal relationship is not merely a phenomenon external to God in God's relationship to creation or in our relationships to one another. Personal relationship is internal and eternal in God. Were God not Father and Son and Spirit in eternal communion of holy love, God would not be. The only God that is, is not a static, inert, mechanical oneness of stuff but a dynamic union and communion of the triune persons. God is eternally loving.[13]

Human being, then, is derived from and given its reality on the basis of the personal covenantal communion of the triune fellowship. We exist in personal covenantal relationship because we are created through and for the Word of the Father. We were created to participate in the same communion that the Son of God enjoyed from all eternity in the heart of his heavenly Father. We were created to be the children of God because we were created through and for the one who is the Son of God. In Christ we are loved with the same love the Son receives. "As the Father has loved me, so I have loved you" (Jn 15:9).

Thus the ultimate grounding for the imperative that we love one another as God in Christ has loved us is the indicative of the love with which the Son has been loved and which has been given to us by the Son. Ultimately our communion with one another is to reflect and bear witness not only to God's communion with us in Christ but also to the eternal triune communion of Father, Son and Spirit.

In this light we discover the full sense in which we were created according to the image of God. We were created in order to mirror in our relationships the same love that is mirrored in the divine Son's relationship to the Father. We were created to personally image in our human relationships the divine love imaged between Father and Son in the Spirit.[14]

In this light it becomes clear why Jesus summed up all the law and the prophets in the two coordinated commands of love. The first command is to love the Lord your God with all your heart, mind, soul and strength. And the second is like it, that is, it is comparable, an image, a reflection, a witness: to love your neighbor as your self. God's own being is constituted by the personal union of holy love. Our own being is first to be constituted by our covenant partnership of love with God and then to be embodied outwardly in a corresponding way in all other creaturely relations, especially among persons. Failure to reflect God's own covenantal and personal love in our relationships misrepresents and thereby dishonors Christ. Worse, it defaces the glorious communion of love that God is from all eternity.

The Fulfillment of Covenantal Being in Relation

Some reflection on the nature of Christ's atoning work is now in order. If the heart of the being of God is personal, loving communion, then the atoning work certainly bears witness to this. The atoning work in Christ can be construed as God's freely chosen act of love to reconcile and so restore right relationship between God and humankind all in order to preserve and fulfill the end for which humanity was created: to enter into eternal union and communion in the triune life. If personal relationship is essentially ontological, then relational brokenness affects our very being; consequently, healing must take place not externally to God or to humanity but within the ontological dimensions of who we are and who we are becoming.[15]

Indeed, this is exactly what we see. The incarnation of the Son of God for us and our salvation is not merely instrumental. The incarnation of the Son of God effected a hypostatic union with humanity. The Son of God (*homoousious* with the Father) became one substance/being (*homoousious*) with us. Our salvation was accomplished not merely by Christ but also in Christ.[16] Our healing took place in him and is shared with us through the restored communion accomplished for us and at God's own expense. "With his stripes we are healed" (Is 53:5 KJV). A wonderful exchange took place in Christ that transforms our being by the transformation of our relationship with God through Christ. We are given new natures. We are being renewed in the image of Christ himself.

Consequently the healing that takes place within the ontological structures of our humanity not only effects a reconciliation with God but also renews and restores our relationships with others and ultimately with all creation. The teaching of Ephesians 2 then becomes clear. In Christ, and not just by Christ, the alienation between peoples has been healed. In place of the once divided humanity (explicitly seen in the enmity between Jew and Gentile in Jesus' day) was created one new humanity. The breach and brokenness between human persons was healed along with our reconciliation to God. And notice that such a healing between persons is not regarded as a potential or a possibility but as an accomplished act. As sure as God has been reconciled to humanity in Christ, so humanity has been healed within its own relationships in Christ. The humanity of Jesus Christ is an all-inclusive humanity.[17]

Only when the being of humanity is grasped as essentially personal and relational, first in its vertical and then in its corresponding horizontal dimensions, can the essential connection between the atonement and racial reconciliation be seen in its proper light and given its proper weight. The connection between the indicative of Christ's incarnation and atonement and the imperative for human reconciliation is not merely a moral one or a functional one. It is ontological, grounded first in the triune life and then in the incarnation and crucifixion. Consequently there can be no disjunction between the reconciliation of God and humanity and the reconciliation among human persons. The indicative of God's reconciling grace establishes the ontological grounding for the imperative of racial reconciliation.

The Shape of Our Covenantal Relationships

The revelation in Christ of the truth of our being in personal covenantal relationships and its ultimate grounding in the triune communion not only indicates that it is so but also illumines the shape of right covenantal relationship. The love of Father, Son and Spirit and God's love for us in Christ define for us the shape of our human relationships—the shape of love.

The normative shape of love is active and apparent in the fulfillment of our human relationship to God in the personal union of the two natures in Jesus Christ. This relationship reached a mature theological expression in the Chalcedonian Creed of 451. The relation of the natures was there delineated as being without confusion, without change, without division and without separation. The logic of the incarnation is the logic of the right loving relationship between God and humanity. Thus it provides insight into the right relationship among persons. As is true in the person of Christ, so among human persons there is to be a unity, a differentiation and a correspondence in right relationship.[18]

In Christ we see a perfected unity of God and humanity—a perfected personal communion of mutual love, glory, knowledge and sharing in one authority and mission. In Christ we see no confusion of God and human nor change of one into the other. In Christ God does not change into a man, nor does a man become God. Neither is there a fusion of both into a third kind of being. The unity does not collapse the distinction. The communion is maintained between divinity and humanity in Christ. In fact, the communion confirms the distinction. The distinction magnifies the unity.[19]

The unity and the distinction work themselves out in a personal correspondence and coordination of one with the other. Beginning in the incarnation of the Son of God and culminating in the faithful obedience of Jesus upon the cross, our humanity is assumed healed and restored as it is brought into conformity with the Word and will of God. In Christ our fallen human nature is brought to the place where it confirms God's judgment and confesses its sin, where with thanksgiving it receives forgiveness and its adoption as a child of God, and where it takes up God's mission in the world.[20] In this way the divine and human become corresponding covenant partners in Christ.[21] What was lost in Adam is restored in Christ. For Christ is the true Adam.

Human covenantal love is then ordered by this pattern. Wherever the unity is undone by the distinctions or the distinctions are obscured by the unity there is a distortion of love. Wherever there is a failure of harmony, correspondence or cooperation throughout a personal interaction, there is a betrayal of covenant love.

Again, the ultimate grounding for this pattern of relationship is found within the eternal triune relationships in which the unity of the Spirit, the Father and the Son are eternally distinct yet unified in holy love in one being.[22] There is a coordination and correspondence of Father and Son in the Spirit in that there is a mutual love, a mutual glorification and a mutual knowing, willing and purposing, such that there is a reflection of the Father in the Son and of the Son in the Father (Jn 17). Human being then can be said to be personal being in relationship essentially with God and correspondingly with others in which the covenantal love of God is manifested. This covenantal love is personal, transforming and extensive, and it exhibits a unity, difference, and correspondence of persons in relation.

Implications for Persons in Racial Reconciliation
Having now laid the groundwork, we can draw out some of the implications of such a trinitarian theological anthropology for racial reconciliation.

1. Since humanity was created for being in a communion that reflects and so glorifies the triune communion, then reconciliation will be at the heart of God's eternal purposes wherever there is broken relationship. Resisting reconciliation is not just a violation of an abstract commandment; it is resistance to the essence of who we are and who God is. Resistance can only mean the rejection of the grace of God, and it constitutes a threat not just to the relationships among the races but also to our being and becoming. It is a rejection of God's essential purposes. Those unreconciled cannot enter the kingdom of God.

2. As crucial as racial reconciliation is, human identity cannot be grounded ultimately in race. The human being is essentially constituted by its relationship to God as the creature, reconciled sinner and glorified child of God. Who we are is determined in and through this relationship, and on the basis of this identity we are called to relate to others as those who also belong to God in this threefold way. The basis for racial reconciliation cannot be race but must be our renewed personhood before God.

Consequently the essential evil of racism is manifest not when someone prefers one race and denigrates another but whenever race itself is idolized.[23] Whenever race is absolutized and made the ultimate basis of human identity and value, whether my own or another's, we are guilty of idolatry. Wherever there is racial idolatry there can never be reconciliation.

Furthermore, the assertion that racial perspective is absolutely and incorrigibly determinative for our worship, theology and relationships constitutes a self-justification of our idolatry. It entails that all religion and ethics are mere mythology and self-projection. It rules out the possibility of repentance and the grace of God. It rules out reconciliation and nullifies our calling to live out our being in personal covenantal relations.

3. The rejection of the idolatry of race does not mean the denial of racial or cultural difference and value. It means that race is given its rightful and relative value as a means of glorifying God, but it is never allowed to become an end in itself. Race is given its proper meaning and enduring value only when it is subordinated to the truth and reality of the one new humanity recreated in Jesus Christ.

Making the significance of race relative does not underestimate the powerful and devastating effects of racism but rather fully acknowledges it by highlighting its true nature as idolatry. For race is never more dehumanizing than when it makes itself absolute and usurps the place of the Holy. Racism can be healed only where there is repentance for idolatry under the worship of the true God—Father, Son and Spirit.

4. Racial reconciliation cannot be accomplished merely by having each race attempt to make itself relative over and against another. This strategy of mutual relativization cannot be distinguished from mutual absolutization. It merely amounts to the promotion of a racial polytheism rather than a racial monotheism, which can only result in a war (certainly between equals) of the survival of the fittest. True reconciliation can be reached only on the basis of each race's acknowledging its ultimate allegiance to the God of all humanity and finding its defining equality not over and against each other but under the inclusive humanity of God in Christ.

5. Wherever there has been broken relationship reconciliation must proceed on the basis of the accomplished work of Christ, which has in principle created one new humanity. Racial reconciliation is not a contingent possibility but a gracious actuality that is waiting to be discovered and made manifest among us. Thus there is no excuse for not pursuing it wherever there is brokenness.

The temptation to increase psychological or moral pressure on a disobedient church by misrepresenting the grace of God as if it were conditioned by our work—a tactic utilized in all branches of the church—must be absolutely resisted. Racial reconciliation can be pursued only by faith, hope and love in the completed work of Christ. In Christ no human is my enemy. All are neighbors. Burnout in the service of racial reconciliation is a theological problem.

6. If we were created and reconciled for participation in and witness to covenantal relationship, then in freedom forgiveness must be requested and given unconditionally by all parties.

While there can be no real reconciliation without justice, making the establishment of justice a condition of offering forgiveness is a betrayal of the gospel and can never lead to reconciliation.

While there can be no real reconciliation without forgiveness, making the offering of forgiveness a condition of justice is a betrayal of the gospel and can never lead to reconciliation.[24]

7. If we were created for a covenantal communion that arises out of a freely chosen, determined and enacted love, then there can be no purely theoretical, speculative, programmatic or even legal approach to racial reconciliation. It must be pursued personally, that is, in and through interaction, communication and experimentation both within and outside institutions. As Karl Barth put it, it must be a real seeing eye to eye, a real hearing and speaking to one another, and a real serving of one another—all done gladly.[25] We will have to have real doings with one another with all the risk that entails. A history of deeper engagement will have to ensue out of faith in the living God.

8. If the norm for the shape of covenantal communion is the communion of Father, Son and Spirit and the communion of God with us in Christ, then both unity by absorption and diversity by autonomy must be rejected. Under the lordship of Christ, where race is granted its proper relative value, the unity of diverse peoples is enriched by the chastened differences, and the differences are harmonized for the sake of a unity that glorifies the triune communion and the reconciling work of God in Christ.

Consequently it should be no surprise that neither extreme of total assimilation nor complete separateness has been adopted in the debate over the problem of race. Rather we have seen an oscillation from one extreme to the other over the past century and a half. In great hope the Christian church should pursue and prophetically encourage a third way in which a true communion of unity, difference and cooperation might come to light.[26]

PART II
Scripture in Black & White

SIX

Wrestling with Scripture

Can Euro-American Christians & African-American Christians Learn to Read Scripture Together?

Michael G. Cartwright

From first to last this has been the work of God. He has reconciled us men to himself through Christ, and he has enlisted us in this service of reconciliation. What I mean is, that God was in Christ reconciling the world to himself, no longer holding men's misdeeds against them, and that he has entrusted us with the message of reconciliation. We come therefore as Christ's ambassadors. (2 Cor 5:18-20 NEB)

Let the word of Christ dwell in you richly" (Col 3:16). These words from the letter to the Colossians challenge the moral imaginations of those of us, black and white alike, who claim to be followers of Jesus Christ. What might it mean for the Word of Christ to dwell among our congregations in such a rich way that our lives, individually and corporately, were constituted by it in the richest, most morally significant sense? This question haunts Euro-American and African-American Christians alike because, in ways that both converge and diverge with one another, "We have been believers."[1] With a sense of delight as well as awe, we have borne witness to the transformative work of God in our lives, and we have testified to our hope that God has "more truth to break forth" from God's Holy Word[2] than what we have thus far discovered.

And yet we have not always followed through on what has been revealed to us. One of the great paradoxes of the history of Christianity in the United States is that Euro-American evangelicalism and the historic black church share a commitment to the centrality of Scripture, but it is precisely these communions that have been divided in American cultural history. For several years this verse from the letter to the Colossians has been an inspiring as well as haunting reminder for me of what God expects the church to look like—a reconciled body—in contrast to what most churches in America appear to be when we gather at "the most segregated hour of the week—eleven o'clock on Sunday morning," which is one of the most lamentable symbols of the absence of reconciliation between Christians that can be imagined.

As Toni Morrison has shown in evocative ways in her essays *Playing in the Dark: Whiteness and the Literary Imagination,* whether we are black or white it is by no means a straightforward task to begin to come to grips with the effects of racism on our (moral and literary) imaginations. To begin to do what Morrison calls "critical geography" is, among other things, to probe "the wider landscape"[3] of our culture and begin to identify those features of our lives that have been constituted by the mythologies of "whiteness," including the ways we do and do not read the Bible. This kind of critical inquiry cannot but be painful, as black and white alike we confront the illusions of the racist mythologies that populate our imaginations. But as Morrison also stresses, this kind of investigation need not lead only to disappointment and further alienation. At our best we will proceed with a sense of delight in what we unearth and the ways in which our moral imaginations can be enriched as we find "space for discovery, intellectual adventure and close exploration"[4] of other facets of our lives and thereby discover sources for renewal, healing and reconciliation.[5]

As Morrison's work suggests, some of the most fruitful fields for exploration of the effects of whiteness on our moral and literary imagination can be found close to home. Therefore I begin this chapter with a personal example. In 1966 I became an RA, a "Royal Ambassador for Christ" (based on the Pauline image of 2 Cor 5:20), at First Baptist Church, Mountain View, Arkansas. I can remember how excited I was as an eight-year-old to wear the uniform, to get the achievement awards (I still have my RA "shield" medallion) and to participate in various service projects of this Southern Baptist discipleship training program for boys. As I became a "Squire" and began my "Crusader Quest" up the mountain of life, making stops along the way in the "castles" of home, church and state, I learned something about what it means to be a disciple of Jesus Christ. Although this was not my only spiritual formation as a Christian, it was certainly the church program that captured my imagination as I embarked on my "Christian Adventure." Not coincidentally, it was during this time that I first made a commitment to follow Jesus. In those Wednesday-night RA chapter meetings, I learned to "serve others in Christ's name" (the RA motto) and was taught that missionary activity is central to the Christian life for those whom God has "entrusted . . . with the message of reconciliation" (2 Cor 5:20 NEB). Certainly these are significant images of discipleship for a little boy to learn.

I also learned other things in the Southern Baptist congregations of my childhood. I participated in religious ceremonies and heard sermons about the superiority of being Southern, and often I heard folks in and out of the church say that "the South shall rise again." Although my Christian education took place a century after the Civil War, vestiges of the "Lost Cause" still were present, and so I learned that the world would be a better place if folks like us—Southern Euro-Americans—were (back) in control. Along the way I also learned that most of the Christians in these congregations also believed in the segregation of the races, a belief for which I was told there was support in the Bible. After all, "the Bible says, 'birds of a feather flock together'" the old folks said. (In fact, my father had taken a 15 percent pay cut and my parents had moved across the state to a county in the Ozark hills, where few if any African-Americans lived, to avoid court-ordered busing of elementary school children to achieve racial integration.)

The same congregations that helped to form me as a person of faith were constituted in ways that effectively prevented me from imagining why it was necessary to be reconciled with African-Americans who were also Christians. Worse still, the same congregations that taught me to imagine myself as a Royal Ambassador for Christ also taught me, by precept and example, to look upon African-Americans as deficient, inferior, ugly and dangerous. It is with profound sadness that I note that it was not on the playground or in the bowling alley but in a Christian church that I remember first hearing a Euro-American adult claim that "the Bible says that interracial marriage is an abomination before God." For me this statement—and all the would-be saints of God who surround it in my memory—constitutes a landmark in the reconstruction of the critical geography of my own struggle with the mythology of whiteness.

Ultimately I left the Southern church of my childhood in large part because I came to realize that the racism within (myself and others) was not being challenged by these congregations that proclaimed to be based on the Bible but whose moral imaginations had been captured by an ideology of racial hatred. As I have come to think of this period of my life, it is as if the voice of God (the Word) was being squelched by the ideological distortions of human beings whose interests it serves that the "wildness" of the Word be domesticated and channeled and the status quo thereby remain untouched, undisturbed and unchallenged. As Dietrich Bonhoeffer might have put it, we had lost the capacity to read the Bible "against ourselves"[6] as the Word beyond our human words.

I came to believe that I had to leave the church of my childhood not only to continue to be a Christian but also to discover more about what the journey of Christian discipleship involves. In the process I have discovered other images of the Christian life that enrich my conception of the possibilities of what it might mean for me to be a royal ambassador for Christ in the fullest sense, but I have also discovered that the Christian adventure is not so much about medieval images of knighthood and crusades as it is about learning to live in the world as a community that knows what it means to live "out of control" because we bear witness to another kingdom. To live this way involves learning to see the church as a different kind of community from what I first encountered in the segregated churches of my childhood. And that in turn involves what I call wrestling with Scripture in the midst of the gospel mandate to be reconciled with one another and with God.

Can Euro-American and African-American Christians Read Scripture Together?

As the foregoing discussion suggests, I believe it is a profound mistake to attempt to answer the hermeneutical question in isolation from the question of the cultural sources and structures of our moral imaginations. This is a haunting and difficult question for anyone who knows the intertwined histories of racism and Christianity in American culture. From the Richard Allen-led exodus from Old St. George's Methodist Episcopal Church in Philadelphia in 1792 to the exclusion of an interracial couple from Barnett's Creek Baptist Church in Thomasville, Georgia, in 1996, the story of the segregated gospel is a sad litany of Euro-American failure to embody the gospel of reconciliation in the midst of the persistent refusal of African-Americans to give up hope that God's Word is operative in the world to bring about the possibility of reconciliation. There are many ways to register the failure, and at times it seems there are too few stories that embody the hope.

I deliberately began this chapter by highlighting the pathos of our situation. That I should begin in this way should not be taken as an indication that I think that Euro-Americans and African-Americans are incapable of reading Scripture together. Far from it! My argument will be that it is possible as well as necessary for us to read Scripture in communion. From the beginning we found ourselves wrestling with Scripture in the midst of our interracial struggles with one another as blacks and whites. The broader outlines of the story of the origins of the African-American Christian tradition of biblical interpretation lie in the Great Awakening that swept the American republic during the late eighteenth and early nine-teenth centuries. As Albert Raboteau, Donald Matthews and other histori-ans of Afro-American religion have shown, African slaves "responded to the Europeans' evangelical preaching and piety, especially the emphasis on conversion experience as the sign of God's acceptance of the worth of the individual, and the often spontaneous formation of communities of the converted for fellowship and mutual affirmation."

> Because testimony regarding personal experience with God was the single most important criterion—relativizing, though not obliterating social status and racial identification—for entry into the evangelical communities, and because that criterion held the promise of a degree of egalitarianism and affirmation, it was no wonder that the Africans began to respond in great numbers.[7]

So great was the power of the gospel message that African-American converts dared to imagine being reconciled with those who enslaved them, as several extant slave narratives clearly show. But as historians have also discovered, the egalitarian promise of the First and Second Great Awaken-ings was rarely realized in the interracial congregations of the North and the South.

In *Slave Religion* Raboteau recounts the story of one such interracial congregation on the American frontier in the early days of the Second Great Awakening.

> When the Forks of Elkhorn Baptist Church in Kentucky held its monthly church conference on the second Saturday of January 1806, Brother Palmer brought before the church a complaint against Brother Stephens and his wife *"for not dealing with Nancy their Negroe Woman and bringing her before the Church and for putting her in Irons."* Brother Stephens was acquitted of the charge. A second charge was brought against Sister Stephens *"for giving their Negroe Woman the lye."* Sister Stephens was acquitted of both charges. But Brother Palmer and the slave member Nancy didn't let the matter rest there: on the second Saturday of April 1806 Palmer once again *"brought a complaint against Bro. Stephens and Wife for not leeting [sic] Nancy come to see her Child. . . ."* This time Sister Stephens countered with a complaint against Nancy for falsely reporting that *"Brother Stephens said he would give her a hundred stripes and every Six stripes dip the Cow hide in Salt and Water—And saying while she was in Irons she*

suffered every day for [want of] Fire, Victuals and Water—And for saying when ever she and the Children fell out they would not hear her, but believe the Children and whip her. . . ." Decision on the charges was delayed until the next meeting, at which time Brother Stephens and Sister Stephens were once more acquitted. Nancy was found guilty and excluded from church fellowship.[8]

This incident can be taken as representative of the kind of moral problem that many Christian congregations faced in the antebellum period.[9] While the particulars in question may or may not be distinctive, many of the elements in the account are familiar: here is an asymmetrical account in which the slave is treated as less than a full member of the congregation and therefore needs someone to be her advocate in order to get a hearing before the congregation. Yet, at the same time, Nancy is regarded as a moral agent to be held accountable when her mistress wants to bring charges against her.[10] Or to use the pious language of the Second Great Awakening, she is at one and the same time a "sister in Christ" (in the "spiritual" sense as one who has responded to the gospel) and "no sister" (socially, ecclesially). What I have described hardly constitutes a reconciled community.

What happened to this "sister in the wilderness"[11] is a chilling reminder of the tragically impoverished moral imaginations of Euro-American Christians in that era. But arguably what is most remarkable about this incident is that "Sister" Nancy dared to confront the evils of the slavocracy in the context of this Baptist congregation and thereby evoked a congregational conversation in which Euro-American Christians began to confront one another about the inherent abuses and injustices of slavery. And thereby "Sister" Nancy, whether she realized it or not, raised the question of the church in relation to the world.

As Raboteau observes in his perceptive commentary on this incident,

Though she failed, it is interesting that Nancy attempted to seek recourse for her problems with her master and mistress in the church. Even though she had to do so indirectly, through a white spokesman, Brother Palmer, who voiced her accusations for her. Even so, she apparently had reason to hope that the church would intervene on her behalf or at the very least serve as a forum for her complaint. (One can only wonder if she succeeded in embarrassing Brother Stephens and Sister Stephens, and at what cost.) The church, after all, did take up her charge instead of dismissing it out of hand.[12]

Despite the fact that the congregation did eventually render its decision in this case, there is a strong sense in which this account displays the unfinished character of the church's ongoing dialogue with Scripture. I have come to think of Nancy's attempt(s) to "tell it to the church" (Mt 18:17) as a microcosm of the history of unreconciled relationship between Euro-Americans and African-Americans.[13] As such it is a haunting reminder of the church's never-ending conversation with Scripture and therefore also displays the ongoing struggle of Euro-American Christians and African-American Christians to act, to use and to embody Scripture in the midst of a culture that continues to be torn by racial strife. That is, it is about our common struggle with Scripture.

"Sister" Nancy's story also suggests some of the ideological factors that have sharply limited not only who participates in this ecclesial conversation (Nancy was given voice only through the interventions of Brother Palmer) but also the ways these ideologies can and do shape the church's conversation with Scripture, not to mention the ways we do and do not imagine ourselves being reconciled and with whom we are obligated to seek reconciliation. Then as now, Euro-American Christians and African-American Christians find it difficult to read Scripture "over against" ourselves,[14] and therefore we confront the need to continue our conversation with Christian Scripture. Moreover, this account displays the moral agency of "Sister" Nancy in attempting to "tell it to the church" (as in the famous church discipline passage of Mt 18:15-20). However much Euro-American Christians may have tried to distort the gospel, slaves like Nancy recognized the power of the Word of the gospel and simply joined the "never-ending congregational conversation"[15] with Scripture, thereby calling attention to the limits of the moral imaginations of their Euro-American counterparts.

Obviously the example that I have presented hardly constitutes a faithful performance of Scripture by the congregation in question. But then much of what we see in American congregations at present is also quite unattractive and arguably just as unfaithful. The question yet to be addressed is, What, if anything, can we learn from such incidents as this one? This is not the occasion for saying all that I think I have learned from my ongoing study of the historic black church's tradition of biblical interpretation. However, I am prepared to say at least this much: here we see a striking example of a "conflict of interpretations" in which divergent performances of Scripture are made visible in the midst of interracial struggle between Christians. This interpretive conflict is all the more remarkable precisely because of the shared ecclesial practices of fraternal admonition and church discipline.

While there is much that is unclear about this incident, it is clear that Nancy's master and mistress believe that the Bible supports them in their dealings with their slave woman, whereas (illiterate) "Sister" Nancy obviously is engaging the gospel in a way that transcends social boundaries. And while this narrative displays a community of faith whose moral sensibilities are seriously impaired, such poverty of moral vision has almost nothing to do with the prescriptive use of Scripture associated with the practices of church discipline and fraternal admonition. In fact, I would argue that it is precisely when we explore the conflicts of interpretation that surround these practices that we begin to confront the heart of the matter: the ecclesiological issue of what it means for the church to be a "social embodiment"[16] of Scripture, which among other things has to do with the embodiment of reconciliation as the body of Christ in the world.

The fact that I place this issue simultaneously as an ecclesiological problem and a hermeneutical problem, as well as a problem at the heart of American culture, is intended to signal that I think it is tricky to answer the question *Are we reading the same Bible?* in a straightforward way without misrepresenting something important about ourselves, our relationships and our moral imaginations. Or to put the matter more pointedly, I believe that the most significant divisions between Christians in American culture are moral and theological; but in claiming this to be the case, I do not want to appear to be disacknowledging the racial divisions that have existed and continue to exist. Rather, I want to interpret the racial, as well as racist, divisions in relation to the moral failures and theological hopes. In the second part of this chapter I want to explore some of these moral and theological discontinuities, even as I try to articulate why I continue to maintain that African-American and Euro-American Christians can learn to read Scripture together, despite the fact that at times it appears as if we have been reading different Bibles.

What It Will Take to Begin Reading Scripture Together

In the conclusion of this chapter I will have more to say about the notion of the never-ending conversation with Scripture and how such a conversation needs to be focused congregationally and cross-racially. In this part of my argument I want to focus on some of the reasons why Nancy and her master and mistress could agree that it was important to "tell it to the church" (a shared practice of discipleship) but could not agree about how to interpret the Bible so as to bring the gospel to bear on the situation in which they found themselves. In the process I hope to provide a more careful explanation why I as a Euro-American Christian continue to have hope that racial reconciliation can come about in the midst of the historic failures or why I would insist that Euro-American Christians and African-American Christians can learn to read Scripture together. I have limited myself to seven claims, though these affirmations and cautions hardly exhaust the subject.

Recognizing and exposing hidden histories. Euro-American Christians and African-American Christians can learn to read Scripture together, but only if we begin to recognize and expose the hidden histories that constitute our identities as white and black in this culture. I have deliberately begun by calling attention to examples of local congregations and communities where the unreconciled state of the community of faith is at issue. I do so in part because it is local history of congregations like the Forks of the Elkhorn River Baptist Church that Euro-Americans are most tempted to forget. But as much as we would like to divorce ourselves from such scenes of the past and present, these are the contexts that oftentimes are most constitutive of our identity and therefore the contexts that most distort our Christian witness in this culture.

The problem that I am describing is what the historian and cultural critic Michael Kammen has identified as the problem of nostalgia (in relation to tradition) in American culture. As he has argued, "American culture contains a dualistic tension where myths are concerned. We can be iconoclastic [especially about European traditions] but we are much more likely to be permissive and self-indulgent about myth."[17] In *The Mystic Chords of Memory: The Transformation of Tradition in American Culture,* Kammen explores the problem of American amnesia in relation to or as a function of "the American inclination to depoliticize the past in order to minimize memories (and causes) of conflict."[18] I believe Kammen's thesis helps to account for much of what we see in our culture, especially with respect to Euro-American Christian denials of the depth of the racial fissure in American culture.

Let us not mince words but speak truth in love. The memories are very painful—so painful that most white Americans will do almost anything to avoid confronting them. Most of us who are Euro-Americans find it difficult to hear the Derrick Bell conclusion that "Racism is a permanent feature of American life."[19] But we cannot afford to deny that racist practices continue to be reproduced inside as well as outside our congregations. The question is, How do we come to grips with this cultural dynamic? Charles Long has offered one of the most trenchant analyses of this problem that I have ever read: "The religion of the American people centers around the telling and retelling of the mighty deeds of the white conquerors. This hermeneutic mask thus conceals the true experience of Americans from their very eyes."[20]

If Long is right, then we should take more seriously than we sometimes do the heuristic power of popular culture portrayals of the relationship of Euro-Americans and African-Americans, because in such portrayals interpretive masking occurs at the level of myth and symbol. James Baldwin identifies D. W. Griffith's 1915 film *The Birth of a Nation* (which was based on the Thomas Dixon novel *The Clansman*) as one of the most important popular culture mediations in this complex process of concealment. At our worst, those of us who are Euro-Americans see the world in terms of racist stereotypes portrayed in such films, narratives that mediate a picture of the world in which black men and white women are structured within what Baldwin calls the "legend of the nigger"—the image of black males as sex-starved rapists who prey upon innocent white women.[21]

So it is no accident that our relationships are so deeply conflicted in American culture, because the relationships between African-Americans and Euro-Americans are socially constructed in ways that we often find difficult to acknowledge to ourselves. As a result our divergent uses of the Bible are sometimes concealed in ways that we cannot admit, precisely because we are reading Scripture within imaginative structures that are literally peopled with culturally constructed monsters.[22] African-American Christians therefore find themselves having to deconstruct these social constructions of themselves not only in the minds of Euro-Americans but also in their own psyches. To the extent that Euro-Americans have used and continue to use the Bible to reinforce these stereotypical oppositions, African-Americans have had to disentangle Christian Scripture from the literary imagination of whiteness, which among other things means rediscovering the power of the Word as it transcends the cultural constraints imposed upon it by racist practices.

We can learn to read Scripture together if we take seriously that for much of our history Euro-Americans and African-Americans have had a different kind of struggle with the Bible. That is to say, we have wrestled with Scripture in largely separate ways.

One of my favorite examples of this tension is taken from a first-person account by a Lutheran pastor who preached to a congregation of African-American Christians at the Bethel congregation in Charleston, South Carolina. Pastor Chreitzburg found himself perplexed by the meanings ascribed to his 1862 sermon by the black congregation. Speaking of himself rather ruefully (in the third person), Chreitzburg recalled the different way that the congregation read the biblical text that was the basis of his sermon: *"What was figurative they interpreted literally."*

He thought of but one ending of the war; they quite another. He remembers the 68th Psalm as affording numerous texts for their delectation, e.g., *"Let God arise, let his enemies be scattered"; His "march through the wilderness"; "The Chariots of God are twenty thousand"; "The hill of God is as the hill of Basham";* . . . and especially, *"Though ye have lain among the pots, yet shall ye be as the wings of a dove covered with silver, and her feathers with yellow gold."* . . . It is mortifying now to think that his comprehension was not equal to the African intellect. All he thought about was relief from the servitude of sin, and freedom from the bondage of the devil; and as to the wings of silver and feathers of gold, that was only strong hyperbole for spiritual good. But they interpreted it literally in the good time coming, which of course could not but make their ebony complexion attractive, very.[23]

Pastor Chreitzburg's way of accounting for the difference in interpretations of Psalm 68 is fascinating, if ultimately inadequate. The categories of literal and figurative readings do not do justice to the intricate ways in which the African-American Christian congregants were imaginatively reconstructing the text of the Bible in relation to the sermon of this Euro-American Christian pastor. As Chreitzburg's final comment suggests, the way African-Americans read Psalm 68 had the effect of reconfiguring the significance of their own visages not merely as individuals but also as a people.[24]

This reconfiguration of the texts of the Bible in the face of self-serving readings by Euro-Americans is also an example of what I have called the double-voiced character of the African-American Christian tradition of biblical interpretation.[25] By "double-voiced" I mean the assertion of life-affirming readings of the Bible presented in the face of dominant death-dealing interpretations. Where nineteenth-century Euro-American Christians read the Bible "for themselves," African-American Christians imaginatively reread the Bible "over against" the ideological distortions of the slavocracy.

While I believe that the double-voiced reading of Scripture characterizes the black church tradition of reading Scripture—at its best—this is not the only way that African-American Christians read the Bible. In my ongoing effort to reconstruct the tradition of African-American Christian biblical interpretation, I have learned much from an essay by Vincent Wimbush published as part of the collection on African-American biblical interpretation entitled Stony the Road We Trod. In "The Bible and African Americans" Wimbush proposed "a working outline" of five "collective readings" of the Bible by African-Americans that have emerged during the past three to four hundred years. Although each of the readings Wimbush has identified is distinct temporally and hermeneutically, they also can be seen to overlap with one another.[26]

1. *Beginning of African-American experience in the New World.* The first reading corresponds to the earliest experiences of "Rejection, Suspicion and Awe" of the Bible.[27] It roughly corresponds to the denial of African-American presence as enforced by the racist hermeneutic associated with the "curse of Ham" interpretation of Genesis. The Bible is viewed as a kind of distorted icon of the absence of African-American presence. Thus while African-Americans were awed by the power of the Bible, they were also deeply suspicious of the way the Bible was used against them, and to the extent that those uses of Scripture persuaded them that this was what the Bible said, they were also tempted to reject the Bible. More often than not they did not reject the Bible; however, they did reject the racist message imputed to Christian Scriptures.

2. *Beginning of mass conversions in the eighteenth century.* If the first reading is marked by ambivalence and rejection, Wimbush believes the second reading can best be characterized as experiential and transformative. As various historians have observed, it was only after the beginning of the religious revivals in America in the eighteenth century that enslaved Africans began to convert to Christianity in large numbers. In the process of conversion African-Americans began to appropriate the Bible for themselves as a community of faith, especially through the sermons of the slave preachers and the spirituals or slave songs. According to Wimbush, this second reading should be regarded as "foundational"[28] for all subsequent readings of Scripture in the black church tradition. "All other readings to come would in some sense be built upon and judged against it. This reading is in fact the classical reading of the biblical text for African Americans; it reflects the classical period in the history of African Americans (the eighteenth century)."[29]

3. *Beginning of independent church movements in the nineteenth century.* The "Establishment of Canon and Hermeneutical Principle" is the label Wimbush assigns to the third collective reading.[30] With this third interpretive matrix, the shape of Wimbush's "working outline" shifts significantly. Associated with the beginnings of the independent church movement among African-American Methodists and Baptists, the emergence of this third type of biblical interpretation "symbolized the oppositional (that is, primarily anti-racist) civil rights agenda and character of African American religion."[31] Wimbush characterizes the use of the Bible in this period as a "prophetic apology," meaning that African-Americans used the Bible "in

order to make self-assertive claims against a racist America that claimed to be a biblical nation."[32] During this era Galatians 3:28—"There is neither Jew nor Greek, slave nor free, male nor female, for you are all one in Christ Jesus"—becomes the *locus classicus* of what would become their central "ethical and moral principle."[33]

4. *Esoteric readings in the early twentieth century to the present.* With the fourth reading, which he describes as "Esoteric and Elitist Hermeneutical Principles and Texts," Wimbush turns to a set of twentieth-century developments that are related to a diverse collection of groups "with little or no formal ties to one another."[34] Wimbush calls for "a typology that can more accurately register the religious diversity among African Americans," and in some senses his own essay can be seen as meeting this criterion. Wimbush correlates this fourth pattern of interpretation with the reading strategies of "the Black Muslims, Black Jews, the African Orthodox, the Garvey Movement, the Holiness/Pentecostal churches, and the Reverend Ike's United Church and Science of Living Institute,"[35] all of which, while differing from one another, claim esoteric knowledge and principles of interpretation that in turn reflect their rejection of the boundaries that are accepted by "mainstream" black churches. But as Wimbush also points out, the appeal to esoteric sources of interpretation and knowledge is not the only way that the black church tradition has been challenged in the twentieth century.

5. *Late twentieth-century fundamentalism.* The fifth reading of the Bible that Wimbush identifies is said to be "largely confined" to the late twentieth century and reflects "a crisis of thinking, of security" experienced by African-Americans, prompted by the cumulative effects of a variety of social changes that have occurred since the end of the nineteenth century. Because of the magnitude of the numbers of African-Americans flocking to fundamentalist churches, Wimbush speculates about some of the reasons for this embrace of fundamentalism. "Their crisis has to do with their perception of the inadequacy of culturalist religion—African American religion—to vouchsafe, or guarantee, the traditions that are 'Christian.'" Therefore this reading of the Bible is marked by "the intentional attempt to embrace Christian traditions, specifically the attempt to interpret the Bible, without respect for the historical experiences of persons of African descent in this country."[36] Wimbush sees this turn away from history toward some "timeless" iteration of the Gospels as a development that poses grave dangers for the historic black church, as well as for the wider community of African-Americans, precisely because it disengages from the historic struggle with Euro-Americans about the persistence of racist practices in

this culture. This fifth reading constitutes a denial of the historical situation of African-Americans in American culture.

When they are taken together, these five readings display the diversity of African-American biblical interpretation as well as hint at the complex patterns of what Theophus Smith has described as the "biblical formations of black America."[37] At the same time these five readings remind us that there is another set of traditions of reading the Bible that must be taken into account—a set of Euro-American Christian readings that exists in a structured and largely oppositional relationship to each of these African-American Christian readings.

Coming to grips with conflicting interpretations. Euro-Americans and African-Americans can learn to read Scripture together, but this will not happen if we do not take into account the different ways that we have read Scripture in the past and the ways these different practices of reading Scripture help to constitute our largely segregated present. We must come to grips with the conflict of interpretations in which both African-American Christianity and Euro-American Christianity continue to be constituted.

In ways that are obvious as well as subtle, Euro-American Christian readings of the Bible and African-American Christian readings of the Bible can be said to exist alongside one another as largely segregated practices of biblical interpretation. Not incidentally these patterns of interpretation exist in relation to the social practices of our still largely segregated congregations. Of course this is not an uncommon occurrence in American popular religion.[38] However, I would argue that the peculiar ways in which ecclesiological, cultural and hermeneutic issues converge with one another demands that this conflict of interpretations be analyzed carefully. All too often, however, historians and theologians have tended to discuss these issues as if the hermeneutic issues are primarily cultural, without giving adequate attention to the ecclesiological dimensions of the interpretive conflict.

With this observation in view, I want to return to Wimbush's typology of readings. As I think Professor Wimbush would agree, the typology of five African-American readings of the Bible can also be said to serve as a kind of argument about what is most central hermeneutically for African-American engagement with the Bible. In this respect the central opposition between the third and fifth readings in his typology cannot be missed. The fifth reading (fundamentalism), which in certain respects is the most recent of the readings to come into being, is the reading that Wimbush appears to regard as the most pernicious, whereas the third reading (the black independent church movement), which is deeply embedded in the historic black church tradition, is the most favored or most significant hermeneutical model of reading for engaging the problems facing African-American Christians. At several points Wimbush makes clear that the third reading is the interpretation that has the most import for the present.

> This reading of the Bible among African Americans extends at least from the nineteenth century up to the present. It has historically reflected and shaped the ethos and thinking of the majority of African Americans. If the period of enslavement . . . represents the classical period, the nineteenth century represents the period of self-conscious articulation, consolidation, and institutionalization.[39]

Professor Wimbush also links the third reading with the African-American tradition of liberation.[40] Thus the cultural problematic associated with African-American identity comes to be seen as most central for the hermeneutical task, according to Wimbush's analysis of the hermeneutical conflict. Accordingly, Wimbush lines up passages from the writings of David Walker and Frederick Douglass, which, when grouped with the episcopal statement introducing the A.M.E. motto "God our Father; Christ our Redeemer; Man our Brother" and comparable statements made by the president of the National Baptist Convention in 1922, begin to look very much like a canonical tradition of moral wisdom that is deeply embedded in the African-American tradition. And this canonical tradition of moral wisdom Wimbush sees being rearticulated in the black theology movement, albeit with new slants and new emphases, from new positions (in the academy) in American culture.

I have found Wimbush's outline of African-American readings of the Bible to be suggestive for my own ongoing attempt to reconstruct the black church hermeneutic in relation to the interpretive practices of Euro-American Protestantism. What intrigues me about Wimbush's outline is that his own typology of readings can be said to be constructed within the context of a complex conflict of interpretations: an ongoing conflict between African-American Christianity and Euro-American Christianity (although Wimbush does not appear to realize that this is the case). It is also important to notice that Wimbush's own disposition to this conflict of interpretations has been shaped in a positive sense by the black theology movement, which he sees in substantial continuity with the third reading, and negatively by his reaction to black evangelicals. As such, Wimbush's outline needs to be expanded in several senses precisely because of the conflict of interpretations that it both presupposes and at least to some extent obscures.

This becomes clearer when Wimbush's earlier article " 'Rescue the Perishing': The Importance of Biblical Scholarship in Black Christianity" is brought into view. In that essay Wimbush identified the interpretive problem in a similar way, except that he characterizes the problem more oppositionally as a conflict between being black and evangelical. He sees the latter orientation as traducing all that is exemplary in the African-American tradition of biblical interpretation. Wimbush opines:

> A strange and frightening thing has happened to black people—including black Christians—on their way to progress and liberation. As the larger society has eased a bit its oppressive grip on the black community, granting, for example, limited educational opportunities, a very unfortunate specter has appeared—the white specter of doctrinalist Christianity in the black community.[41]

Wimbush concludes "Rescue the Perishing" by offering the following provocative diagnosis of the problem facing the black church: "Black evangelical Christianity, for example, is more *evangelical* (read: doctrinalist, traditionally nonblack) than *black*."[42]

I have puzzled over this statement since I first read it several years ago, not because the statement itself is unclear but because it is not clear what kinds of practices it is supposed to describe. What is obvious about the statement is that Wimbush thinks contemporary African-American evangelicals are largely fundamentalist (or monological as opposed to double-voiced) in the way they read Scripture. But what is less clear is what social practices Wimbush has in mind that presumably would make someone like William E. Pannell or Ronald C. Potter less black because these men are clearly identifiable as evangelical in the way they live the Christian faith. In correspondence with Professor Wimbush I have tried to clarify this issue by inquiring about how he understands this circumstance to have come about. He responded to my query this way:

> As for fundamentalism, I am convinced that Black religion, always conservative evangelical, was never before the last couple of decades, allowed the luxury of being defined in any of its diverse parts as fundamentalist. This is because of virulent racism in the United States. So black religion had always ultimately to be racialist—in response to dominant culture. Only the last couple of decades allowed a relaxation such that Black religion could relax on race issues. But then it found itself stuck with the conservative evangelical language! And some—this is the rub—have begun to take this seriously. That is, to define the black religious world according to the rhetorics and language of Protestant

evangelicalism and fundamentalism. The Black culturalist aspect got underplayed or lost. None of this means that there was not black fundamentalism in the early twentieth century. But lynchings, etc., did not allow blacks to make their religious world anything other than anti-racialist.[43]

I find Wimbush's remarks helpful because they bring into view the cultural history that informs his judgment. Surely he is correct to remind us of the ways in which "the ethics of Jim Crow"[44] constituted a reign of terror for African-American Christians in the late nineteenth and early twentieth centuries. In that respect he does advance our understanding of the interpretive conflict by locating fundamentalism as a reaction to a particular cultural situation. And surely Professor Wimbush is also correct to call attention to the pathos of African-Americans who describe themselves and the God they worship in such dehistoricized ways.

I am concerned, however, that Vincent Wimbush's reaction to this state of affairs appears to thrust African-American evangelicals into an overdetermined dilemma, one in which there appears to be no ecclesial resources available for resolution of the dilemma. If we take Wimbush at his word, then black evangelicals do not have the conceptual resources available—except through liberatory biblical scholarship, it would seem—to engage the problem of racism. Quite literally Wimbush points to biblical scholars, not the Holy Spirit or the interpretive practices of the black church, as the means by which African-Americans can be "rescued" from the destructive patterns of reading the Bible displayed in the esoteric and fundamentalist readings of the Bible.

In effect, if not in intent, Wimbush appears to deny the possibility of a theological reading of Scripture that would resituate both the cultural reading that he advocates and the fundamentalist reading that he clearly finds to be inadequate. I regret that space does not permit me to unfold several such alternative readings. But in some sense it may not be necessary for me to do so, because African-American Christian theologians such as Willie Jennings and Cheryl Sanders (as well as others represented in this volume) are beginning to enunciate readings that not only are oriented within richly ecclesiological and pneumatological practices and embodiments of the gospel but also engage the cultural issues that cause Wimbush such concern.[45]

I have highlighted this issue because it is clear that Wimbush is describing a recent development, which in his view diverges sharply from the reading of the Bible that he thinks is most central to the black church

tradition (namely, the third reading). Yet it is not the kind of claim that I
believe can be said adequately to characterize the situation of the second
reading (the experiential and transformative readings of slave religion,
which are perhaps best represented by the tradition of "the spirituals"),
where there is clearly a rich overlap between Euro-American Protestants
and African-American Christians. To put the matter somewhat differently,
I fear that Wimbush has overstated the continuity between the third reading
and black theology while understating the continuities that exist between
the first and second readings, as well as ignoring the distinctive connections
between these readings and the ways African-Americans in the Holi-
ness/Pentecostal tradition read Scripture. (One might even argue that by
locating these churches as part of the "esoteric reading," Wimbush ignores
both the imaginative creativity and the faithful performance of Scripture
that has often occurred in the congregations of the Holiness/Pentecostal
churches.)

While Wimbush clearly says that the second reading is foundational, I
would argue that it is only as the third reading is resourced by such
hermeneutically rich resources as "singing of spirituals" and "preaching of
the Word" that the so-called prophetic apology can be said to continue to
be effective. In other words, Wimbush not only accepts the segregated state
of biblical interpretation in the black church but also extends it in a way that
separates it from the very practices in relation to which African-American
Christianity came into being in the context of the evangelical revivals of the
First and Second Great Awakenings.

My own assessment takes a different trajectory from Wimbush's polemical
account, although I do find his typology to provide a basis for building upon.
First, I argue that it is important to situate all of these readings in relation to
Euro-American readings, both in terms of the areas of overlap and the areas of
distinction. When we do so, we discover that there are more than five readings.
(Thus far I have identified at least six sets of readings.) In each case an
African-American reading can be correlated with a Euro-American Christian
reading, either in the sense that the former is a reaction to the latter or as a
response or a refutation. At the center of this tradition is what I call the
double-voiced hermeneutic of the black church tradition, which I have argued
is embedded in the practices of singing the spirituals and preaching the Word,
practices that not only are characteristic of the independent black churches
(Wimbush's third reading) but also can be found in the "invisible institution"
of slave religion, as well as in contemporary evangelical black churches and
African-American Holiness/Pentecostal congregations.

Whereas Wimbush traces continuity in the political ethic of African-American culture, I would trace continuity in the more dialogical reading of Scripture that is embedded in the ecclesial practices of the black church tradition. Because at least some of these practices of the black church are shared with many Euro-American Christians, there is an overlap between these two traditions of biblical interpretation, an overlap that cannot be ignored precisely because it highlights the moral conflicts that exist among and between congregations that are primarily African-American and pre-dominantly Euro-American congregations. All of this means that the conflict of interpretations that exists between Euro-American Christians and African-American Christians is at one and the same time cultural and ecclesial, as well as hermeneutical. This brings me to my fourth affirmation.

Charting linkages of interpretation. We can learn to read the Bible together, but only if we understand that the "chains" of biblical interpretation can never be frozen precisely because readings of the Bible are always linked with other utterances, diachronically and synchronically.

Not to recognize this is to deny the social character of our own reading practices. That is to say, contrary to what we may initially think, traditions of interpreting Scripture are not hermetically sealed off from one another; they are more like the confluence of streams of influence. They are always moving and melding, clashing and splashing over one another, and therefore can be said to influence one another, even if the interpreters, critics and analysts are not always aware of this fact. When we take the time to chart the linkages that exist across time (diachronically) and at any given point in time (synchronically), we begin to discover the ways in which the "chains of signification" still exist between the historic black church and Euro-American Christianity.

To illustrate this point, I want to gesture toward some nineteenth-century developments that are roughly contemporaneous and that initially may appear to have little to do with one another but, I would argue, have much to do with the ways biblical interpretation in the black church and Euro-American Christian congregations came to be segregated from one another. I have chosen to focus on the period of time immediately following the Civil War, a time of great social upheaval for African-Americans and Euro-Americans alike, as well as a time when Christians in America, black and white, found the shape of their congregations and practices changing in a variety of ways.

The first example, oddly enough, is architectural and musical. Memorial Hall at Fisk University stands as a monument to the extraordinary cultural achievements of the justly famous Jubilee Singers, whose tours throughout the United States and Great Britain during the 1870s and 1880s did much to make the traditions of "the spirituals" famous as well as to provide new embodiments of African-American identity during the early years of Reconstruction. For many Euro-American Christians, the tours of the Jubilee Singers marked an important moment in the way Euro-American Christians viewed African-Americans as a people; this shift occurred when they stopped seeing African-Americans as inferior beings and began to see them for the first time as a people with gifts for culture, a moment of imaginative reorientation and dislocation for black and white alike that has best been captured by Arna Bontemps.[46]

This was also the period in which the spirituals first came to be known outside the "invisible institution" of slave religion. For African-Americans the tours and the related publications of the spirituals (with arrangements by Euro-American composers) marked a shift in the performance of the spirituals. This created a kind of dissonance for some African-American Christians as the "sorrow songs" of slavery became packaged for a wider public and over time began to be appreciated as a kind of cultural contribution not unlike the cultural offerings of the peoples of Europe. As W. E. B. Du Bois would articulate later, at the end of the nineteenth century, these songs could be seen as the most sublime expression of the "souls of black folk" and therefore "the gift of the race" to world culture.[47] Given all that transpired during the tours of the Jubilee Singers, it is appropriate that a building memorializes their national and transatlantic tours.

Memorial Hall at Fisk University is also an example of an architectural style known as frozen music—a style of brickwork that gestures to the musicality of the group of singers it was designed to commemorate. Visitors notice the way in which the vertical and horizontal lines of the building appear to move despite the fact that the bricks and mortar are set. Obviously it is not possible fully to capture the musicality of the Jubilee Singers in architecture any more than it is possible to fully capture the dynamic encounter with the Word that characterizes the practices of "singing the spirituals" and "preaching the Word" in the black church tradition. *Mutatis mutandis,* I would argue that it is a mistake for Euro-American Christians and African-American Christians to think that the dialogue with the Bible can ever be frozen. Yet that is what Euro-American readers of the Bible have often appeared to do. (And as Vincent Wimbush might argue, the fact that some African-American readers are being tempted to adopt fundamentalist readings suggests that this problem is not confined to Euro-American Christians.)

For now I want to probe into the emergence of a particular pattern of Euro-American interpretation of the Bible that epitomizes the notion of a frozen hermeneutic. The example that I have chosen to explore is dispensationalist premillennialism,[48] a hermeneutical schema that has been fairly prominent among Euro-American evangelicals and fundamentalists throughout much of the twentieth century but began to attract the attention of Euro-American evangelicals in the years immediately following the Civil War. It is intriguing to note that while there are some instances of premillennial interpretation of the Bible in the black church in the late nineteenth century, there are no instances that I have been able to uncover of premillennial dispensationalist interpretation of the Bible.[49] While I can only speculate about why this is the case, in the discussion that follows I will try to suggest some possible reasons for this divergence.

In my judgment no one has provided a more penetrating analysis of the ways in which nineteenth-century Euro-American evangelicals struggled with themselves and with God—not to mention how they wrestled with Scripture—than has Douglas Frank. In his remarkably synthetic study *Less Than Conquerors: How Evangelicals Entered the Twentieth Century,* Frank has done an admirable job of delineating the complex of interpretive practices that supported the interpretive web that we have come to know as dispensationalist premillennialism. Although he does not attempt to assess the implications of this struggle for the way evangelicals engaged and disengaged from the struggle with racism, I believe Frank's analysis provides several clues that suggest there may have been more of a relationship between the emergence of fundamentalism and "the ethics of Jim Crow" than has been noticed heretofore.

First, Frank calls attention to the change that begins in the mid-nineteenth century, when Euro-American evangelical Protestants in both the North and the South began to see their position in the culture shift in ways that they did not like. The cumulative effect of the influx of new European immigrants, the upheaval wrought by the recent Civil War, and industrial and governmental changes left them feeling that they were losing control of the culture. Frank argues that "the wildfire growth of premillennialism in the decades after the Civil War really represented a bold move on the part of evangelicals to recapture their control of history."[50] For premillennialists there could be no surprises. The fears of losing control were thus transformed into claims of possessing control. As Frank goes on to demonstrate, premillennialism alone came to be thought of as inadequate as a way of using the Bible to make sense of history. "Sometime during the 1880s and

1890s, it seems, most premillennialist evangelicals also adopted dispensationalism."[51] This is precisely the point at which John Nelson Darby's influence peaks.

Frank observes: "The genesis of Darby's unique understanding of Scripture seems to have come in the midst of his deep disillusionment with the established Church of England."[52] Darby felt that the established church was implicated in his own lack of spiritual power and his works orientation in the days before his deliverance. This assessment led Darby to offer a slightly different articulation of the declining times from the one provided by John Wesley in the eighteenth century. Darby's judgment of the situation was blunt: "The Church is in ruins." Socially speaking, Darby recognized that the church had become the world, but, oddly enough, Darby's critique of the church did not lead him to call for reform. "In his opinion, the church was beyond repair. Believers might better forsake the established church and separate themselves from this embodiment of evil, keeping their worship pure by assembling instead in small groups where, without ritual or hierarchy, they could symbolize the unity of the true church in Christ Jesus."[53]

It is equally significant that Darby thought that it was not possible to predict when the Second Coming would occur. Darby based this belief on a principle that he believed that he had discovered in the Bible. "Historical premillennialism," as Darby thought of it, viewed the church as "the spiritual successor of Israel as the people of God, comprised both of Jews and Gentiles."

> For Darby, Israel was God's earthly people and the church his heavenly people. God had pledged himself to make Israel a great nation, through which all the world would be blessed. Even though the Jews were unfaithful in keeping the Law of Moses, God was going to keep his promise, foretold in the prophets, of giving them an earthly kingdom of peace and prosperity under his personal rule. According to Darby, Jesus came to offer that kingdom and himself as Israel's long-awaited king. When the Jews rejected Jesus, God determined to create a "heavenly" people, a church made of Gentiles who acknowledged Christ as their Savior, and who lived not under law but under grace. This church would be the witness of God's salvation in the interim—of unknown duration—between Jesus' First and Second Comings. Although by this means God was postponing the establishment of the kingdom, he was not to be thwarted in fulfilling his promise to Israel. In the end, Jesus would return to establish an earthly kingdom for the Jews, to be centered in Jerusalem.

This would be the long-awaited millennium.[54]
With these conceptual distinctions in place, Darby argued that Israel and the church were located in entirely different historical dispensations. By introducing a set of Platonic distinctions, Darby refigured the relationship between the church and Israel at the same time that he set the stage for a rationalist hermeneutic.

Accordingly, Darby believed that all the Old Testament prophecies and Jesus' predictions regarding the last times referred only to Israel, not to the church.

> The church is a wholly new thing, he said, not the beneficiary of the prophecies of Israel; the church is heavenly, not earthly. This means that predicted future events are irrelevant to the church. But how could this be so? Won't the church be at least mildly affected by the unfolding of God's judgment and God's promise to the Jews? It would not, according to Darby, because of a most ingenious "biblical" teaching: the secret, pretribulational rapture of the church. Before the unfolding of the specific events of the last times, Christ will return in the air for his saints. He will secretly remove them from history, and take them with him to heaven. Then the predicted events will occur on earth: the rise of the AntiChrist, the persecution of believing Jews, the attempted destruction of Israel by the armies of the world, and the battle of Armageddon in northern Israel. Finally, at the time of this battle, after seven years of absence, the church will return to the earth with Christ at his Second Coming. The AntiChrist will be thwarted, Satan bound, the nations judged, and the millennial kingdom established in Jerusalem. Jesus will reign for a thousand years, after which he will have put down one last Satanic rebellion before the Resurrection of the Dead, the Last Judgment, and the creation of a new heaven and a new earth for his redeemed ones.[55]

With this historical eschatological schema in place, dispensationalists were able to "read each Scripture passage with a view toward putting it into its appropriate doctrinal category so that they could be sure of understanding its implications for history and prophecy aright. Their system is an intricately woven cloth with few loose threads."[56] As George Marsden and others have observed, this hermeneutic turns out to be a strange amalgam of Baconian science and Scottish commonsense realism. As Frank observes, "it was just this quality of dispensationalism—its rationalistic neatness and systematic comprehensiveness—that recommended it to the [Euro-American] evangelicals who, during the perilous times at the turn of the nineteenth century, were casting about for some means to bring history back under their control."[57]

Dispensationalism assumed the Bible to be a thinly disguised guidebook to human history: all one needed in order to decode its message and thus to acquire God's master scheme, according to dispensationalism, was a commitment to a commonsense, literalistic reading of Scripture and the assumption that Israel and the church were two very distinct entities. Using these tools, one could essentially take Scripture apart, verse by verse, and rearrange it into a tight, coherent system of truth—one, for example, that could be displayed graphically on a carefully drawn chart and hung in front of the church auditorium for all the faithful to see.[58]

C. I. Scofield of Dallas Theological Seminary capitalized on this interest in dispensationalism. Scofield stressed the importance of the "Doctrine of the Ages" for teaching students to read the Bible: "It has the same relation to the right understanding of the Scriptures that correct outline work has to map-making."[59] As Marsden has noted, dispensationalists like Scofield were predisposed "to divide and classify everything." Building on Marsden's observation, Frank probes this hermeneutical orientation to the text of the Bible.

All the better to control it. In Scofield's hands, the Bible shed its mysteries and became a jigsaw puzzle that men like Darby had fortunately figured out just in time to let Christians in on the secrets of the ages. To many evangelicals . . . Scofield's notes and dispensationalism generally came with the force of a revelation: so this is what the Bible is about! So that is why the Sermon on the Mount sounds different from Paul's gospel! The beauty of Darby's "postponed kingdom" and his secret rapture as techniques for fitting together Scripture's inconsistencies must have thrilled the souls of many a sincere believer. What a privilege: to possess in one's hand the key of all history, handed down by God himself! For many, the Bible must have seemed like a whole new book that was suddenly clear in its application to history for the first time. . . . As a way to identify with the God who was still clearly in control of history, and to be assured that the control would work to the benefit of the righteous like oneself, Scofield and his dispensational teachings were unparalleled.[60]

What we find here then is the equivalent of a frozen chain of signification in which the geography of the moral imagination has excluded the very social struggles that Euro-American evangelicals had found to be so unsettling.

The codification and canonization of dispensationalism in the Scofield Reference Bible, first published in 1909, brought about a situation in which Euro-American Christian readers came to understand that passages of the Bible have meaning or significance primarily in relation to the categories in which they are placed. As a result the dynamic of an ongoing encounter with Scripture is lost, and with this frozen hermeneutic in place, I would argue that the capacity to read Scripture over against ourselves has been largely eliminated. As Frank observes, for the reader of the Bible who thinks of himself or herself as "rightly dividing the word of truth,"[61] there are "no surprises" within dispensationalist premillennialist readings of the Bible. And, I would add, where there are no interpretive surprises there is no need to wrestle with Scripture in the midst of a nation in which the Reconstruction had been stopped, the Jim Crow regime had taken over and the hegemony of whiteness had once again reasserted itself in the imaginations of Euro-American Christians.

In effect, what Frank has sketched is a portrait of Euro-American Christians who, like biblical Jacob, find themselves wrestling with God (Gen 32:24) in the midst of their disengagement from the consequences and effects of their active evasion of the sufferings of those around them. Frank provides a fascinating as well as insightful psychosocial profile of several Euro-American Christian leaders, comparing them to the position in which the Hebrew prophet Habakkuk found himself struggling with God in the midst of a troubling era of Israel's history. As Frank shows, like Habakkuk, nineteenth-century Euro-American evangelicals had hoped to control history by using God. But they met a bigger and freer God than they expected. But whereas Habakkuk—who was not only puzzled but also anguished about the unfaithfulness of the people of God—struggled through and learned something profound about the surprising way that God was working in history to save Israel from itself, advocates of dispensational premillennialism appear to have been more interested in maintaining control than they were in discovering something new about the God who surprises.

In sum, the problem is not just that the hermeneutic of Darby, Scofield and other dispensationalists is overly tidy, abstract and narrowly focused in terms of inductive patterns of commonsense reasoning. The real problem with the dispensationalist hermeneutic is that it constitutes a way of disengaging from the historical struggle between the church and the world. More serious still is the way this hermeneutic enables Euro-Americans to escape from history, particularly the history of human suffering. Further, dispensationalist premillennialism promises that Christians will not have to suffer. That is to say, what we are dealing with is a kind of cultural fantasy in which the way that Euro-American Christians are taught to read the Bible leads them to disengage from the history of earthly struggle in the church and in the world.

But as Frank goes on to make clear, the "social vision" of the dispensationalists was also "diametrically opposed" to that of the prophets of the
Old Testament. Frank concludes his analysis with an observation about one
of the consequences of the dispensational premillennialist readings of the
Bible.

> It seems a pity that the dispensationalists so segregated the Old Testa-
> ment from the New that they inevitably diminished the importance of
> the Psalms to the church. Had they heard these cries for help as their own
> cries, they might have come to know the God that Habakkuk knew. They
> might have heard a surprising word from that God, one their common
> sense could not believe, a word of suffering but by the same token a word
> of grace. They might have recognized themselves, as Habakkuk knew
> himself, as poor and needy rather than as the controllers of a history that
> exempted them from judgment. In other words, had they heard the
> Psalms, they might also have heard the gospel in them.[62]

Lest it be missed, I would call the reader's attention to Frank's wording in
the previous paragraph. The problem stemmed from the segregation of the
Old Testament from the New, of Israel from the church, of the people of God
from human history—and by implication from those who have no choice
about whether they will suffer or not, which in that era would include the
newly freed African-American men and women who struggled in the midst
of that "unfinished revolution" known as Reconstruction.

Drawing on Frank's earlier argument, we can extend our analysis further. The problem is the result of a pattern of commonsensical thinking
about the Christian life that assumes that there is an ultimate as opposed to
a penultimate separation between Israel and the church, the kingdom of
heaven versus the kingdom of God, and so forth.[63] This kind of "spiritual
segregation" converges with and indirectly can be taken to support various
forms of social segregation that were reemerging during the era of Jim Crow.
Various kinds of prohibitions of interracial marriage, often presented as an
"abomination" before God (thereby supposedly warranted by the Bible),
are but one example that can be cited. Euro-American Christians in both
the North and the South consented to and often actively supported attempts
to segregate social spaces ranging from housing to churches to bathrooms.

Ideological segregation also converges with segregation of church practices. This is also the era when the liturgical practices of the black church
and Euro-American evangelicalism began to be so segregated. If Sandra
Sizer's analysis of the practice of singing during this period can be taken as
valid, then there is also evidence that fundamentalists were sealing them-

selves off from the practices that were so strongly present in the black church. According to Sizer, during the era of Moody and Sankey, hymns of praise were diminishing in importance. Instead, sentimental prayer hymns and exhortations to conversion increasingly were being sung by Euro-American evangelicals. Frank's conclusion focuses on the correlation with the "nest rattling" that evangelicals were experiencing in this era. "The experience . . . had taken some of the joyous praise out of the mouths of evangelicals."[64]

Make no mistake about it, the dispensationalist view of the church required just this kind of historical, eschatological and social segregation. As we have already seen, Darby's conception of "the true church" was erected upon an elaborate eschatological and historical schema cast within a set of Neo-Platonic distinctions. But it depended on an elaborate doctrinal structure as well. For Darby the true church is the "heavenly" entity, composed of "heavenly" people whose true place is with Christ in glory. As such they are "in the forefront of Christ's interest" and "the *ultimate*" of God's plan for humanity.[65] As Darby put it:

> It is this conviction that the Church is properly heavenly, in its calling and relationship with Christ, forming no part of the course of events of the earth, which makes the rapture so simple and clear: and on the other hand, it shows how the denial of its rapture brings down the Church to an earthly position, and destroys its whole spiritual character and position.[66]

This is a frozen chain of signification indeed! Consider that most powerful symbol of the Jim Crow era: after *Plessy* v. *Ferguson* (1896) there were courtrooms where African-Americans were asked to swear on a different Bible from the one that Euro-Americans swore on. Here too they bore witness to a different truth. One is tempted to say that in this case they were in fact reading a different Bible precisely because they were worshiping a different god.

In retrospect it is not too difficult to chart the ways that dispensationalist readings of the Bible contribute to the misreading and the misapplication of the gospel mandate to participate in the ministry of reconciliation in the world. The more challenging task is to explore the critical geography where cultural narratives have shaped religious practices, often in alliance with fundamentalist readings of the Bible.

Disentangling cultural and ecclesial conflicts. We can learn to read Scripture together, but not until we Euro-American Christians and African-American Christians learn to disentangle the cultural conflicts from the ecclesial conflicts and therefore recognize that as Christians we have been and are now wrestling with "the principalities and powers of this dark age."

This is a difficult matter with which to come to grips, not only because of the seeming intractability of the ecclesial conflicts in which Christians black and white find themselves, but also because of the profound sense in which we have yet to grasp the moral significance of the racial divisions within our culture. For most of us the conflicts that constitute our lives are so intricately entangled that we do not fully realize where the roots are and how these social structures distort our experience of Christianity and therefore our capacity as African-Americans and Euro-Americans to even imagine ourselves being reconciled with one another.

To begin to disentangle the two sets of conflicts requires us to make judgments that strike so close to home that those of us who are Euro-American Christians cannot bear to listen even when our African-American "brothers" and "sisters" in Christ dare to speak the truth in love to us. It is a difficult thing to have to acknowledge that what you think you are about is not what you are doing with your life. It is one thing to begin to realize the social dislocations that have contributed to compartmentalized readings of biblical texts such as 2 Corinthians 5:19-20; it is quite another to begin to realize how pervasively one's conception of Christianity has been captured by ideological structures.

Earlier in this chapter I described the significance of my having become a Royal Ambassador for Christ at eight years of age, an image of Christian identity that has stayed with me for more than thirty years and that in significant ways continues to inform how I think of myself as a Christian. I also noted that I was raised in an ethos that was strongly determined by the Lost Cause, a narrative of Southern history and particularly of the War Between the States that is marked by a distinctive moral perspective, particularly with respect to personal honor. In the wake of the Confederate defeat in 1865, many Southerners discovered an important religious lesson from their defeat in a holy war: "God's chosen people did not give up that chosen status when defeated." At one and the same time the religion of the Lost Cause manifested itself in "a paradoxical blend of fatalism and a heightened sensitivity to combat evil."[67] Interestingly, unlike dispensationalist premillennialism, the myth of the Lost Cause did not deny the necessity of suffering but placed suffering in a different context of divine purpose, as the following prayer illustrates:

> Arouse yourselves, children of God; and while you humble yourselves under the mighty hand of God, forget not that you are Christ's servants,

bound to do His work in the church militant upon earth, and to advance His kingdom wherever He may spread the banner of the Cross. Instead of permitting suffering to overcome your faith, let it rather lead you on to perfection.[68]

As early as the 1870s, educational efforts targeted children, particularly boys, with the purpose of inculcating fervor for this amalgam of religious and cultural piety. Southern Baptist ministers like J. William Jones preached a gospel that was populated by the heroes of the Confederate cause, and children and adults alike were exhorted to imitate those "Christian knights" of the Lost Cause, Stonewall Jackson and Robert E. Lee. Space does not permit me to provide the full genealogy that links the Southern Baptist Royal Ambassadors discipleship training program for boys with the efforts of Jones and other advocates of the religion of the Lost Cause; however, the imaginative connections between the two complexes of ideas clearly converge at several levels. Vestiges of the cultural fantasy of the Lost Cause focus the attention of Southerners in ways that encouraged them to ignore the reality of racial injustice.

One of the earliest, longest and perhaps most significant of the apologia for the Lost Cause was written by Edward A. Pollard, a Virginian who articulated a spiritual geography for Southern Christians that invited the defeated Confederacy to reimagine itself as God's chosen people. The final paragraphs of Pollard's peroration provide an example of the determined social resistance that the myth of the Lost Cause evoked in the years immediately after the Civil War and even today continues to evoke in some quarters.

The War has not swallowed up everything. . . . The South . . . must submit fairly and truthfully to *what the war has properly decided.* But the war properly decided only what was put in issue: the restoration of the Union and the excision of slavery; and to these two conditions the South submits. But the war did not decide negro equality; it did not decide negro suffrage; it did not decide States Rights, although it may have exploded their abuse; it did not decide the orthodoxy of the Democratic Party; it did not decide the right of a people to show dignity in misfortune, and to maintain self-respect in the face of adversity. And these things, which the war did not decide, the Southern people will still cling to, still claim, and still assert in them their rights and views.

This is not the language of insolence and faction. It is the stark letter of right, and the plain syllogism of common sense. It is not untimely or unreasonable to tell the South to cultivate her superiority as a people; to maintain her old schools of literature and scholarship; to assert, in the forms of her thought, and in the style of her manners, her peculiar civilization and to convince the North that, instead of subjugating an inferior country, she has obtained the alliance of a noble and cultivated people, and secured a bond of association with those she may be proud to call brethren.

In such a condition there may possibly be a solid and honourable peace; and one in which the South may still preserve many things dear to her in the past. There may not be a political South. Yet there may be a social and intellectual South. But if, on the other hand, the South, mistaking the consequences of the war, accepts the position of the inferior, and gives up what was never claimed or conquered in the war; surrenders her schools of intellect and thought, and is left only with the brutal desire of the conquered for "bread and games;" then indeed to her people may be applied what Tacitus wrote of those who existed under the Roman Empire: "We cannot be said to have lived, but rather to have crawled in silence, the young towards the decrepitude of age and the old to dishonorable graves."[69]

This statement is remarkable for several reasons. This is a notable attempt to freeze the transmission of the traditions of culture at a time when change is already occurring in ways that would prove to be disorienting for blacks and whites alike in the South. It is also fascinating to note the parallelism with the structures of thought that populate dispensationalist thinking, for Pollard was calling for the maintenance of a "social and intellectual South" that is not embodied as such in political institutions. His invocation of common-sense reasoning in combination with a reading strategy anchored in the plain sense of texts also locates additional areas of convergence with the hermeneutic of that former Confederate soldier from Tennessee, C. I. Scofield.

Perhaps most telling is the fact that Pollard's closing statement is prefaced by an explicit invocation of "the Christian world" that the author not only considers himself to be a part of but also clearly believes the South to be one of the foremost cultural representatives of. This is no accident. According to the historian Charles Reagan Wilson, religiosity "was at the heart of this dream"[70] of the Lost Cause. Even more significant for my purposes is the fact that Southern white clergy were among the most active proponents of this mythology. In fact, Wilson observes that Southern clergy "saw little difference between their religious and cultural values, and they promoted the link by constructing Lost Cause ritualistic forms that celebrated their regional, mythological, and theological beliefs."[71] In effect the religion of the Lost Cause provided Southerners with a renewed sense of chosenness and the possibility of spiritual victory in the aftermath of the Confederacy's political defeat. Wilson probes the powerful imagery associated with this mythology when he calls attention to the ways in which the Southern churches believed themselves to have been "baptized in blood." More significant still, these white Southern Christians also believed that if they would be faithful to their calling, they would "rise again" to greater spiritual heights.[72]

It would be a mistake to think that the mythology of the Lost Cause is a relic of the past. There are Christians in American culture today who can be found participating in the rituals, celebrations and ceremonies of this nostalgic narrative.[73] Clearly this particular ideology of whiteness continues to generate itself in the midst of new ideological challenges.

The post-Civil War mythology of the Lost Cause not only displays the accuracy of Michael Kammen's thesis about the role of myth in relation to the transformation of tradition in American culture but also provides an example of the social appeal of what I have described as a frozen hermeneutic at a time when the identity of African-Americans was being reconfigured. Although this mythology was not directly shaped by premillennialism, as Wilson has shown, the dispensationalist hermeneutic was sometimes used in the service of the religion of the Lost Cause.[74] Elsewhere William Leonard has described the significance of this mythology for Southern churches, particularly the Southern Baptist Convention,[75] but to my knowledge no one has charted the connections between the mythology of the religion of the Lost Cause and the hermeneutical schema of dispensationalist premillennialism.

It is beyond the scope of this chapter to chart all the similarities that could be noted between these two hermeneutic schemas; however, I do not think it is an accident that both of these conceptions appeal to commonsense readings of texts and that both have eschatologies that involve the triumph of the righteous chosen ones and the punishment of the wicked reprobates. Most tellingly, both provide the kind of "hermeneutic mask" (to use Charles Long's phrase) that allows Euro-Americans to hide from the facts of the matter. While the religion of the Lost Cause can be seen to deal with "the problem of the color line" more explicitly (if only by denying, as Pollard did, claims of "negro equality") than did the dispensationalist hermeneutic of Scofield and others, the dispensationalist paradigm also can be said to have negative implications for African-Americans. Well into the late twentieth century, one can find examples of "prophecy belief" interpretations of the Bible that place the black peoples of "Cush" (Gen 9—10) among the forces of Gog[76] and among the reprobate peoples who will perish during the tribulation, while white Christians are transported to heaven at the time of the rapture.[77]

I have used examples that are historically specific, personal and regional for a reason. In addition to adding insight to the ways cultural narratives influenced the religious tradition that was most determinative in my youth, it displays the displacing effect, particularly for the issue of racial reconciliation, that emerges when the Bible comes to be read in light of these kinds of ideologies with their attendant practices. As Wilson noted, the Lost Cause was not simply articulated in rather obscure historical tomes like that of Pollard; it was also transmitted in more popular ways through the liturgies and ceremonies of churches, which means that in some sense it became part of the way that young girls and boys (like me) growing up in the Southern United States were formed as Christians. When "being a Christian" and "being a Southerner" come to be so closely identified in the imaginations of church members and it is not possible for most Christians to discern the corruption of their faith by the mythology of the Lost Cause, our conception of Christian reconciliation loses much of its power as a radical force in the world, and texts like 2 Corinthians 5:19-20 lose much of their potency as the Word of God.

In this kind of situation I believe that we must begin to register the power of ideological structures in our midst, which is another way of recognizing that what we wrestle with may be larger than we think. For me this point has been made most poignantly in the following passage, which was written by a Christian living in Ruleville, Mississippi, at a time when the victories of the civil rights era had been eclipsed by the reality of racial intransigence in both the North and the South.

> We have to realize just how grave the problem is in the United States today, and I think Ephesians 6:11 and 12 helps us to know how grave the problem is, and what it is that we are up against: "Put on the whole armor of God that ye may be able to stand against the wiles of the devil. For we wrestle not against flesh and blood, but against principalities and powers, against the rulers of the darkness of this world, against spiritual wickedness in high places."[78]

The words are Fannie Lou Hamer's, but the judgment is as relevant today as it was twenty-five years ago when she first uttered this poignant judgment.

I believe that we will continue to struggle with one another and with the Bible, precisely because—whether we fully grasp the significance of the matter or not—not only are we wrestling *with Scripture* in the midst of wrestling *with one another* as black and white Christians living in American culture, but also we are wrestling with the principalities and powers (Eph 6:12) of our own time. This, I believe, is the sense in which those of us who are Christian, black and white alike, should read Derrick Bell's contention that racism is "a permanent feature of American life."[79] To invoke the strange mythological language of the New Testament is to remind ourselves that the struggle goes beyond ideological constructions of "whiteness" and theories of "ontological blackness"—and even beyond contemporary proposals and counterproposals of what it might mean to speak of "postmodern blackness"[80]—to engage a very different kind of struggle, the struggle between *church* and *world.*

But to engage this struggle requires us to learn to think outside the structures of Constantinianism. For most of us, black and white alike, this is one of the most formidable challenges we face in the reconstruction of our moral imagination. And I have come to believe that it is one of the most significant steps we can take in fulfilling our mission as Christ's ambassadors to a world in which reconciliation is so rarely evident.

Transforming our vision of the church in the world. We Euro-Americans and African-Americans can learn to read Scripture together, but we will not be able to do so unless or until we disavow Constantinianism and resolve to bring the church into visibility again as the social embodiment of a reconciled people standing over against as well as for the world. When we do so, our vision of what it means to be the church in the world is transformed and with it our imagination of what it looks like to be royal ambassadors for Christ.

One of the most challenging tasks that lies before us in exploring the critical geography of racial reconciliation is to learn to imagine the church as something different from the Constantinian image of a community of faith focused in terms of the nation-state. "Constantinianism" describes the situation of the church in relation to the nation-state in which the church succumbs to the temptation to baptize national purposes in such a way that the social embodiment of Christian peoplehood is blurred to the point that the difference between being a Christian and being an American (or Euro-American or Southerner) is no longer recognizable. It is important to observe that Constantinianism does not exist as a monolithic opposition[81] but instead constitutes an ongoing temptation wherever churches find themselves in the position in which they are tempted to wield official power or political clout. It is precisely in these kinds of situations that Euro-American Christians have been most tempted to make interracial reconciliation secondary to other objectives. Paradoxically, these other objectives include the proclamation of the gospel in evangelism, as if Christianity could be communicated and lives transformed independent of the church's social embodiment of the gospel.

The recent recommendation of the United Methodist Church's General Commission on Religion and Race to the 1996 General Conference of the UMC that persons who hold racist views not be barred from church membership in that denomination (a decision that would in effect overturn a decision of the 1992 General Conference) provides a good example of the kind of Constantinianism in which church membership becomes little more than a poor representation of discipline; as a result the social embodiment of the gospel is rendered invisible. Predictably, the "theological rationale" for this decision calls attention to the "all-inclusive" nature of God's grace and the sinfulness of all humanity, as well as the ever-present "possibility of repentance and growth in grace."

But I find it especially noteworthy that the petition on "Membership in the United Methodist Church and in Supremacist Groups" specifies that "the church, as representative of the fullness of interaction between God and the world, must open its doors to all who would enter and join in its community."[82] This is Constantinianism pure and simple. The tension between church and world has been collapsed in favor of accommodating the latter in the name of an inclusivity that Bonhoeffer would have understood to be "cheap grace." Significantly, this decision represents yet another departure from the historical Wesleyan practices of discipleship. Where once upon a time Methodists received everyone "fleeing from the wrath to come" and enjoined them to keep the "General Rules" or be turned out, it would appear that contemporary United Methodists have lost the sense of what it means to be the kind of holy people in whom reconciliation is embodied in disciplined forms of discipleship.

Of course the United Methodist Church is not the only American denomination that is making Constantinian concessions with respect to race and church membership. The Southern Baptist Church has only recently begun to express regret for its own responsibility for racism, and many Euro-American evangelical Protestant leaders have yet to express regret for their lack of leadership in the area of racial reconciliation. In my judgment the disavowal of Constantinian forms of Christianity by black and white alike is one of the most important steps that Euro-Americans must make. Here we have much to learn from the churches of the historic peace traditions, who have long struggled with the distorting effects of Constantinianism on the way the Bible is interpreted.[83]

Until recently there have been few engagements between those who have struggled against racism as part of the civil rights movement and those who have tried to live out the "free church vision" of discipleship.[84] An interesting exception is provided by Will Campbell. In "Footwashing or the New Hermeneutic?" Campbell provides a suggestive reminder of the social significance of "footwashing" as a powerful reminder of what royal servanthood should look like among the people of God (as opposed to Constantinian conceptions of royal ambassadors in which Southern whites remain in control and therefore regard themselves as the arbiters of what "serving others in the name of Christ" looks like). Campbell's essay provides a suggestive reminder of the ways that reading the Bible in the light of such a practice provides a real alternative to the inadequacies of the hermeneutic of Protestant fundamentalism as well as to whatever version of modernist New Hermeneutics we happen to be confronting at a given time.[85] Although Campbell does not develop the point as carefully as one might want him to do, his basic insight is certainly on target. Namely, with respect to racial reconciliation, the ultimate test of the adequacy of any hermeneutic theory is whether it helps us to put out the fire of racial hatred.

Campbell is also candid about another matter that many of us, black and white alike, shy away from admitting. And that is this: in the kind of world in which we live, racial reconciliation quite often is going to look "sectarian" when it is compared to those Constantinian embodiments of church where the color line is not crossed. As Brother Will explains: "But what hope is there among us, within us, the church? . . . Whatever ways for witness that we may find as Christians will be witness of *church,* or it will not be witness at all."[86] Here I would argue that we cannot underestimate the significance of what it might mean in the context of American culture to embody a mode of reconciliation that runs counter to the all-too-common practice of segregation by race. We need to recover the radically biblical sense of what it means to be a gathered community in the midst of our social differences, for only then will we begin to rediscover the signs and wonders of Christian racial reconciliation.[87] Here I have in mind communities of faith as distinctive and as socially significant as Voice of Calvary Fellowship in Jackson, Mississippi, and Azusa Christian Community in Dorchester, Massachusetts, churches (in the sense of Campbell's usage) that in different respects have disavowed the establishment idols of Euro-American Protestant Christianity as well as African-American versions of Constantinianism.[88]

To make visible our unity in Christ, then, requires that we leave aside the temptation to become chaplain to the world in favor of becoming the kind of ambassadors for Christ who bear witness to the reign of God. A good example of the way this alternative ecclesiological conception can be articulated at the level of congregational life is found in Samuel Hines's challenge a quarter of a century ago to the congregation of Washington, D.C.'s Third Street Church of God (Anderson) to become "Ambassadors for Christ in the Nation's Capital."

> We are ambassadors for Christ in the Nation's Capital, committed to be a totally open, evangelistic, metropolitan caring fellowship of believers. To this end, we are being discipled in a community of Christian faith, centered in the love of Jesus Christ and administered by the Holy Spirit. We are covenanted to honor God, obey His Word, celebrate His grace, and demonstrate a lifestyle of servanthood. Accordingly, we seek to proclaim and offer to the world a full cycle ministry of reconciliation and wholeness.[89]

As Cheryl Sanders has noted, among other things, what it means for this congregation to "offer the world a full cycle of ministry of reconciliation and wholeness" is to cross the lines of race and class and national identity. No less significant, Sanders argues, is the fact that this congregation embodies a "three-dimensional holiness ethic, mandating not only holy living for individuals but also holy worship in the churches and holy justice in the social order. . . . In the Sanctified church tradition, the possessing Spirit is the Holy Spirit, the pursuit of social justice is a holy mandate, and the purity of the saint is a testament to God's holiness."[90] Obviously the social embodiment of what it means to be a royal ambassador for Christ in this congregation is quite different from what I was taught in the Southern churches of my childhood! Significantly, as a result of having a "three-dimensional" embodiment of ethics, the congregation is able to imagine a wider set of possibilities for its ministry than do congregations whose imagination of ministry is limited to one or another of these dimensions of Christian living.

This is where I believe that Sanders's discussion of the ecclesiological significance of the practices of "the Sanctified Church" can be helpful. In *Saints in Exile* Sanders articulates the ecclesiological significance of the biblical concept of exile for the Holiness/Pentecostal strand of the black church tradition. "The exilic concept allows for honest appraisal of and response to white racism, without, at the same time, having one's own identity totally shaped by it; the dialectical understanding of existence need not become totally collapsed under the weight of oppression."[91] Sanders concludes her study with an extended discussion of the ecclesiological significance of the congregations like Third Street Church of God in Washington, D.C.

> As a faith community whose dual heritage is rooted in the evangelical imperatives of holiness and unity associated with the egalitarian Holiness movement and the fires of Azusa Street that set the Pentecostal revival ablaze in the twentieth century as a global, multicultural phenomenon, the Sanctified church in America is challenged to sustain a socially conscious and profoundly spiritual Christian witness. The worship and music of the Sanctified churches embody a host of ethical responses to the exilic existence imposed on African-Americans as a consequence of white racism, both in the church and outside of it. The genius of this embodied ethics is that it promotes racial reconciliation without obliterating racial identity.[92]

Sanders is not unaware of the "imperiled future" of the Sanctified church in a North American context marked by a wide variety of practices, including practices that look much like African-American forms of Constantinianism. Her response is to claim the hope that comes from embracing the calling to be an exilic people who display distinctive (Holiness/Pentecostal) practices of discipleship and liturgy in the midst of a cultural situation that she describes as "this North American Babylon."[93]

I believe that Sanders's discussion of the non-Constantinian approach of the "saints in exile" suggests a way forward for renewed conversation between African-Americans and Euro-Americans about what it means to embody the church in the world. Indeed Sanders's own adaptation of a typology originally developed by a Euro-American evangelical, the Episcopal priest and theologian Ephraim Radner,[94] suggests that at some levels the renewed dialogue between African-American Christians and Euro-American Christians that I and others are seeking may already have begun. But we dare not underestimate the obstacles to sustaining such dialogue between Euro-American and African-American Christians. Sanders herself notes that while several Euro-American Christian theologians have rediscovered the power of the Pentecostal tradition in recent years, "the appeal of the exilic metaphor to white Christians remains problematic."[95] The reason, I would argue, has everything to do with the continuing grip of Constantinian habits and practices in the congregations of predominantly Euro-American congregations.

Reconciliation as an ongoing process. We Euro-Americans and African-American Christians can learn to read Scripture together, but we will not be able to do so until we recognize that reconciliation is an ongoing process. Reconciliation must always take place first among the people of God, in whom the world's renewal has begun, and this may happen only as we recover and reconstruct the practices of fraternal admonition and church discipline as disciplines of discernment and reconciliation.

Racial reconciliation is one part of that ongoing process by which the lives of Christians are being transformed by God's grace. Racial reconciliation is one stage in the ultimate restoration of all things, but it should not be thought of as a stage that can be deferred. To quote a line from *A Declaration on Peace,* a little book jointly authored by representatives of the historic peace churches, "In God's people, the world's renewal has begun." More pointedly, "When the people of God embodies the way of peace now, it becomes a sacrament of salvation for the world."[96] This is what it means to be ambassadors for Christ, and anything less than such social embodiment is to opt out of what we have been called to be in the world. We must resist the Constantinian temptation to participate in practices of royal domination masked as servanthood. This is why the kinds of ministry taking place in such places at the Third Street Church of God, Azusa Christian Community in Dorchester, Massachusetts, and in Jackson, Mississippi, are so important for Euro-Americans to take seriously. Those of us who are Euro-American Christians must reimagine what it means to be Royal Ambassadors for Christ, and the way this will take place is through the practice of disciplines of discipleship like "fraternal admonition," which makes truth-telling normative for what it means to be church.

Among other things, to aspire to be a non-Constantinian church means to turn aside from variants of the cultural fantasy of "the once and future" church (the nostalgic remembrance of the apostolic era as a dehistoricized context) in favor of the here-and-now struggle to engage the apostolic mandate to embody the gospel in the world and, where necessary, over against the world. It involves congregations learning to take responsibility for our own discipline, which means that we are going to have to rediscover what it means to engage in moral "reproof" and "fraternal admonition" within and across congregations. Although these practices do exist in residual forms in various Protestant traditions, they largely exist in debased forms, and where examples can be found, they are often ignored even when articulated in provocative ways.

For example, several years ago in an article published by *Christianity Today,* Billy Graham expressed regret about his own role in neglecting the issue of racial reconciliation, but Graham's *mea culpa* on this matter came more than twenty-five years after two fellow Southern Baptist ministers wrote an open letter in which they admonished Dr. Graham as their "Baptist brother" about the meagerness of his actions in the area of racial reconciliation, given the opportunities he had to speak truth to power. James Holloway and Will Campbell did not accuse Graham of racism per se. They would have known about some of Graham's stands in the 1950s, the early days of the civil rights movement, and no doubt they appreciated the significance of those actions.[97] Rather, they admonished Graham about the way he and others went about dealing with problems like racism in relation to the ministry of evangelism.[98]

From the point of view of Holloway and Campbell, Graham was allowing his status as "court prophet" to the American presidency to structure his approach to racial reconciliation; this is the focus of the fraternal admonition by Campbell and Holloway. Graham and the "new evangelicals" had gone to great lengths in the 1950s to put themselves in the position of cultural power that they had achieved.[99] Drawing on what "the Bible says" about the role of the prophet in 1 Kings 22:1-38 (most of which they reproduced in the text of their letter), Holloway and Campbell reproved Graham for his role as court prophet in the tradition of Zedekiah, son of Kenaanah, and called on him to stand forth as a prophet of God without concern for the loss of political power and influence.[100]

Of course this is not the way Graham and many other new evangelicals have tended to think about the problem. So it is quite possible to admit, as Graham does in *Peace with God*, that "the church has failed in solving this great human problem," and shortly thereafter say, "But in the final analysis the only real solution will be found at the foot of the cross where we come together in brotherly love. The closer the people of all races get to Christ and his cross, the closer they will get to one another. . . . The ground is level at the foot of the cross."[101] But to say this kind of thing without embodying it in practice in the context of congregational life is to disengage from the reality of the struggle to be reconciled with African-Americans. It is to perpetuate the notion, advocated by Darby and others, that the church on earth really is not that important. To borrow and reapply a title from Carl F. H. Henry, this form of Constantinian disengagement might be said to be one source of the "uneasy conscience" of contemporary evangelicals. Because many Euro-American evangelicals continue to interpret the Bible within the context of a dispensational premillennialist eschatology, they do not regard the "ruin" of the church as a racially segregated body to be a terribly difficult problem, and therefore they do not engage the problem of racism in the church, because from this framework nothing "ultimate" is at stake.

Our goal as people of God who are engaged in the project of reading the Bible in reconciliation with one another should not be to be chaplain to the world. We must resist the temptation to baptize ideological commitments and programmatic projects even as we look for opportunities to engage the principalities and the powers in our own time and place. Only as we engage the world from the vantage point of the reconciled body can we proclaim the Good News to the principalities and powers and thereby live out the vocation to which we are called in hope, as ambassadors of the reconciliation that God began in Jesus Christ and that continues wherever the church is socially embodied as the reconciled body of Christ.

Reading in Reconciliation—The Church's Never-Ending Dialogue with Scripture

"Let the word of Christ dwell in you richly" (Col 3:16). This admonition by the author of Colossians describes the matrix for the ongoing conversation that Christians past and present, African-American and Euro-American alike, have had and will continue to have with Christian Scripture. Of course, what it means for the "word" of Christ to "dwell" in a community of God's people, while suggestive, is by no means straightforward. There is a sense in which it is easier to say what it does not mean than it is to convey what it could mean in the fullest or richest sense. However, I do believe that it means that the church's ongoing conversation with Scripture is constituted by the "always already" character of our relationships as the people of God whose very life together is constituted by the presence of the transformative Word of Christ.

It is in that sense that I now return to my earlier suggestion about the unfinished character of our conversations with one another and with Scripture. I suspect that the temptation will always be with us to cut short our dialogue with Scripture by creating a grid with a frozen chain of signification, whether in some version of the New Hermeneutic or within the framework of dispensationalist premillennialism. I have already noted the problem with rationalistic evangelicalism's commonsense reading (Douglas Frank) and its failure to grasp the richness of books like the Psalms with their cries of anguish and suffering. And I have tried to explain why I think that the black church's double-voiced tradition is much richer hermeneutically than the monological readings of Euro-American Christians. But I have also argued that it is possible for Euro-American evangelicals to read

Scripture in double-voiced ways;[102] our failure to do so is largely the result of truncated imaginations nurtured by the temptation of prematurely concluding our conversation with Scripture.

This possibility reminds me of a comment by C. H. Mason (an evangelical who was both black and Pentecostal), the great "Scriptural Episcopos" of the Church of God in Christ, who was fond of saying that "the church is like the eye: it has a little black in it and a little white in it, and without both it cannot see."[103] What a stunning explanation for the stunted growth of our moral imaginations in the racist climate of our culture! I have found Bishop Mason's statement to be a suggestive if oversimple image for what I have described as the never-ending congregational conversation with Scripture. By this I mean that we as Christians, black and white alike, are never at a point where we can claim to have exhausted the meanings of the Bible; that is, the chain of signification can never be frozen in time. For, as Bonhoeffer understood so well, it is "only in the infiniteness of its inner relationships" that the wholeness of God's revealing word is to be discovered.[104]

Without in any way conflating the here and now with the new Jerusalem, I think it is possible to understand Christian racial reconciliation as situated within a never-ending dialogue with Scripture, a specifically if not exclusively ecclesial kind of moral conversation that is, and I would argue should be, polyphonic precisely because it is pneumatologically centered and therefore directed by the abiding presence (Mt 18:20) of a Word outside itself. I think this is not unrelated to the kind of directionality of the Pauline counsel (1 Cor 14:26-33), which makes clear that the multivoiced congregational response to the Word is to be oriented within and purposed toward the edification of the community of disciples. "For God is not a God of disorder [confusion] but of peace" (1 Cor 14:33). "Peaceable polyphony" strikes me as one good way of describing both the directionality and the moral focus that can be linked with various chains of signification of the black church tradition, not to mention those that are to be found within the Pauline writings, the four Gospels, the Acts of the Apostles or the Apocalypse of St. John, as all of these play off the Scriptures of the Hebrew Bible.

The defining context of a faithful hermeneutic for Christian ethics (and therefore for Christian approaches to racial reconciliation) is to be discussed not only in light of the question of whether we are "loyal to the story of God's past actions," as Wayne Meeks has argued;[105] the issue is also to be engaged with respect to the question of whether we are prepared to follow in the direction of the "works of God" that "go on beyond Easter" (to invoke Gerhard Lohfink's wonderful image) precisely in the sense that "the es-

chatological, definitive, all-encompassing work of Jesus' resurrection manifests and unfolds itself now in history as the work of building the church."[106]
Therefore, synchronic polyphony and diachronic directionality need not to
be thought of as mutually exclusive. The question is: Can we fathom the
mystery that the way the church engages in moral conversation is always
already constituted not only by the various sociological and racial configurations of our historical and political situation but also, and most significantly, by the presence of the "word" of Christ in our midst? Ultimately the
richness or poverty of our "performances" of Scripture is to be measured
by the degree to which our conversation is oriented by this constitutive
Word of Christ that comes to us (from outside ourselves) to dwell in our
midst.[107]

But as L. Gregory Jones and Stephen Fowl have suggested in *Reading in
Communion,* we cannot pretend that we are being constituted by this transcendent Word if our congregations are constituted in such a way as to shut
out or silence those "outsiders" who may be in our communities and
neighborhoods.[108] Thus the greatest tragedy of the congregation of the
Elkhorn Baptist Church in 1806 may be that it lost the opportunity to bear
witness to the gospel in black and white. That is to say, the world might
have seen the presence of the evangel in the royal servanthood of an
interracial congregation in which brotherhood and sisterhood extended
beyond the color line in such a powerful way as to destroy the institutions
of slavery.

The challenge in our own time is to (re)discover and (re)imagine disciplined forms of congregational life together that are oriented within the task
of reconciliation. As a suggestive indicator of what it might look like to
participate in such a never-ending congregational conversation with Scripture, I conclude this essay with an anecdote about congregational church
discipline, this one from the era of the First Great Awakening. In *The
Autobiography of Ben Franklin* there is an account of an exchange between
Franklin and Michael Welfare (Wohlfart), leader of the Ephrata community,
which broke away from the Brethren in Germantown, Pennsylvania,
around 1730. Welfare appears to have written to Franklin to complain that
his community had been slandered and misunderstood by other groups
living in eastern Pennsylvania. Franklin had written back to suggest it would
be advisable if they would publish a copy of their discipline for all the world
to see. Michael Welfare's response to Franklin's suggestion is intriguing to
consider in view of the notion of a never-ending conversation with Scripture
that I have proposed as one basis for Euro-Americans and African-Americans

to think about how they might read Scripture together. Welfare writes that this possibility had been considered at an earlier point, but had been rejected:

When we were first drawn together as a society, it had pleased God to enlighten our minds so far as to see that some doctrines, which we once esteemed truths, were errors, and that others, which we had esteemed errors, were real truths. From time to time [God] has been pleased to afford us farther light, and our principles have been improving, and our errors diminishing. Now we are not sure that we had arrived at the end of this progression, and at the perfection of spiritual or theological knowledge; and we fear that, if we should feel ourselves as if bound and confined by it, and perhaps be unwilling to receive further improvement, and our successors still more so, as conceiving what we their elders and founders had done, to be something sacred, never departed therefrom.[109]

If I had more space, I would try to tease out several lessons from this statement by one of the Believers' Church congregations of the eighteenth century. As Donald Durnbaugh has suggested, Welfare's comments can be correlated with the principle of openness (to further light) that is found in the Quaker tradition.[110] In addition to this insight, I want to suggest a slightly different reading of Welfare's statement, one that I hope applies to the role of theology in racial reconciliation. Only congregations that are already practicing reconciliation can sustain the patient practice of discernment that takes place when we locate ourselves in the never-ending conversation with Scripture. This requires the kind of hermeneutics of discernment and reconciliation that recognizes that while the canon of Scripture may be closed, there is no end to our reading of Scripture, just as there can be no end to the work of reconciliation this side of the new Jerusalem.

The task of racial reconciliation, like the work of discernment, is an ongoing struggle that must be engaged in all places and in every generation. We can never presume that we have exhausted the riches of Scripture, because we have never read it fully. And that is another way of saying that this side of the new Jerusalem all our readings of Scripture are at best penultimate. That is to say, we know now in part (1 Cor 13:10), even with respect to Scripture, but we will read the text better when we read it in communion with one another as a witness to the capacity of the gospel to reconcile us. I do not believe that we will ever come to the point when we will stop wrestling with Scripture. To do so would be to suggest that we have domesticated Scripture, at which point it no longer comes to us as a

Word outside ourselves but only a word that we have captured within one or another ideology. To stop wrestling with Scripture is to forget what it means to read Scripture over against ourselves. To do so would be to give up on our ongoing struggle with the principalities and powers of this dark age and thereby forsake our proper vocation as ambassadors—royal servants—of the God in whom reconciliation was first embodied in our Lord and Savior Jesus Christ.

PART III
Reconciliation in Black & White

SEVEN

The Gospel & Racial Reconciliation

Craig S. Keener

Glenn Usry is one of my former students at Hood, the A.M.E. Zion seminary; he is also my coauthor of *Black Man's Religion*. The two of us used to joke about whether the Nation of Islam or the Klan would be first to kill us for that book. I am afraid that it currently looks like Glenn may win the bet, since a Muslim already warned him that someone may need to kill him for circulating information unflattering toward Islam.

But the Nation of Islam is not wrong on everything. Most of us disapprove when Black Muslims call white people "devils" for the way they have treated black people.[1] Yet we Christians often read right past Jesus' words on a related topic. According to Scripture, all people are children of the devil and bearers of his nature, until we are born again (Jn 8:44). True to what this might lead us to expect, individuals and groups throughout history have sought power over others and exploited that power once they achieved it; and white American slaveholders and racists have proved no exception. Yet granted that the racial history of the United States provides abundant illustrations of the biblical principle of human depravity, Christians also affirm the transforming power of the gospel. In other words, granted that the Nation of Islam is partly right in denouncing the white majority's general treatment of African-Americans, we might hope that history provides at least a few examples of individuals transformed by the gospel who sacrificially crossed racial boundaries. Or, if history testifies only to human depravity and not to the transforming power of the gospel, we ought to be able to demonstrate that history indicts Christians' disobedience to the gospel rather than the gospel itself.

But can the gospel genuinely prove relevant to contemporary racial questions? After all, the New Testament addressed a world quite different from ours, where differences in skin tone and other physical features were noticed but rarely understood in a prejudicial manner.[2] Nevertheless, "racism" in the sense of various cultures' viewing themselves as superior was widespread. Greeks considered non-Greeks to be barbarians,[3] and Jewish people correctly regarded the vast majority of non-Jews as idolatrous pagans. The historic barriers white oppression has created between black and white differ from the ancient barrier between Jew and Gentile, but if the gospel transcends a barrier that God himself established in Israel's history, then how much more (to borrow a rabbinic line of argument) must it transcend all other human barriers we have erected among ourselves? Because Paul focuses most fully on the gospel of reconciliation, I will address Paul's teaching in the bulk of this chapter and survey only briefly the perspectives of some of the other New Testament writers at the conclusion of our examination of Paul. After that I will provide some brief examples from U.S. history of Christians who crossed racial barriers because of their commitment to Christ. Finally, I will include a few remarks about some soteriological questions in the Bible and how the cause of racial reconciliation is hampered when the church ignores them.

The Shattered Barrier

In Ephesians Paul[4] seeks to bring unity to a church divided in part along Jewish-Gentile lines. He begins by assuring Gentile Christians that God has grafted them into the people of God, applying to the whole church many Old Testament designations concerning Israel (Eph 1:3-14; e.g., predestination; inheritance; possession).[5] As he prepares in Ephesians 2:20-22 to discuss the new temple composed of both Jew and Gentile,[6] he declares that Christ made both Jew and Gentile one (Eph 2:14). Especially when we consider Paul's social context, such a claim was entirely remarkable: not long after Paul dictated these words, riots broke out in Caesarea, the city of Paul's earlier imprisonment, with Jews and Syrians slaughtering one another.[7] Racial reconciliation sometimes demands saying what most of one's contemporaries do not wish to hear.

Paul goes on in Ephesians 2:14 to announce that Christ has shattered the dividing wall of partition between Jew and Gentile. He writes as if his hearers[8] will immediately understand the dividing wall to which Paul refers, and it does not take us long to imagine how Paul's hearers would have understood his point.

Tempting tempers in the temple. Paul's audience in the region around Ephesus would have known exactly why Paul was writing to them from prison; they were aware of the charge that he had transgressed a "dividing barrier" in the temple. The Old Testament had welcomed Gentiles to the temple alongside God's people (1 Kings 8:41-43), but by the first century the temple was a segregated institution. Because of new purity regulations,[9] the "outer court" had become the Court of Israel, limited to Jewish men; on a lower level and farther from the priestly sanctuary there was the Court of Women, beyond which Jewish women could not pass. Still farther from the sanctuary and on a lower level was the new outer court, beyond which Gentile seekers of Israel's God could not pass. Signs posted at appropriate intervals between the outer court and the Court of Women announced to Gentiles that any Gentile passing beyond that point would bear responsibility for his or her own death.[10]

Some Jews who knew of Paul's interracial ministry in Ephesus recognized an Ephesian Gentile with Paul near Jerusalem's temple and decided that Paul must have followed to its conclusion his ideal of breaking down ethnic barriers.11 Paul had actually entered the temple on an errand of racial reconciliation, affirming his Jewish identity for those who thought that he had accommodated the Gentiles too much (Acts 21:21-26).12 Nevertheless, his opponents were wrongly convinced that Paul had brought a Gentile past the dividing wall into the temple. Once word spread, a riot quickly ensued (Acts 21:27-30).13

Once the guards atop the Fortress Antonia on the Temple Mount recognized that a riot was forming, soldiers from the Roman garrison rushed down the stairs into the outer court and seized Paul from the crowds (Acts 21:31-36).[14] In the racially tense situation, the Roman commander assumed that Paul was a notorious Egyptian Jew whom he wrongly associated with a group of "assassins" (Acts 21:38).[15] (Under cover of the crowds in the temple, these "assassins" stabbed Jewish aristocrats, whom their attackers apparently viewed as the Uncle Toms of ancient Judaism.)[16]

But Paul made use of all the cultural resources at his disposal. Most Palestinian Jews were probably bilingual, but few were proficient in a

second language.[17] Thus when his interrogator heard Paul's good Greek
and learned that he was a citizen of a prominent city (Acts 21:37, 39),[18] he
allowed Paul to address the crowd—which Paul proceeded to address in
Aramaic (Acts 21:40).[19] Impressed by his fluency in the nationalistic tongue
of their ancestors, the crowd decided that the person addressing them
deserved their hearing (Acts 22:2). In his speech Paul emphasized every
possible point of identification with his nationalistic hearers, including
having been raised in Jerusalem at the feet of Gamaliel and receiving
ministry from a law-abiding Jewish Christian (Acts 22:3-5, 12).[20] Probably
because the Jerusalem church had identified so effectively with its own
culture, no one took offense as Paul narrated his encounter with the risen
Christ (Acts 22:6-20); in contrast to earlier years (Acts 12:2-3), simply talking
about Jesus no longer stirred much violence, just as talking about "salvation" does not in some segments of culture today.

But then Paul said something that lost his audience, even though he was
still expounding the *narratio*, the opening narration of his speech. Paul had
earlier appealed to Stoic values in Acts 17, finding common ground with
his hearers through much of his speech before the Areopagus (Acts 17:22-
29). He had offended many members of his audience, however, when he
pushed forward to an essential part of the gospel he could not accommodate
to his hearers' worldview (Acts 17:30-32). Now Paul again lost his audience,
but the essential part of the gospel to which he pushed—undoubtedly to
the public embarrassment of the local Christians—was that it included the
Gentile mission (Acts 22:21). On hearing this, his nationalistic audience,
who had suffered so much from the Romans and were so sure that God was
on their side, resumed their riot (Acts 22:22-23). Paul ended up in prison,
first in Caesarea and then in Rome, because he refused to compromise an
opportunity to proclaim the full implications of the gospel.

When Paul wrote to Christian congregations around Ephesus about reconciliation between Jew and Gentile, they understood what he meant by a
"dividing barrier." For Paul and for the Jewish and Gentile Christians of
western Asia Minor, no greater symbol of the barrier between Jew and Gentile
could exist than the dividing barrier in the temple. Paul declares that in the
new temple of God's Spirit, the cross of Christ has abolished that barrier.

How to have a Christian riot. Paul was not the first New Testament person
to pay a price for challenging nationalism in Jerusalem's temple. Jesus did
as well.[21]

The day the Rodney King verdict came back and the streets erupted into
violence, some members of our African-American Bible study group at

Duke University questioned the Bible's relevance to this nation's racial problem. No one much felt like having a Bible study; the preferred option was joining a protest march (which some of us later did). But when I timidly suggested the possibility of staging a Christian riot, someone demanded incredulously, "How can you have a Christian riot?" The consensus was that we could not, but some of us did stay long enough to discover that the Bible does have something to say about a rather overt act of protest Jesus staged in the temple courts.

Some scholars have traditionally doubted that Jesus could have foretold his death as the Gospels report, but the best historical evidence we have concerning Jesus indicts their skepticism. Jesus not only foretold his death; he deliberately provoked it. Some people threatened Jeremiah with death for merely prophesying against the temple (Jer 26:8-9); in the first century, the Sadducean aristocracy urged the Roman procurator to execute Joshua ben Hananiah for prophesying against the temple. Because Joshua was harmless, the governor spared his life but had him scourged until his bones showed.[22] For Jesus not only to prophesy against the temple but also to march through the outer court overturning tables meant that from that day on he was a marked man.

Scholars have proposed various reasons for Jesus' act in the temple, but Jesus provided at least a partial interpretation of his act in the Scriptures he cited. In Mark 11:17 he quotes two texts: Isaiah 56:7 and Jeremiah 7:11. The first text indicates God's ultimate purpose for the temple: a house of prayer for all nations. The Herodian temple, unlike Solomon's, segregated Gentiles from other worshipers.[23] Further, the outer court had become a site more for business transactions than for multiethnic prayer.[24] It is thus possible that Jesus was protesting the segregation of God's house. A biblical scholar would not dare venture to ask what the Lord might feel about many of our houses of worship.

The second text refers to Jeremiah's diatribe against the temple. God's people thought that the temple would protect them (Jer 7:4), but Jeremiah warned that if they did not abandon their acts of injustice toward the poor, toward crime victims, toward their spouses and toward immigrants, God was going to destroy his house (Jer 7:5-15). He would no longer allow his temple to be their "den of robbers" (Jer 7:11), the place where robbers gathered their loot assured of safety. He would make the temple like Shiloh (Jer 7:14), where his ark had once been captured and the tabernacle may have been destroyed (1 Sam 4:4, 11). Like Jeremiah, Jesus promised swift judgment on God's house where the religious leaders tolerated injustice;

some forty years later the temple lay in ruins.[25] A biblical scholar would surely not want to guess what implications such a text might have for today.

Salvation by Grace or by Race?

When Paul first met Aquila and Priscilla, they had left Rome because the emperor Claudius had commanded Jews (or on some readings, Jewish Christians) to leave (Acts 18:2).[26] When he greets them at the end of his letter to the Roman Christians, however, they have returned to Rome (Rom 16:3-4), indicating that Claudius's edict is no longer in effect, presumably because he is dead. This greeting also suggests that what had been for some years an entirely Gentile church in Rome had experienced a fresh influx of Jewish Christians. The rest of Paul's letter suggests that these Jewish and Gentile Christians with their quite different customs were not getting along.

Carrying over the prevalent perspective of their own Roman culture, the Gentile Christians seem to have despised Jewish Christians' food laws and holy days (Rom 14:1-6).[27] Many of the Jewish Christians, conversely, probably questioned the orthodoxy of Gentile Christians who did not observe the laws God had established in the Bible. Thus Paul argues for the first eleven chapters of his letter that Jew and Gentile come to God on the same terms, and neither has an automatic preference regarding God's grace.

First, Paul establishes that all humanity is equally damned. In Romans 1:18-27, Paul proves what probably no one in the church was disputing: non-Christian Gentiles were lost. He focuses on the examples of idolatry and homosexual behavior, which Jewish people considered almost exclusively Gentile sins,[28] but quickly turns to a vice list that includes sins that Jewish people also acknowledged as their own (Rom 1:28-32).[29] Romans 1 is ultimately a setup for Romans 2, in which Paul establishes that his own people are also damned, so that he may conclude in Romans 3 that all humanity is equally damned and in need of Christ (Rom 3:23-31).

Second, Paul shows that God has provided salvation for all people on the same terms. Jewish people commonly believed that they would be saved by virtue of their descent from Abraham, but Paul emphasizes that spiritual rather than merely physical descent from Abraham was what mattered (Rom 4). God had, after all, chosen Abraham when he was still a Gentile (Rom 4:10-12), as Paul's contemporaries also acknowledged.[30] But regardless of who was descended from Abraham, all of us have descended from Adam and share Adam's sin and death (Rom 5:12-21). This too was an argument that should have carried weight with the Jewish Christians.[31]

Paul did not deny that the law was a special gift to Israel (Rom 3:2) or that the law was good (Rom 7:12, 14). But no one can be made righteous by observing the law, because human nature is too sinful to keep the law adequately in its own strength. If approached through faith, the law could become God's gift of righteousness written in his people's hearts (Rom 3:27; 8:2; 9:30-32; cf. Jer 31:33; Ezek 36:27); but this was accomplished by grace, not by human merit. Paul depicts life under the law as a struggle resembling Greek depictions of reason versus one's passions[32] or Jewish traditions concerning the good and evil impulse.[33] The law enables one to know what is good but cannot transform the human heart to be good. Thus Israel's possession of Torah did not guarantee them salvation more easily than the Gentiles—a proposition that would have horrified his contemporaries.

Third, Paul closes his extended theological prologue by treating the relationship between Israel and the Gentiles more directly in Romans 9—11. Jewish people believed that God had chosen them in Abraham, but Paul establishes that not all descendants of Abraham in the Bible qualified for the promise (Rom 9:6-13). He argues that God is so sovereign that he can choose on any basis he pleases—in this context, not simply on the basis of one's ethnicity but rather on the basis of one's response to his Christ (Rom 9:24-33).[34] Jewish people could not trust their ethnic Jewishness for salvation.

Neither should Gentile Christians trust their more recently adopted Gentile Christian subculture for salvation. (Such a warning might have relevance to some modern evangelicals who assume that they are saved by virtue of being evangelicals rather than by being what evangelicals should be, that is, followers of Christ.) Paul points out that Gentiles were saved by being grafted into the people of God, but if God could break off unbelieving Jewish branches who fit into that heritage more naturally, he could certainly break off the foreign Gentile branches (Rom 11:17-22). Further, Paul believed that someday God would bring a great harvest of Jewish branches back to the tree, preparing them for Christ's return (Rom 11:23-27).[35]

Finally, Paul worked out the practical implications for the Roman Christians. They must serve one another like one body with many diverse members (Rom 12), recognize that the epitome of the law is love (Rom 13:8-10), respect one another's customs so long as they are used to glorify God (Rom 14) and embrace models of ethnic reconciliation like Christ (Rom 15:8-12) and Paul himself (Rom 15:25-27). Paul's closing exhortation is to beware of those who sow division (Rom 16:17).

Reconciliation Elsewhere in the New Testament

Although our biblical focus has been Paul, we should mention in passing that ethnic reconciliation is not a solely Pauline agenda but an issue that the ancient Mediterranean world frequently pressed upon the early Christians. The New Testament often addresses reconciliation between Jew and Gentile in the context of the Gentile mission. The book of Acts testifies eloquently to the prejudices against Gentiles that had to be overcome to secure their evangelization (e.g., Acts 10:28; 11:17-18).[36] Gentiles seem to fulfill the same function in Acts as "sinners" and other outcasts did in Luke's first volume, his Gospel. Acts opens where Luke closes, with a commission to evangelize the nations (Lk 24:47; Acts 1:8) and concludes with Paul in the heart of the Roman Empire, emphasizing the Gentile mission (Acts 28:28).

Matthew, writing to predominantly Jewish Christians, likewise lays a decisive emphasis on the Gentile mission (Mt 2:1-2; 3:9; 4:15; 8:11-12, 28; 10:15; 11:23-24; 12:40-42; 15:24-28; 16:13; 24:14; 25:32), beginning with four interracial marriages in Jesus' genealogy (Mt 1:3, 5, 6) and concluding with Jesus' final commission (Mt 28:19).[37]

Because Jesus only rarely encountered Gentiles, sometimes the Gospel writers addressed the issue of reconciliation in terms of his encounters with Samaritans. Luke addresses one encounter in Luke 17:16 and through Jesus' parable about a Samaritan being one's neighbor that one ought to love (Lk 10:29-37). John likewise shows Jesus crossing three barriers with the Samaritan woman. Much to his disciples' astonishment (Jn 4:27), Jesus crossed a gender barrier: men were not supposed to be talking with women outside the home,[38] especially in an ambiguous social setting like a well.[39] He probably also crossed a moral barrier: that she came to the well alone (Jn 4:7) probably suggests that she was not welcome to accompany the other women, presumably because of her marital history (Jn 4:18).[40]

But most important for our purposes, Jesus clearly crossed a cultural barrier by talking with a Samaritan, as she herself recognized (Jn 4:9). Because strict Jewish pietists considered Samaritan women continually unclean,[41] drinking from her vessel would also communicate ritual impurity, yet Jesus requested a drink (Jn 4:7). The narrative probably includes some allusions to the history of conflict Jews and Samaritans shared: the woman reminds Jesus that Jacob was the Samaritans' father—as if to counter the Jewish notion that he was their own (Jn 4:12).[42] Later she speaks of her people's worship on Mount Gerizim in the past tense, presumably an allusion to its destruction by a Jewish ruler about two centuries earlier (Jn 4:20).[43] Although Jesus affirms Israel's priority in salvation history (Jn

4:22), he quickly transcends the ethnic issue and identifies her as someone the Father is seeking to worship him in the Spirit (Jn 4:23-24). That John invites his audience to apply these principles to their own cross-cultural Christian relationships may be implicit in Jesus' prayer for unity among all who would believe through the apostolic witness (Jn 17:20-23).

Some Examples of Reconciliation in U.S. History

Although racial division and white oppression of blacks is dominant in U.S. history, that history nevertheless provides abundant examples that demonstrate the transforming power of the gospel.[44] Many early black churches were interracial, despite the persecution such ministry frequently invited. A white deacon may have also helped George Liele found the Silver Bluff Baptist Church in Savannah, though Liele became the leader.[45] In 1788 former slave Andrew Bryan joined a white and another black Baptist minister to start Savannah's "Ethiopian Church of Jesus Christ."[46] The white Baptist churches of Savannah praised Bryan for his work.[47] Other black Baptists in the South "participated in the rapid growth of legal biracial congregations," some of which belonged to local Baptist associations.[48] Slaveborn African-American David George (1743-1810), who established the first Baptist church in West Africa, earlier faced persecution for baptizing a white woman.[49]

During the Great Awakening, the evangelical revival (especially among Baptists and Methodists) "fostered an inclusiveness which could border on egalitarianism," because it stressed conversion rather than a merely intellectual approach to Christianity.[50] In this period black preachers often preached to white as well as black audiences, sometimes even starting interracial churches.[51] In her first published poem, black poet Phillis Wheatley praised revivalist George Whitefield for the hope his message brought her people.[52] As Lerone Bennett Jr., historian and senior editor of *Ebony*, points out concerning the late 1700s, "Baptists and Methodists strongly condemned slavery," and blacks "like Joshua Bishop of Virginia and Lemuel Haynes of New England pastored white churches."[53]

> For the most part, northern black Christians adhered to the Protestant revivalist doctrines of the antebellum period. Those doctrines tended to brand slavery a sin, thereby making opposition to slavery a sign of holiness and a Christian duty. . . . The American antislavery and reform movements were directly related to the evangelical movement of the early nineteenth century.[54]

Already in 1710, Anglican bishop William Fleetwood attacked American slaveholders for withholding Christianity from their slaves and went on to attack slavery itself.[55] Quakers like John Woolman (1720-1772) developed Christian antislavery arguments.[56] Wesley and all the other early Methodist leaders were committed foes of slavery.[57] Southern as well as Northern evangelicals supported the 1784 Methodist General Conference when it declared slavery "contrary to the golden laws of God."[58] The 1812 General Conference of the Methodist Church ruled that "no slaveholder should be eligible to the office of local elder."[59] By 1827 the Methodists and Friends were the most active antislavery denominations,[60] but many Baptists,[61] Presbyterians[62] and others also joined the cause.[63] The few minutes of Baptist meetings and letters of Baptist missionaries from the 1700s reveal considerable Baptist opposition to slavery.[64]

Some white Christians went further than nonviolent opposition to slavery. Both John Brown and George Boxley led slave revolts,[65] and Northern African-Americans honored Brown.[66] As early as 1741 slaveholders suspected white missionaries of involvement with slave insurrections,[67] and the governor of Virginia in 1831 even blamed white Christian perspectives for influencing Nat Turner's revolt, although he and his contemporaries recognized that black biblical perspectives were still more critical.[68]

One could also list numerous examples of whites who stood for justice after slavery. White statesman Thaddeus Stevens fought in Congress for Reconstruction and chose burial in a black cemetery. His gravestone includes the epitaph he chose for himself:

I repose in this quiet and secluded spot,

Not from any natural preference for solitude,

But finding other cemeteries limited by charter rules as to race,

I have chosen this that I might illustrate in my death

The principles which I have advocated through a long life,

Equality of Man before his Creator.[69]

In the civil rights era, the Reverend Bruce Klunder, a white minister, laid himself in the path of a bulldozer to protest construction of a segregated school in Cleveland, Ohio, and was crushed to death.[70]

Examples of interracial efforts for justice and reconciliation could be multiplied, but if we wished, we could list no fewer examples of Christians' failures to work for reconciliation. History testifies both to human depravity and to the gospel's transforming power, but in most periods it testifies more to the former than to the latter, simply because few Christians express adequate commitment to Christ to stand fully for his values against those of their culture. Thus, for example, while churches in the earliest period did not promote slavery and some actively opposed it, most failed to address the issue,[71] just as most people today, Christian and non-Christian, remain silent on most of the injustices practiced in various parts of the world (including the widespread practice of torture, extrajudicial executions and massive slavery well documented around the world, sometimes with our fellow Christians as the victims).

Likewise, many of the Christian abolitionists feared taking a public stand for "amalgamation"—mixing of whites and blacks in public meetings—lest they be viewed as too radical and thereby hurt the antislavery cause. Most of the male abolitionists counseled the Philadelphia Women's Antislavery Convention in 1838 not to provoke trouble by meeting together as a racially mixed group. The public outcry against the amalgamation was so severe that Philadelphians burned to the ground the place in which the women had met. Nevertheless, the black and white women met again the next day and courageously issued the following statement:

Resolved,

That prejudice against color is the very spirit of slavery, sinful in those who indulge in it, and is the fire which is consuming the happiness and energies of the free people of color.

That it is, therefore, the duty of abolitionists to identify themselves with these oppressed Americans, by sitting with them in places of worship, by appearing with them in our streets . . . by visiting them at their homes and encouraging them to visit us, receiving them as we do our white fellow citizens.[72]

Such examples do reinforce hope for more courageous disciples today.

Other Soteriological Issues Relevant to Reconciliation

Much of the black church has escaped the dichotomy between prophetic concern for justice on the one hand and commitment to evangelism and personal piety on the other that has divided much of the white church since the early part of the twentieth century.[73] Unlike most evangelicals today, most of the abolitionists had a fully evangelical theology that addressed both personal holiness and societal injustice.[74] While many of the white churches abandoned the fuller understanding of the gospel found in much of nineteenth-century evangelicalism,[75] many African-American Christians never had that option.[76]

Some people suppose that the prophetic concern for justice, while important, is not central to our faith as Christians; but they have read their traditions' soteriology into Scripture rather than heeding Scripture's full message. Consider texts like the following:

> "He pled the cause of the afflicted and needy;
> Then it was well.
> Is not that what it means to know Me?"
> Declares the LORD. (Jer 22:16 NASB)

> "Learn to do good;
> Seek justice,
> Reprove the ruthless;
> Defend the orphan,
> Plead for the widow.
> "Come now, and let us reason together,"
> Says the LORD.
> "Though your sins are as scarlet,
> They will be as white as snow;
> Though they are red like crimson,
> They will be like wool.
> If you consent and obey,
> You will eat the best of the land;
> But if you refuse and rebel,
> You will be devoured by the sword." (Is 1:17-20 NASB)

> What use is it, my brethren, if a man says he has faith, but he has no works? Can that faith save him? If a brother or sister is without clothing and in need of daily food, and one of you says to them, "Go in peace, be warmed and be filled," and yet you do not give them what is necessary for their body, what use is that? (Jas 2:14-16 NASB)

Luke is one writer who heavily emphasizes what we would call social concern. When people who have come for John's baptism of repentance ask him what they should do as the necessary fruit of repentance, John declares, "The man with two tunics should share with him who has none, and the one who has food should do the same" (Lk 3:11). Jesus announced, "In the same way, any of you who does not give up everything he has cannot be my disciple" (Lk 14:33). Luke also reports the sacrificial lifestyle of the early Christians, who valued one another more highly than they valued their own possessions (Acts 2:44-45). The only clue for why the rich man in the story of Lazarus was damned is that he allowed Lazarus to starve to death at his doorstep (Lk 16:25). Of course this could never happen to professed Christians in North America today; our society is too sophisticated to let starving people get near our doorsteps. Yet one wonders if knowledge of their need, rather than geographical proximity, is not the real point (2 Cor 8—9).

According to the biblical gospel, saving faith is something on which we stake our lives, not merely a fire escape. Biblical conversion involves salvation from sin's power, not only from hell. This transformation will ultimately produce the Spirit's fruit of love, and love demands a concern for justice once we understand the issues. Some thoroughly evangelical white ministers have told me of congregations they have served where professedly born-again Christians belonged to the Klan. Most black Christians I know have a problem with the idea that an active Klan member is genuinely converted. Which perspective better reveals a biblical soteriology?

For true dialogue to take place, many white churches are going to have to come to grips with their selective piety concerning social and political agendas. Dialogue does not mean that all of us will come to the same conclusions about methods to achieve justice or even the particular issues on which we lay our emphasis, but it does demand that we humbly listen to what our dialogue partners have to say. For the most part white evangelicals have not listened to the perspectives of black church leaders on issues that often affect the black church directly. Is the coercive power of a voting majority that ignores minority concerns less oppressive in principle than slaveholders who imposed their will on slaves? Can we act in such a manner and yet obey the example of Christ, who came to serve and counted not power a thing to be grasped?

Conclusion

Soteriology has important ramifications for ecclesiology. In other words, how we understand the gospel affects how urgently we approach the unity of Christ's body. That biblical writers proclaimed racial reconciliation based on our common means of salvation has practical implications for us. Because they together constitute a spiritual minority in workplaces and schools, Christians of different races and cultures often fulfill those implications, but the implications are more daunting and more disturbing for ministers, professors or denominational leaders whose entire circle of fellowship exists in largely segregated religious institutions.

Many white conservative evangelicals invite dialogue only from black Christians who can speak conservative evangelical language and become frustrated when many of even those black Christians turn out to be less "safe" than they had hoped. If I can extrapolate safely from the circles with which I am familiar, there are probably millions of born-again Christians in black Pentecostal, Baptist and Methodist churches, yet most of them are unfamiliar with the label *evangelical*. Despite a number of notable exceptions, most white evangelicals who talk about reconciliation have not sacrificed the time or the energy to explore relationships in those circles. By limiting the dialogue to African-American Christians who are willing to use "evangelical" labels, white conservative evangelicals essentially limit the dialogue to those African-American Christians who already have intentionally crossed the racial barrier.

If these observations are correct, black evangelicals have borne a much heavier part of the burden in seeking reconciliation than white evangelicals have, although many white evangelicals seem unaware of this situation. White Christians who are serious about reconciliation are going to have to cross ecclesiastical as well as color boundaries, boundaries of longstanding cultural church traditions as well as boundaries of ethnicity. Such barriers can be crossed only if we unite on the basis of our common need before our Lord Jesus Christ, who has reconciled us all to the Father in one body by his cross. May we hear the pain of the One whose body we have dared rend asunder by our prejudices, and may we genuinely heed the truth of his gospel—in the name of the One we claim as Lord.

EIGHT

Acts 10:34, a Text for Racial & Cultural Reconciliation Among Christians

J. Julius Scott Jr.

T he interpretive tradition from which many of us come affirms the relevance of biblical teachings for contemporary situations and issues. There is less agreement on the basis and method for making these applications. I propose an interpretive stance that, although it may be simply stated, is neither uncomplicated in its operation nor universal in its acceptance. Nevertheless, it provides a platform for surveying biblical and theological implications for racial reconciliation in the United States in our day.

Methodological Assumptions
I begin interpretation with the assumption that the Christian faith is not primarily a religion of doctrines, liturgies and laws, although each of these in its proper place has a function. Christianity is first and foremost a favorable, accepting relationship with God made possible through the person and work of Jesus Christ in accordance with the divine plan for redemption and reconciliation. It also involves relationships with others of like faith as the church community and as individuals who are a part of that group. This relationship with God, although it is not earned by human works or behavior, has moral, ethical and social implications. The believer

is to walk or behave worthily, in a manner appropriate to the nature and character of the God with whom he or she is in relation.[1] The Christian ethic is to live in a manner so as to "please God" (1 Thess 2:4; 4:1). The Christian's goals, standards, attitudes and directives are the basic moral and spiritual principles that are rooted in the very nature of God himself. "Good" is that which is in harmony with God's nature and which pleases him; wrong is that which is out of harmony with his nature and displeases God.

The person, nature, will and works of God are made known to us in the Scriptures. In them we see God at work as Creator, Redeemer and the One who lives in relationship with his own people. Of course it is supremely in Jesus Christ that we learn of God; it is in Christ that we see the glory, that is, God's very nature (cf. Jn 1:14).

Occasionally in Scripture God speaks in clear, objective, factual statements about himself, his works and will. More often we learn of God in his acts as Scripture relates them. We see him in action and involved with all kinds of people and situations in different periods of history and geographical locations and within a variety of cultures. From these events and the record of them we come to discern what God requires and what pleases him: namely, those moral and spiritual principles emanating from God's being that must be our directives for life lived in relationship with him. The expression and application of them may differ from time to time and place to place, but the principles themselves are as permanent and unchangeable as God. This means that our present concerns require us to ask about the implications of God's nature for race relations and racial reconciliation.

In this study we will focus our attention upon a single text, Acts 10:34. A contextual examination of this text should yield biblical and theological principles with reference to racial reconciliation. We have selected this verse in part because it clearly links racial and cultural matters with a significant feature of God's nature, and in part for a reason to be noted later.

The Theological Foundation: God's Character of Impartiality

Peter had just arrived in the thoroughly Hellenistic Gentile city of Caesarea on the coast of the land of Israel. He entered the house of Cornelius, a Gentile, an officer in the Roman army of occupation. From the Jewish point of view, Cornelius was a person who was ceremonially unclean and with whom contact could bring ritual uncleanness upon an observant Jew. Peter had come only because of a thrice-repeated vision involving unclean, nonkosher foods in which he had been told, "What God has cleansed you must not call common" (Acts 10:15 NKJV). Furthermore, God had instructed Peter that three men were looking for him and he was to "Arise, go downstairs, and accompany them without misgivings; for I have sent them Myself" (Acts 10:20 NASB). Upon arriving in the centurion's house, Peter said to Cornelius and his friends, "In truth I perceive that God shows no partiality,[2] but in every nation whoever fears him and works righteousness is accepted by him" (Acts 10:34-35, my translation).

Note that Peter takes the lesson he learned from the vision, which dealt with foods, and applies it to persons.[3] As he does so he unites it with a long-recognized aspect of God's nature that for Peter became the basis for attitudes and actions in a new situation.

The impartiality of God4 is a theme occurring in both the Old and New Testaments and in early Christian literature. It has important implications for the attitudes and life of God's people. The initial affirmation of God as one who is wholly impartial is in Deuteronomy 10:17 (NKJV): "The LORD your God is God of gods and Lord of lords, the great God, mighty and awesome, who shows no partiality."5 Clearly God's nature is reflected in his impartiality. This is evidenced by the fact that he takes no bribe. "He administers justice for the fatherless and the widow, and loves the stranger, giving him food and clothing" (Deut 10:17-18 NKJV). Note that the passage not only affirms that God gives justice to disadvantaged citizens but also goes further in affirming his love for the sojourner, the stranger—the ger, the non-Hebrew, the resident alien Gentile who lived in the land of Israel. This is a remarkable Old Testament affirmation of the Lord's universal impartiality.

Of equal significance is that in the broader setting of the passage (Deut 10:12—11:9), the underlying emphasis is upon the unique relationship between the Lord and his chosen, covenant people. Because of this covenant relationship, Israel is to "circumcise the foreskin of your heart, and be stiff-necked no longer" (Deut 10:16 NKJV). An outgrowth of this is that Israel is to "love the stranger" (Deut 10:19 NKJV). God's people not only are to be fair (i.e., just) to the weak of their society but also are to love the foreigner, simply because God does so.

The book of Chronicles also unites the Lord's perfect justice with his impartiality and calls for the same in both the attitudes and the actions of his people. "Let the fear of the LORD be upon you; take care and do it, for there is no iniquity [perversion of justice] with the LORD our God, no partiality, nor taking of bribes" (2 Chron 19:7 NKJV). Elsewhere in the Old Testament[6] the majority of uses of "partial" or "partiality" refer to improper discrimination against people in general[7] or require fairness in judgment within God's covenant community.[8]

In the New Testament the scribes and the chief priests tried to throw Jesus off guard with the insincere compliment, "Teacher, we know that You speak and teach correctly, and You are not partial to any, but teach the way of God in truth" (Lk 20:21 NASB). They were flattering him as one who lived in accordance with the divine ideal. In Romans 2:11 (NASB) Paul characterizes the future divine judgment of both Jews and Gentiles as one in which "there is no partiality with God." In Colossians 3:25 the same point is made.

In Acts 10:34, the passage under consideration, Peter recognizes God's impartiality as the basis for determining proper candidates for inclusion in the Christian community. Ethnic background, race, culture, socioeconomic status and the rest have no part to play. There are no external prerequisites for becoming a Christian, because God is impartial. There can be no requirements for membership in the church, the body of Christ, that God has not made for salvation. Rather, "in every nation [or ethnic group] whoever fears him and works righteousness is accepted by him."[9]

The principle of nondiscrimination and its implications for determining proper candidates for salvation are also firmly recognized by Paul. Romans 10:9-13 (NASB) is a parallel to Romans 2:11, the passage just cited:

> If you confess with your mouth Jesus as Lord, and believe in your heart that God raised Him from the dead, you shall be saved; for with the heart man believes, resulting in righteousness, and with the mouth he confesses, resulting in salvation. For the Scripture says, "WHOEVER BELIEVES IN HIM WILL NOT BE DISAPPOINTED." For there is no distinction betweeen Jew and Greek; for the same Lord is LORD of all, abounding in riches for all who call upon Him; for "WHOEVER WILL CALL UPON THE NAME OF THE LORD WILL BE SAVED."

This then is the biblical context of Acts 10:34 with regard to soteriological concerns involving race and culture. The impartial nature of God that opens salvation to all is also the basis for fellowship within his body. Paul insists that because of unity in Christ, distinctions of birth and social class have no place in the church:

> For you are all sons of God through faith in Christ Jesus. For as many of you as were baptized into Christ have put on Christ. There is neither Jew nor Greek, there is neither slave nor free, there is neither male nor female; for you are all one in Christ Jesus. (Gal 3:26-28 NKJV; cf. 1 Cor 12:13; Col 3:11)

Unity that supersedes external divisions comes from a common relationship with God in Christ. Such unity among God's people is an extension and a reflection of God's nature.

In the New Testament certain relationships are specifically mentioned as those in which there is to be no discrimination among Christians because God is not a respecter of persons. These include the relationships between Christian masters and slaves (Eph 6:9), church administration (1 Tim 5:21) and the esteem and treatment of the poor within the church (Jas 2:1, 9). The principle was so sufficiently grounded within Christian thought that it was cited as a basis for conduct by at least three second-century Christian writers.[10] Has it also implications for race relations in the United States as we enter the twenty-first century? For Christians it does.

The Implied Imperative: The Church's Practice of Nondiscrimination
The implications of what we have said for racial reconciliation in the contemporary church should be obvious. The reality of differences of distinctions of race, culture, social, economic and other external factors is also obvious—and these distinctions are not going away. They are not inherently wrong, nor, as Dr. Jeremiah Wright says, are they "deficiencies."[11] They are a part of what it means to be human. Such human differences have their place.

If human differences have their place, so also does divine unity. For those who are in relationship with God, this unity must, because of God's nature, have precedence over diversity. The simple fact is that for those in Christ such differences, although they are recognized and acknowledged, should not make a difference in the way they relate to other human persons, especially to those of the household of faith. To practice such partiality is a denial of the nature and the expectations of the God to whom the Christian lifestyle must be pleasing.

The New Testament bears ample testimony to the fact that human discrimination remains, even among believers. Whether differences were rooted in race, gender, cultural background, theological leaders or loyalties (as in 1 Cor 1), charismatic experiences (1 Cor 12—14), social class (Jas 2:1-7) or any other reason, the inspired writers, without trying to settle the issues, say, "Cut it out! Your unity, which is rooted in the impartiality of God, must supersede any secondary, potentially divisive factors. You must learn to live acceptingly of diversity, knowing nothing among you except Jesus Christ, the crucified one" (1 Cor 2:2, my translation). To do otherwise, as the epistle of James implies, is to operate on a basis different from that which God used in choosing those who would be his own (Jas 3:5).

As we employ the hermeneutical postulates we outlined at the beginning of this chapter and apply the theological principles revealed and displayed in Scripture to the present situation, we may arrive at a number of conclusions.

Discrimination on the basis of external factors is wrong for those in relationship with God, who is himself not a respecter of persons. This should not be confused with the need for moral discernment on theological or moral grounds. The biblical writers do not tolerate the assumed existence or rights of other alleged deities or the claims that there are ways of becoming acceptable to God other than by grace through faith in Jesus Christ. They are also unyielding in their condemnation of conduct that is not in harmony with an appropriate Christian lifestyle.

Within the framework of an appropriate Christian lifestyle it is not necessary that all Christians adopt a common ethnic culture, strive for a uniform socio-economic level or have identical external religious experience. When theological, spiritual or moral principles are not involved, diversity is acceptable and Christians should be sensitive to the preferences of their fellow believers.[12]

Human nature being what it is after the Fall, acceptance of human diversity may be difficult for many persons, including believers. But the New Testament writers base the necessity and the possibility of doing so on the impartial nature of God. The assumption is that those living in relationship with him should not hold attitudes different from his. Furthermore, the awareness of his nature and the strength that comes from a relationship with him are sufficient to change both attitudes and behavior.

The biblical writers assert that, in the face of possibly succumbing to prejudicial and discriminatory attitudes and behavior, the believer must make a conscious decision and effort to be and do otherwise. These writers assume the presence of the power and renewing work of the Holy Spirit in these matters; nevertheless, they call for positive, conscious commitment on behalf of the individual and community. "Just do it" might be an adequate paraphrase of the biblical attitude toward objections to our protestations of the difficulty of changing long-held attitudes.

We have made theological assertions about the impartial nature of God derived from Acts 10:34 when this text is viewed in its historical, cultural setting. There are other significant features in this text. Let us note a grammatical one. In Peter's statement the verb translated "I perceive," "grasp" or "comprehend" (katalambanomai) is in the present tense, showing action in progress, while the middle voice indicates that the action is upon or for the benefit of the speaker. A better rendering would be, "I am just now in the process of coming to grasp for myself that God is not partial." Peter was aware of the Old Testament statements about the impartiality of God; he had also heard Jesus' command to "make disciples of all nations" (Mt

28:19). Yet the full impact of the implications of these realities had not registered in his mind. In the centurion's home the light finally dawned. His words attest that only then did Peter come to a personal realization of this truth about God and its consequence for the Christian community.

Up to this point, what Peter knew intellectually had not affected him existentially. Racial reconciliation is often more of a growth process than an instantaneous conversion. Christian growth is progressive. So too are the consequences of growth, including spiritual knowledge and understanding. Peter began to apprehend the fact of the impartiality of God and its repercussions in the life and mission of the church only in special circumstances; though he was given divine directives, the implications of them dawned on him only when he found himself in a new location and culture.

Acts 11, Acts 15 and Galatians 2 show that other Jewish believers who had not seen the visions or heard the voice from heaven and who had not experienced what Peter did in the house of Cornelius continued to struggle with the issues of nondiscrimination. The Jewish church as a whole came to accept it only gradually. (And human frailty would again show itself in the second century as, in a startling reversal of roles, Gentile believers discriminated against Jewish Christians.)[13] Even within the house of God, reconciliation among those separated by sociological factors may require time as well as education.

The Personal Application: A Segregationist's Gradual Change of Heart

Earlier I mentioned that there is a second reason for selecting Acts 10:34 as the focal point for this study. It is personal and autobiographical.

I am a fourth-generation Southern white American with deep-running appreciation for and pride in my regional cultural heritage. Still, there are areas of my culture and personal history of which I am ashamed and for which I must and do apologize. My great-grandfather was a slaveholder and an officer in the Confederate army. I, like my grandfather and father, was raised a racial segregationist. I had no animosity toward African-Americans and enjoyed a warm, close, personal relationship with many. Nevertheless, I never thought of the possibility of any other social structure; all those about me, including members of both racial groups, also seemed to accept it. I had a vague awareness that the same situation did not exist elsewhere, but that was where Yankees lived among proportionately fewer persons of other ethnic groups. (They also did not know the superiority of hot homemade biscuits and cornbread over cold, commercial, sliced bread.)

My experiences in Yankeeland, including four years at Wheaton College, did nothing to make me question my views. I believed I had a better attitude toward individual persons of color than did most of the non-Southerners with whom I came in contact. I finished theological seminary before the end of the 1950s; in that institution segregation was sometimes questioned and criticized, but I do not remember solid biblical or theological issues being raised against it. I served as a pastor for more than two years in central Mississippi; although the civil rights movement was beginning, it had little effect on me and those among whom I lived and served.

In 1961 I entered the doctoral program of the University of Manchester in England. My research topic had to do with the church in Jerusalem and the development of internal factions within it. In the process of that work I met anew Acts 10:34. I realized that the issue Peter faced was a racial and cultural one, not unlike that which existed in my home area.[14] I came to an awareness for myself that God does not discriminate on the basis of race or culture. Hence, although I was an admitted respecter of persons, God was not. *I realized I had the choice of either changing my racial and cultural views or giving up my biblically based Christian faith.* To paraphrase Luther, I had no choice but to adhere to the Word of God, which has possession of my conscience. Mine was, I emphasize, a conscious choice, made on the basis of what I had come to understand as the clear teaching of Scripture.

The consequences of that choice were not always easy or pleasant. I faced the disapproval of family and friends. With his special sense of humor, God put me back in Mississippi at the height of the civil rights conflict of the mid- to late 1960s. I directed my energies in racial matters toward my students, my fellow evangelical Christians and my denomination. I reasoned that if we could not address this issue on biblical grounds among fellow believers, what hope did we have among the populace at large? If judgment "begins with us first, what will be the end of those who do not obey the gospel of God" (1 Pet 4:17 NKJV)?

From the enlarged understanding of the nature of God that I had come to grasp from Acts 10:34, I insisted time and again that we cannot make requirements for church membership or Christian fellowship that God did not make for salvation. The role of the Bible and theology in my personal change was completely determinative, and by God's grace, biblical and theological principles continue to be the ideals for my thought and actions, imperfect though they be. I am convinced of the need of theology and biblical teaching, along with a proper hermeneutical approach, in dealing with the need for racial reconciliation in our day, especially among Christians, because I know it can work. Acts 10:34 with its theological implications is a crucial text for the type of cultural and sociological issues we must address in this time and place. I cannot conceive of anything else effecting such a radical change as the way that God brought this verse to bear on the life and experience of the racial segregationist I knew best.

But remember the verb in this verse and its tense. Peter said, "I am just now in the process of coming to realize for myself." The racial reconciliation I most earnestly desire—not that of changing laws and institutions, as important as they are, but of attitudes and hearts—may well come through a process rather than a crisis moment. Legal barriers may be felled with the stroke of a pen, but people may change more slowly. They may not always see things clearly, instantaneously or completely.

My father spent a lot of time with his grandfather, the slaveholder and Confederate soldier. I once asked Daddy if his grandfather had ever discussed his attitudes toward slavery with him. He answered, "No, and I always wondered how a man who was as strong a Christian as my grandfather could have owned slaves." I look back at my father, probably the strongest and most consistent Christian male I have ever met, and wonder how he could have lived out his life as a racial segregationist. Now I wonder what blind spots my children do and will see in me.[15]

PART IV
The Church in Black & White

allslip Request   1/13/2014 11:49:17 AM

equest date:1/11/2014 02:34 PM
equest ID: 43693
all Number:261.8348 OK41
em Barcode:

3 4 7 1 1 0 0 0 9 3 9 4 7 2

uthor:

- Gospel in Black and White : theological
  eration:c.1Year.
     Name:Lisa Jones
     rcode:

5 9 1 5 7 5

  omment:

equest number:

4 3 6 9 3

Route to:
I-Share Library:

Library Pick Up Location:

NINE

How We Do Church

Worship, Empowerment &
Racial Identity

Cheryl J. Sanders

Race has been a constant source of Christian disunity and discord in
U.S. church history. It can be argued that Christian racism is the predomi-
nant factor that has shaped denominational life in North American Protestant churches, many of whom split before the Civil War over the slavery
issue and have yet to be reconciled. Martin Luther King Jr.'s comment that
eleven o'clock on Sunday morning is America's most segregated hour
stands as an indictment of Christian denominational racism, which seems
virtually unaffected by the civil rights struggle and the removal of legal
barriers to racial integration in other social institutions. Racism is the
premier context for the formation of the social consciousness of African-
Americans, because all have been victimized in some way by racial discrimination, regardless of religious affiliation. By the same token, the
Christian church has generally failed to dismantle and disarm the white
racists within its own ranks, again irrespective of denomination.

The Third Street Church of God
The centerpiece of any serious discussion of the role of theology in racial
reconciliation ought to be a critical reflection upon the racially exclusive

ecclesiologies of American evangelicalism. However, I will begin by pre-
senting a concrete illustration of "how we do church" at the congregation I
serve in the city of Washington, D.C., with a view toward highlighting some
practical and theoretical aspects of the ministry of reconciliation.

Since its inception in 1910, the Third Street Church of God has been
aligned with the Church of God Reformation Movement based in Anderson, Indiana. Over its history this urban congregation has embodied a
dialectics of refuge and reconciliation under the leadership of two pastors:
Charles T. Benjamin, who led the church from 1910 to 1967, a span of
fifty-seven years that ended with his retirement at the age of eighty-eight;
and Samuel G. Hines, whose twenty-five-year tenure began in 1969 and
was cut short by his sudden death from a heart attack on January 6, 1995.
Elder Benjamin understood the church to be a refuge from sin and worldly
living, a home away from home for persons seeking employment, education and Christian fellowship in the urban environment. Dr. Hines emphasized reconciliation across class and racial lines so that the hospitality of a
hot meal and a warm welcome could be extended to refugees of the urban
crisis: the homeless, prostitutes, alcoholics, drug addicts and the unem-
ployed. Both pastors sought to cultivate a sound spiritual environment for
winning souls and nurturing believers.

Reconciliation was the central theme undergirding the pastoral leadership of Dr. Hines. He challenged the congregation to become "Ambassadors
for Christ in the Nation's Capital," proclaiming the message of reconciliation as directed by the apostle Paul in 2 Corinthians 5:17-21. In 1972 a
ministry statement was developed and adopted to this end:

> We are ambassadors for Christ in the Nation's Capital, committed to be
> a totally open, evangelistic, metropolitan caring fellowship of believers.
> To this end we are being discipled in a community of Christian faith,
> centered in the love of Jesus Christ and administered by the Holy Spirit.
> We are covenanted to honor God, obey His Word, celebrate his grace,
> and demonstrate a lifestyle of servanthood. Accordingly, we seek to
> proclaim and offer to the world a full cycle ministry of reconciliation and
> wholeness.

Dr. Hines expressed his own commitment to the ministry of reconciliation
in other ways. He gave critical behind-the-scenes leadership to the demo-
lition of apartheid in South Africa by aggressive and focused counseling of
church leaders, political activists and governmental leaders. The church
sponsored other members on short-term visits to South Africa to do work
projects, such as building construction and children's ministry. Closer to

home, he insisted that the weight of biblical evidence places great responsibilities on the church to minister to the poor. The congregation's energies and resources became focused on bringing the powerful and the powerless together in ministry among the urban poor, guided by the conviction that "dogma divides and mission unites."

The daily Urban Prayer Breakfast remains the centerpiece of the church's ministry of reconciliation, now under the direction of David Hines, minister of urban outreach and son of Dr. Hines. What follows is a description of a typical weekday morning at our church, centered around the breakfast.

Worship begins at about 7:30 a.m. The praise team offers contemporary inspirational music—brisk praise choruses and Scripture songs from the white charismatic movement, such as "Come into This House," "Mourning into Dancing," "He Is Exalted," "Celebrate Jesus" and many more. The synthesizer provides complete accompaniment, keyboard chords, solo instrumental voices and rhythmic beat of the percussion instruments. The singing is led by a black woman, two black men and a white man. The seats facing the stage are now mostly filled, and latecomers are directed to fill in the empty seats scattered from front to back. The audience is attentive and responsive but seems not to know most of the songs. But they join in the singing, occasionally lifting their hands, standing on their feet or saying "Amen." A few of the men in the congregation sleep, read the newspaper or otherwise tune out the worship without distracting the others.

After a full thirty to forty minutes of singing, one of the men on the ministry team steps forward to begin preaching. The sermon is not delivered in any rapid, formal manner; the preacher is as casually dressed as the others, and he engages the audience with questions, challenges and observations without being condescending. At several points in the message he exhorts them to seek the kingdom of God, to choose Jesus Christ as Savior and to acknowledge that poverty is no excuse for failing to follow the Lord. The message ends with a prayer and an appeal for the worshipers to come forward for prayer.

The spirit of the gathering is extremely congenial, and one senses a distinct orientation toward mutuality, humility and service. Among the volunteers, most are eager to greet and meet each other informally. The worship leader routinely introduces any groups who are visiting as volunteers, but they mingle on their own among the men and among other volunteers. The ecumenical and interracial nature of the ministry is striking. The volunteers come from many churches and denominations throughout the United States.

It is not so easy to distinguish the volunteers from the "poor"—all are casually dressed in T-shirts and shorts or jeans, and the persons who come in from the streets are not necessarily disheveled or inebriated. Of the 160 who are served breakfast on a typical day, at least 90 percent are young black males. There are fewer than a dozen women, almost all black, and a few men appear to be middle-aged or elderly. The forty or so volunteers include three members of the church, the ministry team composed of persons from three local charismatic congregations (including blacks, whites, Cambodians and Ethiopians), an all-white Young Life group of teens and adult leaders, and five or so black men closely identified with those being served, except that they obviously have roles assisting in the food service and securing the entrances and exits. The daily prayer breakfast program depends heavily upon volunteers, and the only advertisement is by word of mouth among the persons on the streets and in the shelters. There is always a diverse mix of people present—men and women of all races and all ages, except that children are rarely present. On the average, 150 to 200 persons gather each weekday for worship, work and fellowship around a substantial soul-food breakfast, a term aptly applied to both the menu and the ministry.

Although the Sunday-morning congregation at Third Street is also inclusive of the urban poor, there is a more formal order of service, and the majority of congregants dress up rather than down, as is the practice in the churches of the urban working and middle classes. There are more women than men, and many more blacks than whites, with persons of West Indian, Asian and European descent included. All age groups are represented. The order of service includes an intentionally diverse mix of sacred music and performance styles: hymns, choruses, anthems, spirituals and gospel songs. The prayers include the people's petitions for help, the sermons are informed by contemporary interpretations of the Scriptures, and the altar calls encourage individuals to experience personal salvation, spiritual growth, progressive action and mutual empowerment.

Two additional elements of the Sunday worship service take on special significance in a community of believers who are likely to experience alienation in a racist and sexist social order, namely, the reading of announcements and the welcoming of visitors. At first glance these might appear to be mundane matters of marginal importance to the real business of worship. However, the announcements are an important sign of the church's role as a critical forum for the sharing of information concerning both religious and secular events and may bear an implicit moral approval or ecclesiastical endorsement of outside activities. The announcements provide a means for the church to proclaim that particular events, programs and accomplishments merit community attention and affirmation.

Similarly, the welcoming of visitors may seem to be unimportant, but the practice may possess understated ethical significance as an opportunity to reaffirm and underline the open-door policy of the church in the course of the liturgy. In a nation whose history includes the racist exclusion of African-Americans from virtually all social institutions, including the Christian churches, the welcoming and recognition of each visitor by name can be seen as a countercultural act that affirms the oneness of all humanity before God. During the aftermath of slavery, the public announcement of one's name, hometown, home church and pastor in black church services not only was an important means of establishing personal and social identity but also, as Cheryl Townsend Gilkes has noted,[1] served a vital networking function for the reunion of individuals and families who had been sold away from each other as slaves. C. Eric Lincoln has addressed the historical significance of the black church practice of inviting visitors to identify themselves in worship:

> The time was when the personal dignity of the Black individual was communicated almost entirely through his church affiliation. To be able to say that "I belong to Mt. Nebo Baptist" or "We go to Mason's Chapel Methodist" was the accepted way of establishing identity and status when there were few other criteria by means of which a sense of self or a communication of place could be projected.[2]

Lincoln believes that the social identity and self-perception of black people are still refracted through the prism of religious identity. The welcome to visitors in worship offers the individual an opportunity to give voice to this identity in the community of faith; however, it is morally imperative to extend equal hospitality to all visitors, regardless of race, sex, age or economic status. The ethics of the Christian gospel sustains the church's effort to reach out to black people in love and affirm black identity without despising whites and others.

The Broader Ecclesiological Question

Thus far I have tried to describe one congregation's approach to the practical implementation of the ministry of reconciliation in worship and outreach. I would like to conclude by addressing the broader ecclesiological question: How can the church bring members of all races to shared worship, identity and empowerment in Christ? My response to this question is informed by an article that appeared several years ago in *The Christian Century*, "From 'Liberation' to 'Exile': A New Image for Church Mission." The author, Ephraim Radner, is a white Episcopal priest and scholar who outlines an "exilic ecclesiology" based on insights he gained while working in an urban parish in Cleveland. His proposal is directed to his own context, the churches of the white Protestant mainstream. Radner begins with a critique of the inadequacies of liberation theology based on his own experience as a "socially responsible seminarian in the 1970s who concluded that liberation theology was the only show in town":

> Those of us who were uneasy with the simplistic and politically rote conclusions to which liberation theology gave rise had no other examples to follow. Tired North American denominations offered no parallel to the martyrs and confessors of the church in Latin America, Africa, and Asia.[3]

Yet in reality the same churches who address their liberation rhetoric in the form of statements, resolutions, protests, pickets and boycotts have failed to engage the poor directly and have little to offer with respect to the practical task of reforming communities. Meanwhile the poor are excluded from liberal and conservative denominational churches, both black and white:

> Statistics indicate that major denominations—including traditional black churches—have increasingly exclusive memberships, defined along economic, class and ethnic lines. Churches in inner cities and poor rural areas are closing, while those that remain are often composed of commuting members with little interest in the church's neighbors.[4]

Radner prescribes a threefold remedy for churches seeking to engage the poor directly as they address issues of crime, drug use and housing. First, he calls for totalistic transformation. Behaviors, expectations, attitudes and motivations must be addressed in conjunction with any attempt at fostering social change. The black Pentecostals and dissenting Protestants have developed avenues for faithful response to crime and drug use:

> Reaching out and incorporating new members and inculcating in them behaviors and expectations congruent with the vision of the Christian community has been the main activity of the church's mission across the centuries. It has been the means for the transformation of many socially marginal groups in the U.S., from poor rural whites in Methodist and Assemblies of God churches to rural and dislocated urban blacks in Baptist and Church of God in Christ churches. These highly self-conscious groups have deliberately, and on the basis of well-articulated evangelical mandates, provided the means for motivational and educa-

tional upbuilding. In so doing, they have also been the vehicles for upward mobility.[5]

Radner names the secular culture or economic consumerism as a major factor in the church's abandonment of its traditional mission of totalistic renewal. Only so-called sects such as Jehovah's Witnesses and the Black Muslims have maintained the vision and the motivation to seek and transform those outside the economic and educational mainstream. These groups are vilified by the political right for refusing to accept patriotic values and for resisting participation in the political process, and by the political left for uncritical espousal of economic self-improvement and failure to challenge the capitalist system. But these critiques hint at the coherence and integrity of these groups as separate communities capable of totalistic renewal.

The second aspect of Radner's remedy is the idea of the church as an alternative community with an identity of "exile."[6] In this regard he puts his finger on the fundamental ecclesiological fallacy of liberation theology: in their zeal to merge the sacred and secular, liberationists reject the notion of the church as a separate community that evangelizes the people it seeks to serve. Radner argues, "It makes little sense for churches to work at becoming liberating agents when they refuse to become communities that are themselves inclusive of the people they seek to serve."[7] Exile is offered as a more effective theme for the church's mission than liberation. A church with an exilic identity is an alternative community formed by a coherent set of values at odds with the surrounding culture. He notes that the nineteenth-century evangelicals exemplified a truly exilic perspective linked to missionary outreach, which expanded the community of churches to include socially marginal groups.

The third and final element of Radner's proposal is a return to New Testament ecclesiology in support of the exilic identity or the church's mission: "Much of the New Testament calls people out of an existing society into a theocratic alternative that is to continue in the midst of the larger society until the inbreaking of God's own action."[8] He lifts up the first epistle of Peter as the best New Testament example of exilic ecclesiology.

A distinctive Christian identity involves a host of special commitments and "hard confrontation" with secular values, pointing the church to the way of the cross as the social character of exile. But by maintaining its integrity in the face of the dominant culture, the church can rediscover the means to embrace new members from the margins, forming a distinct and enticing place of renewal:

Exile is a move to that realm where divine liberation can begin to take on meaning, because it springs from the longing of a separated people. If the churches cannot groan, God shall never hear. That is the secret of the exodus, and the moment to which we are called to return.[9]

Certainly the "longing of a separated people" is implicit in the sacred song and speech of those urban churches who open their doors to the poor.

Our experience at Third Street Church has been that a simple commitment to ministry among the urban poor has drawn us into partnership with Christian individuals, churches and institutions across the lines of race, class and nationality. In my view the potential for development of credible ministries and ecclesiologies of racial reconciliation in the churches of North America depends largely upon the specific willingness of evangelical Christians to follow the example of Christ by preaching the gospel to the poor.

TEN
Meeting Messiah

Pamela Baker Powell

I am the white pastor of a black Presbyterian church in Lubbock, Texas. If you know anything at all about the state of Texas, you know that it is big, and if you know anything about black churches, you know that they are usually small. This comparison encapsulates the experience of serving an African-American congregation in West Texas.

Where Messiah Is Found

The church that I serve as pastor is Messiah Presbyterian Church of Lubbock, a church of twenty-one adult members, eight children and a constituency of forty-three in an essentially segregated city with a population of 200,000 people. The Anglo population constitutes about 65 percent; the Hispanic, 25 percent; and the black population consists of less than 9 percent (about 17,000 people).

Texas, like a small nation, has its own regional differences. In order to relate my experience of being the pastor of Messiah Presbyterian Church, or "meeting Messiah," as I call it, I must set the church in its context of West Texas.

West Texas exists as its own special place. It is the last of the geographic areas to be settled in the forty-eight contiguous states. It is noted for its flat terrain, the wind that can quickly develop into a tornado, dust storms, and the heartiness of the settlers who came there and stayed. It is a region that is so rugged that it could not be settled until the development of windmills, barbed wire and the six-shooter. People either died or left if they did not like it, and the ethos of the people of the area reflects this kind of tough contentment. West Texas is characteristically a place that is hard on women, the weak and minorities. It is a place where change comes slowly, a characteristic that is not necessarily negative. With strong Southern influences, family is valued above all else, and there are many three-generation families in Lubbock. Children tend to go to college in Lubbock, attending Texas Tech University, and then stay to raise their families. The church is still a real force in the society of West Texas, and people see themselves as mostly conservative Christians and conservative politically. Of course they live in that context with all the contradictions of human life. Texas has the second highest teenage pregnancy rate in the nation, and now, as before, concealed weapons are legally a part of life. Ranchers wear boots and carry rifles because of the danger of rattlesnakes. Natives wear big hats because above them is the "big sky"—much talked about and admired for its beauty.

Texans have a real sense of humor and pride about themselves and their state, and West Texans are no different. When the Texas Tech women won the National Collegiate Athletic Association women's basketball championship in 1994, bumper stickers all over town read: "Texas Tech University—where men are men and women are champions!"

In West Texas people understand a fundamental fact of life on the plains: you never know when a disaster will strike and you will need your neighbor. This "good neighbor" policy of West Texas is a powerful component of the understanding of community. On the highway people wave to one another as they drive past. When I first moved to Lubbock from Los Angeles, I thought the finger raised was an unwelcome sort of communication, but I have since learned that it is entirely neighborly. Still, this is not a sentimental sense of community. As a general rule, like the rugged individualist settlers who are their forebears, people keep their own counsel and solve their own problems. Yet when my husband received a call to the Westminster Presbyterian Church in Lubbock in 1988, we found the manse was filled, floor and counters, with food, flowers and useful gifts. This is an old Southern custom called a "pounding" and a characteristic act of Texan hospitality.

The economy of West Texas is dependent upon cotton farming. Half of the farmers are dry-land farmers (i.e., they have no irrigation system for their crops). Oil wells and cattle ranches make up another segment of the economy. In addition, Lubbock's role as the regional medical and banking center and the presence of Texas Tech University (a state university of twenty-five thousand people) help to make Lubbock's economy more stable than that of most cities its size. The arts are represented in Lubbock. It is the hometown of Buddy Holly and Glenna Goodacre, the sculptor of the women's addition to the Vietnam Memorial in Washington, D.C. Lubbock has a symphony orchestra with a resident conductor, a youth symphony orchestra and two ballet companies.

Yet many would say that Lubbock, Texas, is the outback of America. In many ways Lubbock is an island unto itself. It is a six-hour drive east to Dallas and west to Santa Fe. It is a two-hour drive north to Amarillo, a city smaller than Lubbock, and a two-hour drive south to Midland-Odessa, where they take their oil wells as seriously as their football.

There is a black side of town—the northeast side. The congregation I serve lives there.

How I Met Messiah

I had been living on the white side of town—the southwest side—for five years when I began to serve Messiah. To "meet" Messiah Church at East Tenth Street and Martin Luther King Jr. Boulevard, I leave my house, take the loop around the city for about ten minutes and exit at Nineteenth Street; then I head east into the industrial section of town. I cross Avenue A and the railroad tracks and pass the great one-hundred-feet high cottonseed elevators with their imposing pyramid shapes that push against the horizon. I move toward Martin Luther King Jr. Boulevard, which until a few years ago was named Quirt Avenue—the main street of the black community.

It is not an exaggeration to say that Messiah Church and I are from two different worlds, and even in the best of circumstances, merging these worlds can be complicated for both blacks and whites.

Two years ago, when I began at Messiah, I telephoned the Reverend D. A. Smith of Smith Chapel in Lubbock. Reverend Smith is the president of the Interdenominational Ministerial Alliance, which in popular parlance is referred to as the Black Pastors Association. I told him that I had just come to Messiah Church. Reverend Smith told me that he would call me back. He did call back, in a manner of speaking, two years later, when I was finally invited to the IMA meeting at Smith Chapel. There I was—the only woman, the only clergywoman, the only white woman—in a meeting room filled with black male pastors and one white male Methodist pastor. I know I was there because of Reverend Smith's intercession for my inclusion. And at that meeting I could not have been more welcome.

As the meeting convened, one of the first orders of business was for President Smith to introduce me to the membership. I do not know that I have ever had a more flattering or surprising introduction: "Brothers, this is Sister Powell. She's the pastor at Messiah Presbyterian on Martin Luther King. We all know the good work of Sister Powell in our community. And we welcome her. She's white!" Thus I was introduced to the Black Pastors Association, who in their graciousness made me one of the seven preachers in the following Good Friday Black Community Service.

Here then is the bridge that explains how I became one of the only white women (if not the only white woman) serving as pastor of a black church in the Presbyterian Church (USA), a denomination of nearly 2.75 million members, 10,000 congregations (of which only 485 are African-American) and 20,585 ordained ministers (of which 2,726 are women, and only 85 of these are black women). I am a daughter of Calvin who believes that our sovereign God works in amazing ways. I am a disciple of Jesus Christ who believes that all believers are children of God, no matter what color they are.

When our family moved to Lubbock because of a call that my husband received from the Westminster Presbyterian Church, the largest Presbyterian church in the city, it never occurred to me that I would eventually be serving the smallest Presbyterian church in the city and the only African-American congregation in the presbytery, an ecclesiastical domain that encompasses sixty-five congregations and is larger than the state of Pennsylvania.

But in January of 1994, I received a telephone call from the worship committee chairperson of Messiah asking me to provide pulpit supply through Lent and into Easter. Their black pastor had left, and they were in need of worship leadership. Those forty days of Lenten devotion spent with Messiah turned out to be significant. I was there during February—Black History Month—and listened to the elders present historical vignettes and songs to enrich our understanding of black history. I heard, for the first time, the black national anthem, "Lift Every Voice and Sing." I began to hear talk of Juneteenth. I was there preaching through the last days of our Lord and witnessing real faith in the eyes and the hearts of the congregation. I was there when we faced the resurrection story of new life and new hope, and I saw it in a new way. And when they asked if I would be available to them in the future, I found myself answering yes and knowing that I was called. Officially I became their part-time pastor on May 15, 1994, serving a congregation of seventeen adults. I could remember times in Los Angeles when I was not sure a class was worth teaching if it had fewer than twenty-four people in it.

Immediately I came to grips with two issues. First, I had to face the fact that my life and experience had been very different from my congregation's. This had to do with more than just race. It also had to do with education, socioeconomic class, regional upbringing and even experiences of faith. Second, how would I be at Messiah and who would I be at Messiah?

To address the first issue I adopted the rule of a good pastor—namely, to remember my congregation's life experience. From that point I began to try to relate my own life to theirs. Some experiences are common to almost all people: falling in love, getting married, having children, rearing children, finding and making a home, burying one's parents, paying taxes. Despite variations, these are common experiences. So I began my pastorate by emphasizing what we had in common as brothers and sisters in Christ and in life. And as I did that for what I thought was the sake of Christ and the benefit of my congregation, a surprising thing happened to me. I began to identify with their struggles as African-Americans, which were not really my struggles. I began to hear my white counterparts and colleagues differently as they talked about racial issues. I began to develop and become conscious, somewhere deep inside of me, of the nuances of racism. I worked on remembering how alike we were, and I discovered that is the key reason why prejudice and racism hurt so much. Because we are so much alike, racism is so profoundly unjust.

The second issue had to do with how "careful" I should be. Should I watch what I say? Should I say I "understand" what I can never really understand? Should I try to put on a "black skin"?

The only sensible answer seemed to me to be myself. I had to recover a sense of who I was that had led me to this place. I had to remember that I was the person who had put on my first dossier years ago that I would be willing to serve a congregation of another race. I had to remember that I was the person who had been the only friend of a five-year-old black boy in my kindergarten class, because my mother had given me a firm lecture on racism when this little boy entered our class in 1950. I had to remember that I was the person who had carried an election in high school because I had "gotten" the black vote, though at the time I had no idea how I had done that except to be friends with my classmates. I remembered those things about myself. I remembered that in 1968 my husband and I were the only whites who stopped on an Alabama road to help a black family who had been in an head-on collision with a "white" car. I remembered waiting while two ambulances left empty because they did not carry blacks. Things I had never thought much about now became memories that provided me with an identity in my pastorate.

Of course, I also remembered that I was a middle-aged Yankee woman in a fairly liberal mainline denomination who had had a life of privilege compared to most people, especially compared to the Messiah congregation. I tried to remember it all and be myself. In retrospect I think that my willingness to be real in my relationship with the congregation opened the door for the congregation to begin to be the same with me.

The reality of this struck home early in my pastorate. One of the first pieces of mail that I received was a packet from the black caucus of the denomination. "Dear Black Pastor," it began. It asked that I seek the session's approval to teach a series of adult Sunday-school classes using curriculum that explored the need to become more Afrocentric in worship and theology. At first the entire curriculum seemed incomprehensible to me. I took it to the session and told them that I did not understand it, but I could follow the lesson plans. It was designed to be a discussion class. I could moderate and listen. They said, "Do it."

And so early in my pastorate I had the benefit of listening to my congregation as they explored the sensitive issues of racism in their own experience. I sat back and took notes. It was a gift beyond all gifts for my ministry. I heard stories that I had never heard or imagined before. I saw tears in the eyes of some of the most dignified and decent people I have ever known. I learned something about what hatred and injustice and racism can do to the human heart. These were lessons that I have valued and kept carefully within me. To hear these stories so early in the pastorate was a great advantage to me because it helped me grow in understanding. It also impressed upon me something I have always believed: it is important to listen carefully to people before you even think you may understand them.

When Messiah Stepped In

But sometimes there is hardly time to listen before God says, "It's time to act!" Just a few weeks after I had assumed the ministry at Messiah, I received a letter from a nearby school, Iles Elementary School, inviting community leaders to discuss how the community could be more closely involved with the school. I went. Though the entire area of the city was new to me, when I arrived I met the competent and well-liked principal, about a dozen teachers and several black leaders of the community. The principal announced the goal of the session as an attempt to let the community become involved in the school in order to protect the school population from the encroaching drug and gang leaders.

Then the teachers talked, one by one. A sixth-grade teacher told of his student who was running drugs. The child was making one thousand dollars a week. He had just bought his mother a car and paid cash. He told his teacher that in a year or two he would be able to buy his mother a house. "No," his teacher told him, "I am afraid you won't live that long." And the boy looked at his teacher as if he knew it were true. There is an element at work in the at-risk kids that says, "You won't live long anyway. Do what you want. Do whatever you can."

But the teacher who haunted my memory was a mild-mannered white man who taught second grade. He said that he had a child in his class who was a lookout for a drug dealer. The child was from a poor family, but now he was wearing expensive athletic shoes. All the kids in the classroom were suddenly impressed with him. The teacher was concerned. "What can I do with this kid?" he said, half to himself and half to the rest of us. "He's only seven years old. He doesn't even completely understand what he's doing. He thinks he's making a good choice when he's really making a bad one."

That afternoon I went home and could not get out of my mind this story: a second-grader with the shoes every kid dreams of, running into a life of gangs and drugs and crime with no awareness of any other option, of any other way to live.

The next week Messiah's session met. I brought to the session a mission proposal for the local elementary school. At this meeting—my first one at Messiah—the church took its initial step in one of its finest hours. There I sat, crammed into a small space with six elders at a long table stretched down the center aisle of the sanctuary (which, with a small office, was the extent of the church's building at that time).

When you "meet Messiah," you meet the elders of Messiah.

Elder Brenda Lyles was forty-two years old, beautiful and soft-spoken, with a bachelor of arts degree in journalism from Texas Tech University. She had fought off cancer the year before and now had a rod in her leg to keep her from falling; but she always believed that it was Jesus who kept her from falling. She was the clerk of session and the ranking elder.

Elder Don Jones, to whom everyone deferred out of great respect, sat beside her. Soon to retire from his position as a counselor at the black high school in town, he was the highest wage earner in the congregation, the most committed to the church and the one who kept everything going. He was also the treasurer. He was a person of great dignity and self-possession, and he was the heart and the hands of the congregation—the esteemed one.

Then there was elder Ed Higgins, a retired military man. Ed had been in World War II, in Korea and in Vietnam. He was an army cook and still cooked for the church. He was also a pastor's kid. His wife had died a few years before. Ed could play the jazziest piano you ever heard in worship. He had the gift of evangelism, and he loved his Lord.

Elder Deborah Horton was tall and attractive, single, and in her mid-thirties. Reared in a "functional" extended family, she was a junior-high coach. Deborah is spending her life reaching out to kids. She was there in her quiet faithfulness.

Brenda's brother was elder Bernard Harvey, a handsome, caring forty-year-old, determined to make a good life for himself. He was highly regarded and college-educated, with a good job. He was cherished in the congregation as a rare black man in their experience. Bernard, as usual, cared about his church.

Elder Bettie Iles, eighty-six years old and a widow for twenty years, had not completely recovered from a serious fall that was occasioned by a stroke. Bettie had been a gospel singer. In fact, she grew up as one of thirteen children who all were either singers or preachers. Her daddy had been a preacher and had helped to plant Messiah Church with the Cumberland Presbyterians. Bettie was one of the first women ordained as an elder in the Presbyterian Church in the late 1950s. Bettie now had a walker and no longer could speak plainly. But her eyes were telling. The Holy Spirit was real for Bettie.

In that session meeting, I told them about the meeting at Iles Elementary School, what the teachers said, and that I had felt led to make a proposal. Then I told them the proposal: that we help the school by supplying an incentive for kids to make right choices instead of wrong ones.

My proposal was that Messiah Church offer three kids in each classroom each semester a pair of the best athletic shoes money can buy, if they made right choices by excelling in school. We could reward children for being outstanding in their classroom, whether it be for scholastics or citizenship or athletics. Iles had seventeen classrooms, so that would come to 51 pairs of shoes a semester or 102 pairs of shoes a year. It could cost us as much as ten thousand dollars.

They were silent. I knew very well that we did not have the money. "We will raise the money," I said. *Ten thousand dollars.* I knew what they were thinking. Messiah operated on a shoestring. There were times when the utility bills could hardly be paid. My salary was paid by the presbytery. The "extra" funds for the church came from my husband's congregation, which sent Messiah its fifth-Sunday loose change offering, usually between sixty and eighty dollars a month.

More silence. Then Don said, "Do you think we can raise this money?"

"I think so," I said. "But I've never raised that much money before." I had to be honest.

More silence.

"We should pray," said Bettie. We understood what she said.

We prayed.

They looked up. Bettie's eyes were bright.

"I think the Lord means for us to do this," Don said. The others agreed. It was moved and seconded. (Presbyterians follow *Roberts' Rules of Order* even in the midst of the movement of the Holy Spirit!) The vote was affirmative. Messiah, a tiny church on Martin Luther King Jr. Boulevard, had just caught a glimpse of God's vision for God's kingdom—and voted to go with it. There was not an elder there, so far as I know, who possibly could have come up with that kind of money. It was to be strictly by faith.

We contacted the school, shared the plan and asked if they were interested.

"Are you kidding?" they said. "Of course we're interested, but how can you do it?"

"Only with God's help," we said. And we were not kidding!

This is not one of those stories where we immediately went to the mailbox and found a check for ten thousand dollars. Yet I would mention it to people at lunch, and they would suddenly write a check for one hundred dollars or three hundred dollars. One time I telephoned the denominational offices in Louisville, Kentucky. They thought it was a fabulous idea and were a tremendous encouragement. We called Foot-Locker and Kids FootLocker (owned by Kinney Shoes). They thought it was such a wonderful idea they were willing to give us an initial discount of 25 percent at Kids FootLocker and 15 percent at FootLocker.

At the church we called it the Presbyterian Shoes Ministry. For the public, it was P.S. for Presbyterian Shoes. The motto was "P.S.—Go for It!" By the end of the first semester, the school arranged an all-school assembly.

"Everybody around here knows that you can make a lot of money doing the wrong thing," I said to the children at the assembly. They looked surprised that I would speak the truth. "But these shoes are for kids who are choosing to do the right thing. In the end, more good will come to you for making right choices. And we are here to show you that is true. When you go into FootLocker or Kids FootLocker, you pick out any pair of shoes you want—any pair—because you have done the right thing. Everyone who does the right thing is a winner!"

The names were called out: Shamika Jones, Steve Wells, Soli Ramirez, Tameka Eddington, Aashuantis Johnson, Amber Fair, Nyquisha McConic, Hillary Hutchinson, and on and on. The children came down from the bleachers to receive their certificates, handed to them with congratulations by the elders of Messiah. Then each child stood before the whole assembly, publicly identified as a winner.

A week later, one of the sixth-grade teachers told me that in her classroom after the assembly the other kids said to the three winners: "You just wait. When you get into that shoe store, you won't be able to get whatever you want. There'll be some cheap, junky shoe. Just wait."

That afternoon and evening, forty of the fifty kids went to the mall to get their shoes. The FootLocker managers told me it was the same question with each child who came in: "Can I get anything I want? *Anything?*" And they replied as we had asked them to reply: "Yes, you can, because you are a winner."

That next day in school, the principal said her office was nearly overrun with kids who wanted to show her their wonderful new shoes. She said the whole school was in celebration.

A short time later we received a letter from a mother of twin boys who had won shoes from different classrooms. It read: "I have eleven children. You cannot imagine what a blessing it is to have my two boys have new shoes. God bless you, Messiah."

Although those kids may have received shoes, and their harried, worried parents got a financial break, the people who were really blessed were the folks of Messiah Presbyterian Church.

When the Associated Press picked up the story of the little church that was doing so much for schoolchildren, articles appeared in newspapers all over the world. Then money did start coming in the mail: two dollar bills crumpled up in an envelope with a note written by an arthritic hand that read, "Keep up the ministry for the kids!"; a check for $750 from a colonel in the Air Force in Italy arrived with the note, "I read about your ministry in the *Stars and Stripes* newspaper. Keep up the ministry for the kids!"

Since then, the Messiah elders have stood before several all-school assemblies to award certificates for shoes. In addition, the session adopted another elementary school. We are beginning to be known in the city as the little church that has a heart for kids on the east side. We have bought hundreds of pairs of top-quality shoes. And two years after that first session meeting, we did receive a check for ten thousand dollars—from the national organization Presbyterian Women. We had written them to say: "We don't believe we have to be big to do big things for the kingdom of God." And they wrote back with a ten-thousand-dollar check: "Neither do we!"

Now we are in the midst of preparing to open Messiah's School. It will be an educational latchkey program, designed for particularly needy but promising kids. Every schoolday afternoon they will spend time with a trained Christian teacher. At Messiah's School children will be tutored in the basics, be exposed to the arts and receive Christian education and moral training. We will start with a class of first-graders and stay with them through sixth grade, as much as possible, utilizing an educational technique known as looping. The school district's head of elementary education has committed the district to work with us, and the city mayor has gone on record to find monetary resources for us.

Messiah keeps reaching out—and receiving. In the midst of all this, twenty-two thousand dollars came from a denominational fund to build a fellowship hall, so we have room for our school now. In the midst of this our membership increased by more than 20 percent; now we have twenty-one adult members. And in the midst of this USA Today recognized Messiah Church with an Honorable Mention for conducting one of the sixty best educational initiative programs in the country—and one of the five best in Texas.

The questions I ask myself are *Why am I so surprised? Didn't I always believe that God could do amazing things?* Yes. But I have never been more certain than I am now that I have really "met Messiah."

Learning Theology from Messiah

In fact I have learned much about theology since I have come to Messiah. For instance, we could talk theological theory about "historic slavery as a metaphor for discipleship," and I have learned that it is a lot easier to call yourself a slave for Christ when there is no memory of slavery in your family. How I admire those who are able to embrace this concept without being glib or false and to know that being a slave for Christ is to be sold out to the one Master who will always redeem us.

We could talk theologically about "heaven as a survival resource" in the black community, but I would say that I have been enriched immeasurably by the real hope that exists among black Christians for that great and glorious day.

We could talk about "social pain and the exodus story," and then I would have to relate the stories that have been shared by the women in my church. These are experiences I have never had. I have never been told that I could not try on a dress in a store nor been escorted by the clerk to the very last dressing room. I do not know what it means to be constantly watched when I am shopping. Social pain cuts deep into the lives of Messiah's people, and it interferes with trust and interaction among the races in ways that I am only beginning to understand. Once in a while I get a glimpse of understanding, and then I realize it is no wonder that there exists a desire to get away—to "exodus." The black community is a "community of the diaspora," according to Cornel West.

If we want to discuss the "dynamics of kenosis and the African-American," we must be very careful that we are not glib or facile. Kenosis that has been forced upon people, as it was on the enslaved Africans in this country, is not a holy experience. Whites must be careful not to romanticize what is more profoundly like a rape of the human spirit when it is not a voluntary kenosis.

To talk about "generational poverty and justice blind spots," we must remember that when one is poor and black, one is often at a loss as to how to access the help that society offers.

Some time ago, one of the children in my church got into trouble at school. Rodrick (not his real name) was a sixth-grader. A Hispanic boy in his class called Rodrick a "nigger." Rodrick responded by pushing the boy off his chair. Both boys were sent to the principal's office. The principal is new and white. She had the school police give Rodrick a ticket. When his grandmother called me, I drove over to see it. It was exactly like a traffic ticket.

When we called juvenile court, we found out that Rodrick had to appear in court. We were told that the lowest fine was two hundred dollars. I spoke to the principal at the request of Rodrick's grandmother. The principal informed me that Rodrick had been getting into "scuffles" at school. I asked to see the reports of the scuffles, but when she began to go through the papers, she found that she could not find a report saying that Rodrick had ever been expelled. The fact is that he never had been expelled. Rodrick had never even been in a day-long school-based detention. The principal and I both knew that these were remedies taken before a police ticket was issued. She realized she had mistakenly labeled Rodrick a "troublemaker."

Nevertheless, he was going to have to pay the price. I explained to the principal that if Rodrick got a two-hundred-dollar fine the family would be in a financial crisis. Rodrick's grandmother seldom used her clothes dryer, which she bought with insurance money after the death of one of her children, because she could not afford to pay the power bill. Would the principal rescind the ticket on the basis of her own error? No. She told me she could not do that. I later discovered that she could. Would the principal consider coming to court to speak to the judge on Rodrick's behalf? Yes. But she had many meetings, and it would have to be convenient.

As it turned out, it was not convenient. Rodrick made not one trip to the courthouse, but two. He had a hearing before a judge who was impressed that Rodrick had so many church members at the courthouse to support him. Because of his community, she declined to impose a monetary fine on Rodrick. Rodrick's punishment was to do twenty good deeds in his neighborhood, all verified in writing by the neighbors, with the completed list due at the courthouse within one month.

But Rodrick suffered through this situation in a way that a twelve-year-old child who had been provoked into a foolish scuffle should not have had to endure. His grandmother and I fear that having once been to court, he will consider a return inevitable. Maybe it will turn out all right. I pray it will be. And Rodrick does seem better. But my point is that if Rodrick had had a powerful family, if Rodrick had had influence, and most likely if Rodrick had not been black, he never would have been in court at all for such a childish offense.

An impoverished grandmother rearing four grandchildren and trying against all odds to provide a decent home so that these children "won't be poor like I was" now worries over twelve-year-old Rodrick who pushed a boy and went to court. His grandmother is banking everything on these children that they might at least have a chance in life. My guess is that there are Rodricks everywhere in our society. The church should be praying for them. And the church should be helping them.

The church must open its eyes to see and understand poverty. It is eye-opening to be with people who are not using their clothes dryer because it is too expensive to run. It is eye-opening to be with families who have loved ones in prison due to crimes that are related to their poverty. It is eye-opening to witness the hand-wringing concern of grandmothers and mothers over whether their young black boys will stay alive. It is eye-opening to realize that many of the families in my church have been touched by murder. It is eye-opening to discover that poverty has its own rules and its own world. Those who are not fortunate enough to have eyes opened by "meeting Messiah" should at least read the book on poverty by Ruby

Payne.[1] For lack of experiences, such books help us to understand the differences in the world of poverty.

Finally, we could discuss "biblical dynamics for transcultural paradigms." They are found in the story Jesus told of the good Samaritan. They are found in caring for others who are so different from you that you would never know them unless you were willing to stop by the road and look; unless you were willing to touch what others will not touch; unless you were willing to pay with your effort, your schedule, your time, your money, your respect and your understanding; unless you were willing to set aside pride (either white or black) and embrace God's people in all their various hues. Messiah's participation in the J. C. Penney Golden Rule Award ceremonies in Lubbock was a visible demonstration of the fact that this group of Christians has heralded a new paradigm of ministry in West Texas culture: a black congregation that is reaching out to black and white alike because this congregation is doing unto others what they would have others do unto them.

When I first met Messiah, I was in line to be president of the board of directors of one of the city's ballet companies. Because of this I was able to obtain a group of free tickets to *The Nutcracker* one Christmas. I distributed them to the church. During that year, one of the visiting families to Messiah had been the symphony orchestra's conductor and his American-Dutch family. No one in the congregation thought of them as anything other than interested Christian friends. At the Christmas ballet one of the elders, Ed Higgins (the piano player), came up to me at intermission and said, "Did you see? That's George down there in front conducting the orchestra!" Ed smiled, lowered his voice to a confidential tone and whispered to me, "Well, I said to myself, *Now, there's one of ours!*"

In the most profound sense, being able to say to one another "There's one of ours!" whatever our color or our socioeconomic class, is a tremendous testimony to the power of Jesus Christ to bring us together in Christ's body, the church.

I was once in a crowded general store near the church. There was so much merchandise in the store that things were piled from floor to ceiling. As I approached the counter and waited to be helped, I looked down at my feet, and there was a large framed picture of a virile, powerful, fierce-looking black man. His long hair was braided in multistrands, and he was sitting, surrounded by children. Black children were all around him—on his lap and at his feet and side. The toes of my shoes were almost touching the picture, so I stepped back. I was startled when I saw it, and my first thought was *Who is that supposed to be?*

But then something happened. Something deep inside me caused me to look again—to look again and to see. And there I saw my Lord differently. For the first time in my life, I saw my Lord in black skin, and in my heart I praised him.

When I first met Messiah, I drove to another part of town and found people who were strange and different to me. But now that I have met Messiah, I find something has happened—and I am at home in a new way in God's world.

Notes

Introduction/Okholm

[1]J. Gresham Machen, "Christianity and Culture" (pamphlet), cited by George Marsden at a conference sponsored by the Institute for the Study of American Evangelicals at Wheaton College, Wheaton, Illinois, April 18, 1997.

[2]Glenn Usry and Craig S. Keener, *Black Man's Religion: Can Christianity Be Afrocentric?* (Downers Grove, Ill.: InterVarsity Press, 1996), p. 16.

[3]The conference was the fifth annual Wheaton Theology Conference, held at Wheaton College, Wheaton, Illinois, April 17-20, 1996.

Chapter 1: The Responsibility of Evangelical Intellectuals in the Age of White Supremacy/Rivers

[1]Joel Kovel, *White Racism* (New York: Columbia University Press, 1984).

[2]Maurice Olender, *The Languages of Paradise: Race, Religion and Philology in the Nineteenth Century,* trans. Arthur Goldhammer (Cambridge, Mass.: Harvard University Press, 1992).

[3]David R. Roediger, *The Wages of Whiteness: Race and the Making of the American Working Class* (New York: Verso, 1991).

[4]Theodore Allen, *The Invention of the White Race* (New York: Verso, 1994).

[5]Alexander Saxton, *The Rise and Fall of the White Republic* (New York: Verso, 1990).

Chapter 2: Race, Theological Discourse and the Continuing American Dilemma/Potter

[1]Gunnar Myrdal, *An American Dilemma: The Negro Problem and Modern Democracy* (New York: Harper & Row, 1944).

[2]C. Eric Lincoln, *Race, Religion and the Continuing American Dilemma* (New York: Hill & Wang, 1984), p. xvii.

[3]Robert Wuthnow, *Communities of Discourse* (Cambridge, Mass.: Harvard University Press, 1989), p. 16.

[4]See Richard Lints, *The Fabric of Theology: Prolegomenon to Evangelical Theology* (Grand Rapids, Mich.: Eerdmans, 1993), chap. 1.

[5]See Arthur F. Holmes, *The Contours of a Christian World View* (Grand Rapids, Mich.: Eerdmans, 1983), pp. 34-35.

[6]Wuthnow, *Communities of Discourse*, p. 3.

[7]See Stanley J. Grenz, *Revisioning Evangelical Theology* (Downers Grove, Ill.: Inter-Varsity Press, 1993).

[8]The concept of "public theology" has been discussed by such theologians as David Tracy, Max L. Stackhouse and Dennis P. McCann. Its most recent articulation can be found in Robert Benne's *The Paradoxical Vision: A Public Theology for the Twenty-first Century* (Minneapolis: Fortress, 1995), p. 4.

[9]Quoted in Carl F. H. Henry, *Twilight of a Great Civilization: The Drift Toward Neo-paganism* (Westchester, Ill.: Crossway, 1988), p. 165.

[10]Henry, *Twilight of a Great Civilization*, p. 165.

[11]Carl F. H. Henry, "The Vigor of the New Evangelicalism," *Christian Life*, January 1948, p. 32.

[12]See Mark A. Noll, *The Scandal of the Evangelical Mind* (Grand Rapids, Mich.: Eerdmans, 1994).

[13]E. J. Carnell, *The Case for Biblical Christianity*, ed. Ronald Nash (Grand Rapids, Mich.: Eerdmans, 1969), pp. 90-91.

[14]Ibid.

[15]Paul K. Jewett with Marguerite Shuster, *Who We Are: Our Dignity as Human—A Neo-evangelical Theology* (Grand Rapids, Mich.: Eerdmans, 1996).

[16]James H. Cone, *God of the Oppressed* (New York: Seabury, 1975), p. 46.

[17]See Peter Paris, *The Social Teaching of the Black Church* (Philadelphia: Fortress, 1985), p. 10.

[18]William E. Pannell, *My Friend the Enemy* (Waco, Tex.: Word, 1968), p. 34.

[19]William H. Bentley, "Our Engagement with Black Power," a paper read at the National Negro Evangelical Association convention, Chicago, Illinois, April 1968.

[20]Lerone Bennett Jr., *The Challenge of Blackness* (Chicago: Johnson, 1972), p. 36.

[21]These critical questions are adapted from J. Richard Middleton and Brian J. Walsh, *Truth Is Stranger Than It Used to Be: Biblical Faith in a Postmodern Age* (Downers Grove, Ill.: InterVarsity Press, 1995), p. 11.

[22]"Interview with Dr. James H. Cone," *Enquiry*, March-May 1971, p. 55.

Chapter 3: Wandering in the Wilderness/Jennings

[1]Shirley Guthrie, *Christian Doctrine*, 2nd ed. (Louisville, Ky.: Westminster John Knox, 1994), p. 7. Emphasis added.

[2]William, C. Placher, *Narratives of a Vulnerable God: Christ, Theology and Scripture* (Louisville, Ky.: Westminster/John Knox, 1994).

[3]Paul Tillich, *Theology of Culture* (New York: Oxford University Press, 1959), p. 47.

[4]Douglas John Hall, *Thinking the Faith: Christian Theology in a North American Context* (Minneapolis: Augsburg, 1989), p. 19.

[5]In using the term *West* I am referring to those cultures and societies that would claim the Enlightenment and the history of colonialism and industrial capitalism as part of their heritage or lineage.

[6]Enrique Dussel, *The Invention of the Americas: Eclipse of "the Other" and the Myth of Modernity*, trans. Michael D. Barber (New York: Continuum, 1995).

[7]Immanuel Kant, *Foundations of the Metaphysics of Morals* (New York: Continuum,

1995); cf. Immanuel Kant, "What Is Enlightenment?" in *Foundations of the Metaphysics of Morals*, trans. Lewis White Beck (New York: Macmillan, 1959), pp. 85-92.

[8]Kant, "What Is Enlightenment?" p. 91.

[9]Ludwig Feuerbach, *The Essence of Christianity*, trans. George Eliot (New York: Harper & Row, 1957), p. 336.

[10]Ludwig Feuerbach, *Lectures on the Essence of Religion*, trans. George Eliot (New York: Harper & Row, 1967), p. 28. These lectures were originally given in 1848-1849 in Heidelberg.

[11]Ibid., pp. 26-27. Cf. Melvin Cherno in the introduction to *The Essence of Faith According to Luther* (New York: Harper & Row, 1967), pp. 10-13.

[12]Feuerbach, *Lectures on the Essence of Religion*, p. 29.

[13]Dussel, *Invention of the Americas*, p. 22.

[14]Émile Durkheim, "Elementary Forms of Religious Life," in *Émile Durkheim: On Morality and Society*, ed. Robert N. Bellah (Chicago: University of Chicago Press, 1973), pp. 204-5. Emphasis added.

Chapter 4: Theological Method in Black and White/Bacote

[1]Stanley J. Grenz, *Theology for the Community of God* (Nashville: Broadman and Holman, 1994), p. 15.

[2]Robert M. Kingdon, "Calvin's Ideas About the Diaconate: Social or Theological in Origin?" in *Piety, Politics and Ethics: Reformation Studies in Honor of George Wolfgang Forell*, ed. Carter Lindberg (Kirksville, Mo.: Sixteenth Century Journal Publishers/Northeast Missouri State University, 1984), pp. 167-80. Elsie Anne McKee has an opposing view, as set forth in her 1982 dissertation, published as *John Calvin on the Diaconate and Liturgical Almsgiving* (Geneva: Libr. Droz, 1984). She argues for a theological explanation instead of an "institutional" one as does Kingdon. I agree with Kingdon primarily.

[3]John Calvin *Institutes of the Christian Religion* 4.3.9.

[4]Kingdon, "Calvin's Ideas About the Diaconate," p. 171.

[5]Ibid., p. 179.

[6]James H. Cone, "General Introduction," in *Black Theology: A Documentary History*, ed. James H. Cone and Gayraud S. Wilmore, 2nd ed., 2 vols. (Maryknoll, N.Y.: Orbis, 1993), 2:1.

[7]Patrick Bascio, "The Failure of White Theology: A Black Theological Perspective," in *New Africa in America*, ed. Mozella G. Mitchell, Martin Luther King Jr. Memorial Studies in Religion, Culture and Social Development (New York: Lang, 1994), 3:4-5.

Chapter 5: Persons in Racial Reconciliation/Deddo

[1]While the growing interest in trinitarian theology can be seen throughout all branches of the church, my synthesis is especially indebted to contemporary theologians such as T. F. Torrance, Colin E. Gunton, Eberhard Jüngel, J. B. Torrance and Ray S. Anderson. These scholars have deliberately aimed to be faithful to the biblical, prophetic and apostolic witness to Jesus Christ and have built on the trinitarian theological developments enshrined in the ecumenical councils of the

first five centuries. They have also been working within the continuities of the Reformed tradition received from Calvin and through Karl Barth. These expressions of trinitarian theology have also been christologically centered and so are also incarnational in character. See Colin E. Gunton, *The Promise of Trinitarian Theology* (Edinburgh: T & T Clark, 1991), for an accounting of this renewed interest.

[2]See Karl Barth, *Church Dogmatics* 3/2, ed. G. W. Bromiley and T. F. Torrance, trans. Harold Knight et al. (Edinburgh: T & T Clark, 1960), pp. 19-54 (§43.2), and T. F. Torrance, *Calvin's Doctrine of Man* (Grand Rapids, Mich.: Eerdmans, 1957), pp. 13-14.

[3]This is the root and source for Barth's *analogia relationis* (*Church Dogmatics* 3/2, p. 220 [§45]). See also Gary W. Deddo, "The Grammar of Karl Barth's Theology of Personal Relations," *Scottish Journal of Theology* 47, no. 2 (1994).

[4]See John D. Zizioulas, *Being as Communion: Studies in Personhood and the Church* (Crestwood, N.Y.: St. Vladimir's Seminary Press, 1985), for the finest exposition of this point as well as a recounting of the centuries-long struggle in which the early Greek church fathers engaged to overcome the inadequacies of Greek forms of thought for expressing the true nature of personhood as being essentially constituted by relationship.

[5]Barth, *Church Dogmatics* 3/2, pp. 142-55 (§44.3).

[6]For a profound philosophical treatment of persons being in relation see John Macmurray's Gifford Lectures, *The Self as Agent* (Atlantic Highlands, N.J.: Humanities Press International, 1991), and *Persons in Relation* (Atlantic Highlands, N.J.: Humanities Press International, 1991).

[7]Karl Barth, *Church Dogmatics* 3/4, ed. G. W. Bromiley and T. F. Torrance, trans. A. T. Mackay et al. (Edinburgh: T & T Clark, 1961), §54.

[8]See Barth, *Church Dogmatics* 3/2, p. 320 (§45), and J. B. Torrance, *Worship, Community and the Triune God of Grace* (Carlisle, U.K.: Paternoster, 1996; Downers Grove, Ill.: InterVarsity Press, 1997).

[9]For an extensive analysis of God's trinitarian becoming see Eberhard Jüngel, *The Doctrine of the Trinity: God's Being Is in Becoming* (Grand Rapids, Mich.: Eerdmans, 1976).

[10]T. F. Torrance, *The Mediation of Christ* (Colorado Springs, Colo.: Helmers & Howard, 1992; Grand Rapids, Mich.: Eerdmans, 1984), p. 67. See also Karl Barth, *Church Dogmatics* 2/1, ed. G. W. Bromiley and T. F. Torrance, trans. T. H. L. Parker et al. (Edinburgh: T & T Clark, 1957), p. 285.

[11]Torrance, *Worship, Community and the Triune God of Grace,* p. 26.

[12]Barth, *Church Dogmatics* 3/4, §54.3.

[13]See Barth, *Church Dogmatics* 2/1, p. 286 (§28.2).

[14]This is Barth's way of construing the *imago Dei*; see *Church Dogmatics* 3/2, pp. 323ff. See also Willie Jennings, "The *Imago Dei* as a Christological Vision," in *Incarnational Ministry,* ed. Christian D. Kettler and Todd H. Spiedell (Colorado Springs, Colo.: Helmers & Howard, 1990); and Ray S. Anderson, *On Being Human* (Grand Rapids, Mich.: Eerdmans, 1982).

[15]This is a strong theme in T. F. Torrance. He calls relations of this sort "onto-rela-

tions." See T. F. Torrance, *Reality and Evangelical Theology* (Philadelphia: Westminster Press, 1982), pp. 43-44, and *The Ground and Grammar of Theology* (Charlottsville: University of Virginia Press, 1980), pp. 174-78.

[16]J. B. Torrance emphasizes this aspect of Calvin's understanding; see *Worship, Community and the Triune God of Grace*, p. 43. It also reflects the insights of Irenaeus and the Cappadocian fathers, who saw the connection of the incarnation and the atonement, summarized in the dictum "The unassumed is the unhealed."

[17]Torrance, *Worship, Community and the Triune God of Grace*, p. 40.

[18]See Deddo, "Grammar of Karl Barth's Theology."

[19]The discussion of the Cappadocian fathers, Athanasius, Cyril of Alexandria, and others, which all contributed to the formulations found in the early church councils, are instructive here. See Philip Edgcumbe Hughes, *The True Image* (Grand Rapids, Mich.: Eerdmans, 1989), chaps. 18-28; also Gunton, *Promise of Trinitarian Theology*.

[20]Torrance, *Mediation of Christ*, p. 79.

[21]Barth, *Church Dogmatics* 3/2, p. 320.

[22]This is the thrust of Colin E. Gunton's *The One, the Three and the Many* (New York: Cambridge University Press, 1993). The Trinity ultimately sheds light on the solution to the problem of the one and the many and provides the ultimate grounds for hope in human relations.

[23]This insight is prominent in what has remained an important text on a Christian interpretation of racism, George D. Kelsey, *Racism and the Christian Understanding of Man* (New York: Scribner's, 1965).

[24]I am indebted to the teaching of J. B. Torrance for this insight. See J. B. Torrance, "Covenant or Contract?" *Scottish Journal of Theology* 23, no. 1 (February 1970).

[25]See Barth, *Church Dogmatics* 3/2, pp. 244ff. He presents a theological reinterpretation of Martin Buber's "I and Thou."

[26]This is the import of Gunton's *The One, the Three and the Many*.

Chapter 6: Wrestling with Scripture/Cartwright

[1]Here I borrow the title of Margaret Walker's poignant and highly evocative poem about the African-American experience in relation to the history of oppression, often at the hands of those whites who also claimed to be believers. In particular I have in mind the third stanza where Walker employs imagery of reconciliation to describe the indomitable character of African-American belief. "Neither the slavers' whip nor the lynchers' rope nor the bayonet could kill our black belief. In our hunger we beheld the welcome table and in our nakedness the glory of the long white robe. We have been believers in the New Jerusalem." See Margaret Walker's poem "We Have Been Believers," in *For My People* (Salem, N.H.: Ayer, 1990), p. 16.

[2]Donald F. Durnbaugh, *The Believers' Church: The History and Character of Radical Protestantism* (Scottsdale, Penn.: Herald, 1985; New York: Macmillan, 1968), p. 295. Although it is most closely associated with a sermon given to the Pilgrims on the occasion of their departure for America by the English Puritan John Robinson, this affirmation is also associated with the Quaker and Church of the Brethren

traditions, each of which interprets it as a principle of openness to the direction of the Holy Spirit for the congregation or meeting.

[3]Toni Morrison, *Playing in the Dark: Whiteness and the Literary Imagination* (Cambridge, Mass.: Harvard University Press, 1992), p. 3. Morrison uses these phrases to describe the task that she has set for herself in the lectures that constitute this book.

[4]Ibid.

[5]As Vincent Harding, the distinguished historian of the African-American freedom struggle, reminds us, we dare not forget the formative role that spirituality plays in the struggle; for "there is a river" (Ps 46:4) whose streams provide the sources of renewal as well as imaginative moral focus for the struggle toward racial reconciliation. The challenge is to locate the narratives of our lives in relation to that stream, which includes the saga of the lives of those who have gone before us in the struggle. See the moving introduction to *There Is a River: The Black Struggle for Freedom in America,* the first volume of Harding's history (New York: Harcourt Brace Jovanovich, 1981), pp. xi-xxvi.

[6]In *Reading in Communion: Scripture and Ethics in Christian Life* (Grand Rapids, Mich.: Eerdmans, 1991), Stephen E. Fowl and L. Gregory Jones call attention to the moral significance of reading Scripture over against ourselves. They cite Dietrich Bonhoeffer's address to a youth conference in August 1932 in which he called attention to the problem. "Has it not become terrifyingly clear again and again, in everything that we have said to one another, that we are no longer obedient to the Bible? We are more fond of our own thoughts than of the thoughts of the Bible. We no longer read the Bible seriously, we no longer read it over against ourselves, but for ourselves. If the whole of our conference here is to have any great significance, it may be perhaps that of showing us that we must read the Bible in a quite different way, until we find ourselves again" (Dietrich Bonhoeffer, *No Rusty Swords,* trans. C. H. Robertson et al. [London: Collins, 1970], p. 181, quoted in Jones and Fowl, *Reading in Communion,* p. 140).

[7]Vincent Wimbush, "The Bible and African Americans," in *Stony the Road We Trod,* ed. Cain Hope Felder (Minneapolis: Fortress, 1991), pp. 85-86.

[8]Albert J. Raboteau, *Slave Religion: The "Invisible Institution" in the Antebellum South* (New York: Oxford University Press, 1975), p. 182. Emphasis added.

[9]At this stage of the historical investigation of antebellum evangelical congregations, we do not know "how frequently or infrequently slaves sought redress for maltreatment by appealing to church discipline" (Raboteau, *Slave Religion,* p. 183), but there is enough extant evidence to suggest that attempts by slaves to offer fraternal admonition to their slave masters were by no means unknown during this period of American history.

[10]There are numerous accounts of runaway slaves who, upon being returned to their masters, were charged in civil courts with having stolen property (themselves) from their masters. When some of these same slaves inquired why it was not regarded as a violation of the fifth commandment when they were taken from their country and enslaved, they were told that the slave trade did not involve stealing; it was a business.

[11]Here I am borrowing from the title of Delores Williams's study *Sisters in the Wilderness: The Challenge of Womanist God-Talk* (Maryknoll, N.Y.: Orbis, 1993). See especially chap. 5, "Sisters in the Wilderness and Community Meanings," pp. 108-39.

[12]Raboteau, *Slave Religion,* pp. 182-83.

[13]The recent conflict about the burial of an infant of mixed race and the subsequent request of her parents to be married at the Barnett's Creek Baptist Church near Thomasville, Georgia, provides yet another example demonstrating how racial reconciliation remains a challenge for most American congregations. The controversy erupted when one of the deacons of this Southern Baptist congregation told the family of the deceased infant that church leaders wanted the grave to be disinterred and the body of the mixed-race child moved to another cemetery. For a detailed reporting of this incident see the article by Kevin Sack, "Burial of Mixed Race Baby Provokes All-White Church," *The New York Times,* March 29, 1996, p. A8, and subsequent articles.

[14]Here I borrow a phrase from the work of Dietrich Bonhoeffer, quoted in Jones and Fowl, *Reading in Communion,* p. 140.

[15]Here I borrow a phrase from James William McClendon's *Ethics: Systematic Theology* (Nashville: Abingdon, 1986), 1:223. McClendon's discussion of "the politics of forgiveness" in particular and more generally his conception of the way church discipline and reconciliation interact with one another informs much of this chapter.

[16]Wayne A. Meeks uses the phrase "social embodiment" in his essay "A Hermeneutics of Social Embodiment," *Harvard Theological Review* 79 (1986): 176-86, where he argues that "the hermeneutical process has a social dimension at both ends" of the polarity between what it means and what it meant (p. 184). See Michael G. Cartwright, "The Practice and Performance of Scripture: Grounding Christian Ethics in a Communal Hermeneutic," in *The Annual for the Society of Christian Ethics 1988* (Washington, D.C.: Georgetown University Press, 1988), pp. 31-53, in which I use Meeks's essay to argue that the issue of the use of Scripture in Christian ethics needs to be refocused in terms of the ecclesiological issue of what it means to embody the church as the people of God.

[17]Michael Kammen, *The Mystic Chords of Memory: The Transformation of Tradition in American Culture* (New York: Knopf, 1991), p. 26.

[18]Ibid., p. 701.

[19]Derrick Bell, *Faces at the Bottom of the Well: The Permanence of Racism* (New York: Basic Books, 1992), p. 12. As Bell comments more fully in the introduction to his book, the proposition he wants his readers to consider, even though he knows it is "easier to reject than to refute," is this: *"Black people will never gain full equality in this country. Even those herculean efforts we hail as successful will produce no more than temporary peaks of progress, short-lived victories that slide into irrelevance as racial patterns adapt in ways that maintain white dominance. This is a hard-to-accept fact that all history verifies. We must acknowledge it, not as a sign of submission but as an act of ultimate defiance."* Emphasis in the original.

[20]Charles Long, "Civil Rights—Civil Religion: Visible People, Invisible Religion,"

in *American Civil Religion,* ed. Russell E. Richey and Donald G. Jones (New York: Harper Forum Books, 1974), p. 214.

[21]James Baldwin, *The Devil Finds Work* (New York: Laurel/Dell, 1976), pp. 52-69, especially p. 57.

[22]Ibid. In particular see Baldwin's commentary on the cultural potency of the image of the mulatto and how this structure gets reproduced cinematically in such films as *In the Heat of the Night.*

[23]A. M. Chreitzburg, *Early Methodism in the Carolinas* (Knoxville, Tenn.: Publishing House of the Methodist Episcopal Church, South, 1897), pp. 158-59, quoted in Robert T. Osborn, "North Carolina Methodist Theology in Post-bellum Nineteenth Century," in *Methodism Alive in North Carolina,* ed. O. Kelly Ingram (Durham, N.C.: Duke Divinity School, 1976), pp. 99-100.

[24]As Richard Lischer points out, this reading reported by Pastor Chreitzburg also displays what amounts to a double-reverse; that is, African-American congregations heard the text literally despite the fact that the preacher preached it as a figurative meaning. See Richard Lischer, *The Preacher King: Martin Luther King Jr. and the Word That Moved America* (New York: Oxford University Press, 1995), p. 201.

[25]See Michael G. Cartwright, "Ideology and the Interpretation of the Bible in the African-American Christian Tradition," *Modern Theology* 9 (April 1993): 141-58, in which I explore the hermeneutical significance of double-voiced readings of the Bible found in the historic black church tradition.

[26]Wimbush, "Bible and African Americans," pp. 81-93.

[27]Ibid., pp. 84-85.

[28]Ibid., p. 89.

[29]Ibid.

[30]Ibid., p. 90.

[31]Ibid.

[32]Ibid., p. 92.

[33]Ibid., p. 90.

[34]Ibid., p. 93.

[35]Ibid., p. 94.

[36]Ibid., p. 96.

[37]The phrase comes from the subtitle of Theophus Smith's book *Conjuring Culture: Biblical Formations of Black Culture* (New York: Oxford University Press, 1994).

[38]As Edith Blumhofer has observed in a different context, the insularity of popular religion in American culture makes it quite possible for fundamentalists and Pentecostals to remain almost entirely ignorant of one another's hermeneutic. See Edith Blumhofer, "Dispensing with Scofield" (a review of Jack Deere's *Surprised by the Power of the Spirit* [Grand Rapids, Mich.: Zondervan, 1993]), *Christianity Today,* January 10, 1994, p. 57. As Blumhofer goes on to point out, "Vast networks that encompass thousands of American Christians simply do not overlap."

[39]Wimbush, "Bible and African Americans," p. 91.

[40]The possibility that Wimbush and others may have overstated the connection

between black liberation theological reading of Scripture and the third reading is a question that will be taken up in part two of this work.

[41]Vincent Wimbush, "Rescue the Perishing: The Importance of Biblical Scholarship in Black Christianity," in *Black Theology: A Documentary History*, ed. James H. Cone and Gayraud S. Wilmore, 2nd ed., 2 vols. (Maryknoll, N.Y.: Orbis, 1993), 2:212-13.

[42]Wimbush, "Rescue the Perishing," p. 214. It should be noted that Wimbush's claim is put forward in the service of his own apologia for biblical scholarship as essential to the black community. Immediately following his provocative declaration about black evangelicals, Wimbush declares: "The times require the same creative and intellectual energies that gave birth to the black theology movement to address the present needs of the black communities of faith. We cannot go back to more innocent times when faith came by hearing alone. Nor can we assume that all is well if all is quiet. That we have bodies of black Christians is no indication that we have their minds. They must be rescued from the clutches of dogmatic Christianity and led in more constructive, more affirming directions. For this task biblical scholarship is indispensable" (p. 214).

[43]Letter from Professor Wimbush to the author, October 4, 1995, pp. 1-2.

[44]I have borrowed this term from the title of Richard Wright's story "The Ethics of Jim Crow," a semi-autobiographical story of the harsh and cruel ways African-Americans were treated in the mid-South. The story is set in the Delta country of eastern Arkansas.

[45]In particular I would call attention to the work of Willie James Jennings of Duke Divinity School. Jennings appears to be on the track of this kind of alternative reading of Scripture, as evidenced in an unpublished paper he shared with me, entitled "Between a Rock and a Hard Place: Afro-Reading, Black Christian Identity and the Bible." I find Jennings's description of this theological reading to be intriguing: "This would be a reading in which Israel serves not just as a model of an oppressed ethnic community from which we as displaced Africans can continue to gain rhetorical tools and narrative space for the display of our own history of oppression, which in turn would create space for a theological understanding of cultural identity" (p. 30).

[46]Arna Bontemps's novelized account *Chariot in the Sky: A Story of the Jubilee Singers* (Philadelphia: John C. Winston, 1951) probably provides the best account of the psychic dislocation experienced by Euro-Americans and African-Americans alike in the midst of this cultural shift.

[47]W. E. B. Du Bois, *The Souls of Black Folk: Essays and Sketches* (Chicago: A. C. McClurg, 1903; New York: Penguin Classics, 1989). See in particular the chapter "The Sorrow Songs," pp. 204-16.

[48]I have intentionally focused my comments on dispensationalist premillennialism, which is but one strand of the incredibly diverse and complex stream of millennialism that has shaped the interpretation of the Bible in American culture. Some scholars associated with Dallas Theological Seminary have attempted to rescue dispensationalist premillennialism from the problems that I discuss. While I do not find this defense to be convincing, the fact that such an argument for "progressive dispensationalism" is being put forth suggests that there is a

growing awareness of the limits of the hermeneutic put forth by Scofield et al. earlier in the twentieth century. See, for example, Craig A. Blaising and Darrell L. Bock, *Progressive Dispensationalism* (Wheaton, Ill.: Victor, 1993). Where Blaising and Bock would attempt to reform from within, my own argument puts forth an external critique that employs cultural criticism for the purpose of showing how a dispensationalist hermeneutic may serve to conceal racist patterns of thought.

[49]See, for example, Theophilus Gould Steward's double-voiced reinterpretation of Genesis via Psalm 68:31 in *The End of the World* (Philadelphia: A.M.E. Book Rooms, 1888). Steward's hermeneutic was technically premillennialist, but it was hardly compatible with the dispensationalist framework of J. N. Darby or C. I. Scofield.

[50]Douglas Frank, *Less Than Conquerors: How Evangelicals Entered the Twentieth Century* (Grand Rapids, Mich.: Eerdmans, 1996), p. 68.

[51]Ibid., p. 69.

[52]Ibid., p. 70.

[53]Ibid., pp. 70-71; Frank quoting from Darby's text as cited in C. Norman Kraus's *Dispensationalism in America: Its Rise and Development* (Richmond, Va.: John Knox, 1958). As Darby expressed it, "It is positively stated (2 Tim. 3) that the church would fail and become as bad as heathenism; and the Christian is directed to turn away from evil and turn to the Scriptures, and Christ (Rev. 2—3) is revealed as judging the state of the churches . . ."

[54]Frank, *Less Than Conquerors*, pp. 71-72.

[55]Ibid., p. 72.

[56]Ibid., pp. 72-73.

[57]Ibid., p. 73.

[58]Ibid., 73.

[59]Ibid., p. 73.

[60]Ibid., pp. 74-75.

[61]As George Marsden points out, C. I. Scofield, "the great systematizer" of the dispensationalist approach, deliberately used this phrase from the King James Bible as the title of his programmatic study. "Scofield interpreted this phrase . . . to mean that 'the Word of Truth, then, has right divisions . . . so any study of that Word which ignores those divisions must be in large measure profitless and confusing." See George Marsden, *Fundamentalism and American Culture: The Shaping of Twentieth-Century Evangelicalism, 1870-1925* (New York: Oxford University Press, 1980), p. 59.

[62]Frank, *Less Than Conquerors*, pp. 84-85.

[63]Ibid., p. 74. Frank's discussion on this point is insightful.

[64]Ibid., p. 102.

[65]Ibid., p. 94.

[66]Ibid., p. 94, quoting note 58.

[67]Ibid., p. 78.

[68]Charles Reagan Wilson, *Baptized in Blood: The Religion of the Lost Cause, 1865-1920* (Athens: University of Georgia Press, 1980), p. 77. The prayer was offered by Episcopal bishop Stephen Elliott.

[69]Edward A. Pollard, *The Lost Cause: A New Southern History of the War of the Confederates* (New York: E. B. Treat, 1866), p. 752.

[70]Wilson, *Baptized in Blood*, p. 1.

[71]Ibid., p. 11.

[72]Ibid., p. 8.

[73]In some cases the rhetorical twists and turns of Pollard's ur-text have inspired contemporary articulations. For a contemporary invocation of the Lost Cause see "Compatriot" Tim Waggener's remarks on the occasion of Confederate Memorial Day, April 28, 1996, from *The Reveille* (newsletter of the Sons of Confederate Veterans, Jefferson Davis Camp, No. 635) 26 (May 1996): 2-3: "I am honored today to have been asked to offer some remarks on this memorial occasion, as have others before me in unbroken succession since 1865. It is proper and right that we continue to observe this day to honor the Confederate Dead—May it ever so remain.

"It is with appreciation that I am reminded that our Memorial Day for the Confederate Dead remains one of the few unspoiled holidays of American life. Marketing, advertising, unrelated ideology, which have somehow managed to ruin many of our national occasions have largely untouched our special day. . . .

"For our Confederates, true, the Cause was lost. The country was lost. The War was lost. Countless lives were lost. The slaves were lost. The sons and daughters, men-servants and maid-servants, the oxen and cattle were lost. Homes and lands were lost.

"But courage and honor and fidelity were not lost, and on them the foundation of a new world was made!"

[74]Ibid., pp. 64-65. For a specific example, see Wilson's discussion of J. W. Sandell's interpretation of history and the Bible found in Sandell's *The United States in Scripture, the Union Against the States, God and Government* (Jackson, Miss.: n.p., 1907).

[75]William Leonard, *God's Last and Only Hope: The Fragmentation of the Southern Baptist Church* (Grand Rapids, Mich.: Eerdmans, 1990), especially pp. 11-15 and following.

[76]See Paul Boyer, *When Time Shall Be No More: Prophecy Belief in Modern American Culture* (Cambridge, Mass.: Harvard University Press, 1992), pp. 166-67.

[77]See, for example, Hal Lindsey's bestseller *The Late Great Planet Earth* (Grand Rapids, Mich.: Zondervan, 1970), pp. 78-80, where Lindsey encourages his readers to "put together" the various biblical prophecies in a dispensationalist framework in which the opposition between the forces of God and the forces of Satan are identified in terms that place the "black African nations" (contemporary representatives of "Cush") in alliance with Arabs in large part because of their pursuit of the "liberation" cause. In fairness to Lindsey, it is not entirely clear what this would mean for African-Americans, but the fact that his usage of "Cush" in this way converges with the old proslavery arguments at several levels cannot be denied.

[78]Fannie Lou Hamer, "Sick and Tired of Being Sick and Tired," in *The Failure and the Hope: Essays of Southern Churchmen*, ed. Will D. Campbell and James

Y. Holloway (Grand Rapids, Mich.: Eerdmans, 1972), p. 164.

[79]Bell, *Faces at the Bottom of the Well*, p. 12.

[80]In *Beyond Ontological Blackness: An Essay in American Religious and Cultural Criticism* (New York: Continuum, 1995), Victor Anderson argues for a new paradigm, "postmodern blackness," and against the tradition of "ontological blackness."

[81]This point is made most effectively by John Howard Yoder in "The Otherness of the Church," in *The Royal Priesthood: Essays Ecclesiological and Ecumenical*, ed. Michael G. Cartwright (Grand Rapids, Mich.: Eerdmans, 1994), pp. 53-64: "For the early church, 'church' and 'world' were visibly distinct, yet affirmed in faith to have one and the same Lord. This pair of affirmations is what the so-called Constantinian transformation changes (the name Constantine is used merely as a label for this transformation, which began before A.D. 200 and took over 200 years; the use of his name does not mean an evaluation of his person or work). The most pertinent fact about the new state of things after Constantine and Augustine is not that Christians were no longer persecuted and began to be privileged, nor that emperors built churches and presided over ecumenical deliberations about the Trinity; what matters is that the two visible realities, church and world, were fused. There is no longer anything to call 'world'; state, economy, art, rhetoric, superstition and war have all been baptized" (p. 57).

[82]Petition Number 20968-IC-NonDis-0, "Membership in the United Methodist Church and in Surpremacist Groups," as printed in the *1996 Daily Christian Advocate Advance Edition* (Nashville: United Methodist Publishing House), pp. 868-70.

The background of this petition is noteworthy. This petition was prepared by the UMC's General Commission on Religion and Race (GCORR) in response to a petition presented at the 1992 General Conference, which sought to amend paragraph 208 of the 1988 Book of Discipline of the UMC by adding the following sentence: "*However, since membership in the United Methodist Church cannot coexist with membership in racial and ethnic supremist [sic] groups, any persons who holds [sic] membership in racial and ethnic supremist groups shall not hold membership in the United Methodist Church*" (emphasis added). The 1996 General Conference approved the petition put forward by GCORR, thereby agreeing not to bar persons from being members of such groups as the Ku Klux Klan.

It should be noted that the GCORR also made a recommendation in which it acknowledged "the deep inconsistency between the Gospel of Jesus Christ and the philosophy of racial and ethnic supremacist groups" (p. 869). This recommendation parallels other stands of the UMC on such issues as military service, where despite the fact that the church notes that war is incompatible with the gospel of Jesus Christ, it recognizes and accepts those persons who are conscientious objectors to war and those who choose to serve in the military.

[83]Constantinianism takes many guises, and Constantinian practices have infiltrated too many of our habits of reading Scripture. For too long Euro-American Protestants have used the parable of the wheat and the tares (Mt 13:24-30, 36-44) not only as a proof text for amillennialism and against premillennialism but also as a means of fending off the fraternal admonition of the Believers' Church

traditions. Yet these traditions have most to contribute to our understanding of the distinction between church and world.

[84]During the civil rights movement of the 1960s, several theologians involved in the Church Peace Mission (an effort launched by the three historic peace churches) hosted a conference on "Revolution, Non-violence and the Church" at Black Mountain, North Carolina (December 9-12, 1963). On that occasion John Howard Yoder made a presentation on the topic of "The Racial Revolution in Theological Perspective" in which he raised the issue of the distorting effects of Constantinianism in relation to the struggle for racial reconciliation in American society. It appears that the majority of participants in the conference did not grasp the significance of Yoder's presentation, although some years later Will Campbell began to explore non-Constantinian approaches to racial reconciliation. Yoder's presentation, which was not published at the time, is included in his collection *For the Nations: Essays Public and Political* (Grand Rapids, Mich.: Eerdmans, 1997).

[85]Will D. Campbell, "Footwashing or the New Hermeneutic?" in *The Failure and the Hope: Essays of Southern Churchmen,* ed. Will D. Campbell and James Y. Holloway (Grand Rapids, Mich.: Eerdmans, 1972), pp. 106-7. "The real point is that the idols of the sects are not as secure as those of the established church. . . . This may be the hope for renewal if we in the establishment learn to think sect!" It may be significant that after offering this comment, Campbell playfully explains what "think sect" means through a series of double-voiced images (p. 107) of sect over against the practices of the established churches.

[86]Ibid., p. 99. Of course we need not wallow in the shibboleth of "sectarianism"; a better characterization of what is involved would probably be to describe the church as a kind of "polis," as Stanley Hauerwas has tended to do in his important body of work as a theological ethicist. For an important and carefully wrought study of the significance of Hauerwas's "theological politics," see Arne Rasmusson's *The Church as Polis* (Notre Dame, Ind.: University of Notre Dame Press, 1995).

[87]To invoke John Howard Yoder's phrase, this means that we must recover the "otherness" of the church in a culture in which "church" and "world" have become indistinguishable. Of course Yoder has also effectively argued, in the wake of the collapse of the so-called Holy Roman Empire with its one church, that there is no one standard sociological configuration that Constantinianism takes (just as, I might add, there is no one social configuration of racism). Rather, there are various forms of Constantinianism that have adapted to specific cultural situations. The Constantinianism of the Church of England is logically different from that of the Constantinianism of officially disestablished but culturally entrenched Euro-American Protestantism of the nineteenth century, and both of these can be differentiated from the Constantinianism of the religion of the Lost Cause.

[88]For another provocative example of this kind of non-Constantinian approach, see Eugene Rivers's "The Responsibility of Evangelical Intellectuals in the Age of White Supremacy," chap. 1 in this volume.

Here we must remember that while in the most technical of senses the historic black church has always been sociologically a "free church" in American culture, that designation cannot account for the complex social configurations of congregations in the African-American Christian tradition living in a largely segregated cultural context. Moreover, when you take into account the different historical conflicts between Euro-Americans and African Americans, it is not possible to assume that all forms of the black church are non-Constantinian because they are nonmajoritarian. We know that there are forms of authoritarianism and patriarchalism in the black church that reflect dreams of church-state empires that are specifically African-American but hardly constitute the fullness of Christian practice. If we are going to be able to envision moving beyond the veil of racism that has constituted our relationships, then the black church as well as Euro-American Christianity must leave aside its Constantinian habits.

[89]Cheryl J. Sanders, *Saints in Exile: The Holiness-Pentecostal Experience in African American Religion and Culture* (New York: Oxford University Press, 1996), p. 40. This is the text of the 1972 ministry statement of the congregation of Third Street Church of God in Washington, D.C., which has served as a missional purpose for that congregation for much of the past twenty-five years.

[90]Ibid., p. 132.

[91]Ibid., p. 125.

[92]Ibid., p. 150.

[93]Ibid., pp. 150-51. Although Sanders does not use the word *Constantinianism* to describe the practices she lists, the fact that she so carefully makes the distinction between church and world (at several levels) in the context of using the exilic metaphor for what it means for the congregation to be the people of God suggests to me that my use of this designation is not incorrect.

[94]Ibid., pp. 125-32. Ephraim Radner's article was published as "From 'Liberation' to 'Exile': A New Image for Church Mission," *The Christian Century* 106, no. 30 (October 18, 1989): 931. As Sanders notes (*Saints in Exile*, p. 126), Radner's ecclesiological proposals "were directed toward his own context, the churches of white Protestant mainstream, but his allusions and applications related as well to the Sanctified churches on the margins."

[95]Sanders, *Saints in Exile*, p. 150. As a case in point Sanders calls attention to the ambivalence expressed in the conclusion of Harvey Cox's *Fire from Heaven: The Rise of Pentecostal Spirituality and the Reshaping of Religion in the Twenty-first Century* (Reading, Mass.: Addison-Wesley, 1995), pp. 320-21.

[96]Douglas Gwyn et al., sponsored by Church of the Brethren et al., *A Declaration on Peace: In God's People, the World's Renewal Has Begun* (Scottdale, Penn.: Herald, 1991).

[97]James Y. Holloway and Will D. Campbell, "An Open Letter to Billy Graham," in *The Failure and the Hope: Essays of Southern Churchmen,* ed. Will D. Campbell and James Y. Holloway (Grand Rapids, Mich.: Eerdmans, 1972), pp. 109-19. Holloway and Campbell would have known that in the 1950s Graham had moved to integrate his own organization by inviting Howard O. Jones, a young black pastor from Cleveland, to join his evangelistic team. They would have known about Graham's "bold step" of inviting Martin Luther King Jr. to discuss the racial

situation with his team and to lead in prayer at the Madison Square Garden crusade of 1957. And they would have been aware of the fact that Graham had "personally removed the ropes separating the white and colored sections at a Chattanooga crusade" after he had become convinced that segregation is wrong. These and other "socially progressive" actions of Graham are narrated in William Martin's review of Graham's life, "A Workman That Needeth Not Be Ashamed," *Christianity Today,* November 13, 1995, pp. 22-23.

[98]Hollaway and Campbell, "Open Letter," p. 114.

[99]For Graham to baptize Dwight D. Eisenhower shortly after his inauguration was tantamount to having become chaplain to the U.S. presidency, a position that Graham would hold for much of the next four decades.

[100]Holloway and Campbell, *Failure and the Hope,* p. 115.

[101]Billy Graham, *Peace with God* (Garden City, N.Y.: Doubleday, 1953), p. 195.

[102]Dietrich Bonhoeffer's *Psalms: The Prayer Book of the Bible* (Minneapolis: Augsburg, 1974) provides an example of this kind of polyphonic reading of Scripture. Finding in the Psalms the "key" to reading the Bible, Bonhoeffer urges readers not to identify their voice with the voice of the psalm but instead to learn to place their voices in relation to the voices of the psalmist (David) and the voice of Christ.

In a different way Bonhoeffer's study *Life Together* calls attention to the never-ending dialogue that we are to have with the Bible. Bonhoeffer writes: "As a whole, the Scriptures are God's revealing Word. Only in the infiniteness of its inner relationships, in the connection of Old and New Testaments, of promise and fulfillment, sacrifice and law, law and gospel, cross and resurrection, faith and obedience, having and hoping, will the full witness to Jesus Christ the Lord be perceived." Describing this dialogical context of reading in language that suggests symphonic musical analogies, Bonhoeffer observes: "The Scripture is a whole and every word, every sentence possesses such multiple relationships with the whole that it is impossible always to keep the whole in view when listening to details. It becomes apparent therefore, that the whole of Scripture and hence every passage in it as well far surpasses our understanding" (Dietrich Bonhoeffer, *Life Together* [New York: Harper & Row, 1954], p. 51).

I would like to think that Bonhoeffer's conception of reading Scripture owes something to his experience with the black church (for a time he participated in Harlem's Abyssinian Baptist Church) and in particular to his enjoyment of the spirituals.

[103]C. H. Mason, quoted by Joe Maxwell in "Building the Church (of God in Christ)," *Christianity Today,* April 8, 1996, p. 26.

[104]Bonhoeffer, *Life Together,* p. 51.

[105]Contra Wayne A. Meeks, *The Origins of Christian Morality: The First Two Centuries* (New Haven, Conn.: Yale University Press, 1993), p. 216.

[106]Gerhard Lohfink, *The Work of God Goes On* (Philadelphia: Fortress, 1987), p. 26. The focus of Lohfink's meditation is Acts 4—5.

[107]This leads me to my final point, which is that there is an important difference to be drawn between the kind of ad hoc correlation that lies behind the Puritan John Robinson's phrase "The Lord hath more truth to break forth out of His holy

Word," which is pneumatologically oriented, and the Troeltschian conception of correlation which locates the origins or "invention" of Christian morality solely within human culture. The first places the Christian community within the context of a never-ending conversation with Scripture that is pneumatologically authorized and enabled; the second places Christian communities within a never-ending conversation with culture, which among other things invites us to style our witness after something other than the gospel. In the first instance, to practice the peaceable polyphony that is made possible by the Word that dwells in the midst of our words is part of what it means to live provisionally this side of the new Jerusalem; in the second, polyphony is situated politically in human culture. To use the trinity of terms that Meeks employs in his discussion, this political polyphony takes place within the overlapping contexts of "History, Pluralism and Morality." See Meeks, *Origins of Christian Morality*, pp. 211-19.

[108]L. Gregory Jones and Stephen E. Fowl, *Reading in Communion: Scripture and Ethics in Christian Life* (Grand Rapids, Mich.: Eerdmans, 1991); see especially chap. 6.

[109]Michael Welfare's explanation to Benjamin Franklin of why the Ephrata community did not publish its rules of discipline is found in H. W. Schneider, ed., *Benjamin Franklin: The Autobiography* (New York: Liberal Arts, 1949), p. 115. See also Donald F. Durnbaugh, *The Believers's Church: The History and Character of Radical Protestantism* (Scottdale, Penn.: Herald, 1985; New York: Macmillan, 1968), pp. 295-96.

[110]Durnbaugh, *Believers' Church*, p. 296.

Chapter 7: The Gospel and Racial Reconciliation/Keener

[1]David Walker, a black Christian protesting injustice, applied the expression in 1829 to unrepentant white racists. Long before Nation of Islam began (Gayraud S. Wilmore, *Black Religion and Black Radicalism: An Interpretation of the Religious History of Afro-Amerman People*, 2nd rev. ed. [Maryknoll, N.Y.: Orbis, 1983], p. 40), Henry Highland Garnet applied similar language in 1843: see his "Address to the Slaves of the United States of America," in *Witness for Freedom: African American Voices on Race, Slavery and Emancipation*, ed. C. Peter Ripley (Chapel Hill: University of North Carolina Press, 1993), pp. 165-69; the quote is from p. 169.

[2]See Frank M. Snowden Jr., *Blacks in Antiquity: Ethiopians in the Greco-Roman Experience* (Cambridge, Mass.: Belknap Press, Harvard University Press, 1970), and *Before Color Prejudice: The Ancient View of Blacks* (Cambridge, Mass.: Harvard University Press, 1983).

[3]When Paul uses "Greeks and barbarians" to summarize all humanity (Rom 1:14), he adopts a schema standard among Greeks and many who followed their usage (e.g., Isocrates *Nicocles/Cyprians* 50 Or. 3.37; *Panegyricus* 108, Or. 4; *Helen* 67-68, Or. 10; Plato *Alcibiades* 2, 141C; *Theaetetus* 175A; *Laws* 9.870AB; Strabo *Geography* 6.1.2; 13.1.1; 15.3.23; Plutarch *Agesilaus* 10.3; *Timoleon* 28.2; *Eumenes* 16.3; *Bride* 21; *Moralia* 141A; Dio Chrysostom *First Discourse on Kingship* 14; *9th or Isthmian Discourse* 12; *12th or Olympic Discourse* 11, 27-28; *31st Discourse* 20; *32nd Discourse* 35; *36th Discourse* 43; Sextus Empiricus *Against the Ethicists* 1.15; Diogenes Laertius 6.1.2; Athenaeus *Deipnosophists* 11.461b; Tatian 1, 21, 29). Some Roman texts

add Romans as a third category: Juvenal *Satires* 10.138; Quintilian *Institutio Oratoria* 5.10.24), though others are content to use the Greek categories (Cicero *De Inventione* 1.24.35; Seneca *Dialogi* 5.2.1; cf. Cicero *De Officiis* 3.26.99). Although Jews sometimes classified themeselves differently (cf. Philo *De Specialibus Legibus* 2.165), Greeks included Jews among "barbarians" (Strabo *Geography* 16.2.38), and some Jews followed suit (Josephus *Jewish Wars* 1.preamble 3). Jewish writers in Greek often summarized humanity as "Greeks and barbarians" (Josephus *Jewish Wars* 5.17; *Antiquities of the Jews* 1.107; 15.136; 18.20; *Against Apion* 1.201; 2.39; Philo *De Cherubim* 91; *De Ebrietate* 193; *De Abrahamo* 267; *De Vita Mosis* 2.20; *De Decalogo* 153; *De Specialibus Legibus* 2.18, 20, 44, 165; 4.120; *Quod Omnis Probus Liber Sit* 94, 98; *De Vita Contemplativa* 21; *Legatio ad Gaium* 145, 292). The basis for the contrast was sometimes primarily linguistic (e.g., Plato *Cratylus* 409DE; 421D; 425E-426A; Plutarch *De Liberis Educandis* 6, *Moralia* 4A; Sextus Empiricus *Outlines of Pyrrhonism* 3.267; Philo *De Confusione Linguarum* 6, 190).

[4]The authorship of Ephesians is frequently disputed. Against Pauline authorship see A. T. Lincoln, *Ephesians,* Word Biblical Commentary 42 (Dallas: Word, 1990), pp. lix-lxxiii; D. E. Nineham, "The Case Against the Pauline Authorship," in *Studies in Ephesians,* ed. F. L. Cross (London: A. R. Mowbray, 1956), pp. 21-35; C. L. Mitton, *Ephesians,* New Century Bible Commentary (Greenwood, S.C.: Attic, 1976), pp. 4-11; Wilfred L. Knox, *St. Paul and the Church of the Gentiles* (Cambridge: Cambridge University Press, 1939), p. 182; John C. Kirby, *Ephesians: Baptism and Pentecost—An Enquiry into the Structure and Purpose of the Epistle to the Ephesians* (Montreal: McGill University Press, 1968), pp. 3-56. In favor of Pauline authorship see J. N. Sanders, "The Case for the Pauline Authorship," in *Studies in Ephesians,* ed. F. L. Cross (London: A. R. Mowbray, 1956), pp. 9-20; J. A. T. Robinson, *Redating the New Testament* (Philadelphia: Westminster Press; London: SCM Press, 1976), p. 63; Markus Barth, *Ephesians,* 2 vols., Anchor Bible 34-34A (Garden City, N.Y.: Doubleday, 1974), 1:3-60; cf. H. J. Cadbury, "The Dilemma of Ephesians," *New Testament Studies* 5, no. 2 (January 1959): 91-102. I believe that all the elements of this letter's style appear in undisputedly Pauline letters, although by this period in his ministry (cf. Acts 19:9-10) his language in such letters has moved in a more Stoicizing direction (attested also in Philippians). Ancient rhetorical training included the adoption of various styles.

[5]Paul's *berakah* or blessing to God in Ephesians 1:3-14 introduces many of the letter's themes, as was frequent in his letters; see Peter T. O'Brien, "Ephesians 1: An Unusual Introduction to a New Testament Letter," *New Testament Studies* 25, no. 4 (July 1979): 504-16, p. 512.

[6]God's people also appear as a temple (Eph 2:19-22) in some contemporary Jewish documents (e.g., 1QS 8.5-9 [*serek hayyahad* from Qumran Cave 1]; Bertril Gartner, *The Temple and the Community in Qumran and the New Testament* [Cambridge: Cambridge University Press, 1965], pp. 16-46).

[7]Josephus *Jewish Wars* 2.266-70, 457-58. For other massacres in reprisal see *Jewish Wars* 2.458-68; *Life* 25.

[8]I intentionally use "hearers" rather than the less precise "readers": one person in the congregation would read, while others would simply hear, his letter (cf., e.g.,

Rev 1:3).

[9]Purity rules were common in ancient sanctuaries (e.g., inscriptions in Frederick C. Grant, *Hellenistic Religions: The Age of Syncretism* [Indianapolis: Bobbs-Merrill/Liberal Arts, 1953], pp. 6-7). Compare an eschatological idea excluding Gentiles portrayed in Joel 3:17 (Masoretic Text 4:17); Zechariah 14:21; but compare the coming of Gentiles to Jerusalem for homage, tribute or worship in Isaiah 18:7; 60:3-16; Zechariah 14:17; Tobit 13:11-12: *Sibylline Oracles* 3.716-19, 772-74; 1QM 12.14 [*War Scroll* from Qumran Cave 1]. Jesus cites Isaiah 56:3-8, the text most decisively supporting his position.

[10]Josephus *Antiquities of the Jews* 15.417; *Jewish Wars* 5.193-200; 6.124-26. For the extant inscription see Efrat Carmon, ed., *Inscriptions Reveal: Documents from the Time of the Bible, the Mishna and the Talmud*, trans. R. Grafman (Jerusalem: Israel Museum, 1973), pp. 76, 167-68, §169; Josephus, *The Jewish War*, ed. Gaalya Cornfeld (Grand Rapids, Mich.: Zondervan, 1982), pp. 354-56. The penalty probably applied even to Roman citizens like Paul (pace Alfredo Mordechai Rabello, "The Legal Condition of the Jews in the Roman Empire," *Aufsteig und Niedergang der römischen Welt* 10.13.662-762 [Berlin: Walter de Gruyter, 1980], pp. 737-38). Although Romans otherwise withheld the right of capital jurisdiction from subject peoples, they sometimes permitted it for temple violations; one may compare their permission for violation of the Eleusis sanctuary (John J. O'Rourke, "Roman Law and the Early Church," in *The Catacombs and the Colosseum: The Roman Empire as the Setting of Primitive Christianity*, ed. Stephen Benko and John J. O'Rourke [Valley Forge, Penn.: Judson, 1971], pp. 165-86, especially p. 174).

[11]Several paragraphs in this section overlap with chapter six of Glenn Usry and Craig S. Keener, *Black Man's Religion: Can Christianity Be Afrocentric?* (Downers Grove, Ill.: InterVarsity Press, 1996), although I have added more detailed information here.

[12]Paul's activity, if understood, would have appeared virtuous within Judaism: cf. Acts 18:18; 21:24 with Josephus *Antiquities of the Jews* 19.293-94; *Jewish Wars* 2.313-14.

[13]The governor provided extra troops for the Roman garrison in the Fortress Antonia during the crowded festivals. Riots could easily occur in the crowded temple area, leading to the trampling of many people (Josephus *Jewish Wars* 2.224-27); the garrison thus took special precautions during the festivals (Josephus *Jewish Wars* 5.244).

[14]On the fortress see, for example, Josephus *Jewish Wars* 1.118, 121, 401; 5.238-45; 6.68, 74; *Life* 20; Tacitus *Historiae* 5.11.

[15]On this Egyptian Jew, who had recently escaped Felix's grasp, see more fully Josephus *Jewish Wars* 2.261-63. The proposed identification with Ben Stada in rabbinic texts (Joseph Klausner, *Jesus: His Life, Times and Teaching* [New York: Menorah, 1979; n.p.: Macmillan, 1925], pp. 21-22) is fanciful.

[16]By extension the term *sicarii* could apply to any murderers (Quintilian *Institutio Oratoria* 10.1.12), but in this period in Judea it applied specifically to nationalistic Jewish terrorists who frequently carried daggers resembling Roman *sicae*; see Josephus *Antiquities of the Jews* 20.185-89, 208-10; *Jewish Wars* 4.516; 7.253, 262,

437; see further R. A. Horsley, "The Sicarii: Ancient Jewish 'Terrorists,' " *Journal of Religion* 59 (1979): 435-58. It is not surprising that Paul's interlocutor might have viewed various revolutionary movements (*sicarii* and the Egyptian) as related (cf. Josephus *Jewish Wars* 2.259-60).

[17]On bilingualism see, for example, John Meier, *A Marginal Jew: Rethinking the Historical Jesus,* vol. 1, *The Roots of the Problem and the Person* (New York: Doubleday, 1991), pp. 255-68. On the usual lack of proficiency, see G. H. R. Horsley, *New Documents Illustrating Early Christianity* (North Ryde, N.S.W.: Ancient History Documentary Research Centre, Macquarie University, 1989), 5:23-24; Josephus *Antiquities of the Jews* 20.263-64. If Luke refers to the level of Paul's Greek, we must regard as ill-founded Ernst Haenchen's suspicion of Lukan inaccuracy because "the Egyptian Jews spoke Greek by preference" (Ernst Haenchen, *The Acts of the Apostles: A Commentary* [Philadelphia: Westminster Press, 1971], p. 621). Paul would not have needed Latin here; the Roman administration of Syropalestine conducted its public affairs in Greek (see A. N. Sherwin-White, *Roman Society and Roman Law in the New Testament* [Oxford: Oxford University Press, 1963; Grand Rapids: Baker Book House, 1978], pp. 150-51). Romans in the western Mediterranean resented the encroachments of Greek there (e.g., Juvenal *Satires* 6.184-99; on the fluency of Roman Jews' Greek see Harry J. Leon, *The Jews of Ancient Rome* [Philadelphia: Jewish Publication Society of America], pp. 75-92), but in the East it remained the lingua franca (e.g., Apuleius *Metamorphoses* 9.39) and was spoken, albeit not as the only language, in Palestine (cf., e.g., A. W. Argyle, "Greek Among the Jews of Palestine in New Testament Times," *New Testament Studies* 20, no. 1 [October 1973]: 87-89; G. Mussies, "Greek as the Vehicle of Early Christianity," *New Testament Studies* 29 [1983]: 356-69; J. N. Sevenster, *Do You Know Greek? Novum Testamentum* Supplement 19 [Leiden: E. J. Brill, 1968], pp. 176-91). In *Corpus Inscriptionum Judaicarum* more Palestinian Jewish inscriptions appear in Greek than in Aramaic or Hebrew, and even rabbinic texts attest the early use of Greek (e.g., *y. Soṭa 7:1, §4*).

[18]Citizens of cities ranked higher socially than did the numerous resident aliens present (Ramsay MacMullen, *Roman Social Relations: 50 B.C. to A.D. 284* [New Haven, Conn.: Yale University Press, 1974], p. 59); one could be born in or voted in by the citizen assembly (Chariton *Chaereas and Callirhoe* 8.8.13-14). On civic pride or honor see, for example, Aelius Aristides on Rome; Isocrates *Panegyricus Panathenaicus;* Diogenes Laertius *Lives* 7.1.12: Heraclitus *Epistle* 9 to Hermodorus; Quintilian *Institutio Oratoria* 3.7.26; *Rhetorica ad Herennium* 3.3.4; *Genesis Rabbah* 34:15; cf. Dieter Georgi, "Socioeconomic Reasons for the 'Divine Man' as a Propagandistic Pattern," in *Aspects of Religious Propaganda in Judaism and Early Christianity,* ed. Elisabeth Schüssler Fiorenza (Notre Dame, Ind.: University of Notre Dame, 1976), pp. 27-42, especially pp. 27-28: H. J. Cadbury, *The Book of Acts in History* (London: Adam & Charles Black, 1955), pp. 32-33. Local municipal citizenship and Roman citizenship were viewed as compatible by this period (John E. Stambaugh and David L. Balch, *The New Testament in Its Social Environment,* Library of Early Christianity 2 [Philadelphia: Westminster Press, 1986], p. 31). For Paul's wording, compare Rendel Harris, "Did St. Paul Quote Euripides?"

Expository Times 31, no. 1 (October 1919): 36-37; Josephus *Life* 1. Haenchen's skepticism (*Acts,* p. 621) is thus unwarranted.

[19]Some evidence exists for some learning of Hebrew for Scripture study and prayer (e.g., *Epistle of Aristeas* 11.30.38; *Jubilees* 12:25-27: Tosepta *Haggai* 1:2; *Sifre Numbers* 39.2.1; *Sifre Deuteronomy* 46.1.2; cf. J. M. Grintz, "Hebrew as the Spoken and Written Language in the Last Days of the Second Temple," *Journal of Biblical Literature* 79 1960: 32-17). Aramaic was far more pervasive as a spoken language (see, e.g., Matthew Black, "The Recovery of the Language of Jesus," *New Testament Studies* 3, no. 14 [July 1957]: 305-13; Martin Goodman, *State and Society in Roman Galilee A.D. 132-212,* Oxford Centre for Postgraduate Hebrew Studies [Totowa, N.J.: Rowman & Allanfield, 1983], p. 66; cf. Josephus's rhetorical understatement in *Jewish Wars* 1.3; *Antiquities of the Jews* 1.7; 20.263-64). The crowd likely would not have understood a long address in biblical Hebrew.

[20]On the sense of "raised in Jerusalem," see especially W. C. van Unnik, *Tarsus or Jerusalem: The City of Paul's Youth* (London: Epworth, 1962). Emphasizing particular aspects of one's account for a particular audience was standard rhetorical practice (e.g., Callirhoe in Chariton *Chaereas and Callirhoe* 2.5.10-11 omits Chaereas's kick).

[21]Stephen's speech also decentralizes God's presence in Israel's history, challenging traditions about the temple (Acts 6:13). The similarity of the charge against Paul in Acts 21:28 creates suspense, although Paul, unlike Stephen, survives through Roman intervention (cf. similarly Acts 19:30-31).

[22]Josephus *Jewish Wars* 6.301-5.

[23]Josephus *Jewish Wars* 5.194; 6.124-26; *Antiquities of the Jews* 15.417.

[24]It is unlikely that the issue is economic exploitation per se: given varying local currencies, moneychangers were necessary (Goodman, *State and Society in Roman Galilee,* p. 57; E. P. Sanders, *Judaism: Practice and Belief, 63 B.C.E.-66. C.E.* [Philadelphia: Trinity Press International, 1992], pp. 63-65), and the temple moneychangers reportedly made little profit (*m. Šeqalim* 1:6-7], though compare *m. Keritot* 1:7). Some charged the Sadducean aristocracy with corruption (1QpHab 9.4-5; 11.6-7 [*pesher on Habakkuk* from Qumran Cave 1]; Cairo *Damascus Document* 5.6-7; cf. *Psalms of Solomon* 8:11-13: *Testament of Levi* 14:1, if not an interpolation) or false teaching (various rabbinic texts), but Jesus may oppose especially their refusal to recognize his mission (Mk 11:27—12:12).

[25]Various factors support the authenticity of Jesus' prediction. First, some of Jesus' contemporaries shared the expectation (*Testament of Moses* 6:8-9; *1 Enoch* 90:28-29; 11QTemple 29.8-10 [*Temple Scroll* from Qumran Cave 11]; Josephus *Jewish Wars* 6.301, 304, 306, 309); an accurate warning of Roman conquest hardly need be a "prophecy after the event" (e.g., 1QpHab 9.6-7 [*pesher on Habakkuk* from Qumran Cave 1]). Second, if Jewish people recognized the first destruction as judgment (*Psalms of Solomon* 2:1-10; 17:5; cf. *Song Rabbah* 8:12 §1) and many later so recognized the second destruction (e.g., Josephus *Jewish Wars* 6.288-315: *Pesiqta Rabbati* 26:6; cf. *Apocalypse of Abraham* 27:3-7), one has no reason to suppose that a prophet of judgment might not expect the event. Third, one creating a prophecy to fit a past event would likely have conformed it better to historical reality: the

fire, some stone's remaining attached, etc. Fourth, the prophecy fits the criterion of embarrassment in the early period: Jewish Christians continued to respect and worship in the temple (Acts 2:46; 21:26-27). Finally, the point is multiply attested in various forms: a symbolic act of judgment (Mt 21:12), testimony of witnesses later Christians believed to be false (Mt 26:61; cf. Mk 15:29; Jn 2:19; Acts 6:14), and Q material (the house being left desolate—Mt 23:38 parallel Lk 13:35).

[26]Suetonius *Claudius* 25.4. Scholars currently debate the extent of Claudius's expulsion (cf. Dio Cassius 60.6); one may wish to compare the analogous expulsion under Tiberius in Suetonius *Tiberius* 36 but also the relatively uninterrupted Jewish life in Rome (*Corpus Inscriptionum Judaicarum* 1:lxxiii).

[27]Although various schools (Plutarch *Quaestiones Romanae* 95, *Moralia* 286D; *Eating of Flesh* 1.1, *Moralia* 993A; Philostratus *Vita Apollonii* 1.8; Diogenes Laertius *Lives* 8.1.12-13; 24.8.19), cults (e.g., Plutarch *Isis* 2, 5, *Moralia* 351F; 352F; Apuleius *Metamorphoses* 11.21), rituals (e.g., *Papyri-Graecae Magicae* 4.52-55, 3079-81) and ethnic groups (Herodotus *Historiae* 3.100; Epictetus *Discourses* 1.11.12-13; 1.22.4; Artemidoris *Oneirocriticon* 1.8; Plutarch *Quaestiones Romanae* 21; *Moralia* 268E; *Isis* 7, *Moralia* 353C; Lucian *Syrian Goddess* 54; Sextus Empiricus *Outlines of Pyrrhonism* 3.220-25) practiced diverse food customs, Greeks and Romans particularly mocked Jews for these (Plutarch *Table-Talk* 4.4.4, *Moralia* 669C; Molly Whittaker, *Jews and Christians: Greco-Roman Views* [Cambridge: Cambridge University Press, 1984], pp. 73-80: John G. Gager, *The Origins of Anti-Semitism: Attitudes Toward Judaism in Pagan and Christian Antiquity* [New York: Oxford University Press, 1983], p. 57; J. N. Sevenster, *The Roots of Pagan Anti-Semitism in the Ancient World, Novum Testamentum* Suppplement 41 [Leiden: E. J. Brill, 1975], pp. 136-39). Gentiles likewise ridiculed Jewish practice of the sabbath (Plutarch *On Superstition* 8, *Moralia* 169C; cf. Ex 5:8, 17).

[28]For denunciations of idolatry, which was largely though not exclusively a Gentile sin see, for example, Bel and the Dragon; Epistle of Jeremiah; *Epistle of Aristeas* 134-38; *Sibylline Oracles* 3.8-35; 4.4-23; *Testament of Solomon* 26; *t. Bekorot* 3:12; *Pe'a* 1:2; *Sanhedrin* 13:8; *Sifra Vayyiqura Dibura Dehobah* par. 1.34.1.3; *Sifre Numbers* 112.2.2; *Sifre Deuteronomy* 43.4.1; 54.3.2; *'Abot de Rabbi Nathan* 40A. Jews regarded homosexual behavior much more exclusively as a Gentile vice, virtually inconceivable among themselves in this period (e.g., *Epistle of Aristeas* 152; *Sibylline Oracles* 3.185-86, 596-600, 764; 4.34; 5.166, 387, 430; *t. Horayot* 2:5-6).

[29]Sins such as envy (e.g., Wisdom 6:23; *Epistle of Aristeas* 224; Josephus *Antiquities of the Jews* 2.13; *Jewish Wars* 1.77: Philo *Quod Omnis Probus Liber Sit* 13; *Sibylline Oracles* 3.660-64; *Testament of Gad* 7:2; *Testament of Simeon* 3; *Testament of Solomon* 6:4), pride (e.g., 1QS 4.9 [*serek hayyahad* from Qumran Cave 1]; Sirach 3:28; 10:7, 12-13; 13:1, 20; 22:22; 25:1; Philo *De Posteritate Caini* 52; *Testament of Reuben* 3:5; *Testament of Judah* 13:2; *Testament of Job* 15:8-10) and slander (e.g., 1QS 7.15-16 [*serek hayyahad* from Qumran Cave 1]; Philo *De Specialibus Legibus* 4.59-60; *Sifre Deuteronomy* 1.8.2-3; 275.1.1; *'Abot de Rabbi Nathan* 9; 40A; 16, §36; 41, §116B) also appear in condemnations of Jewish vices or warnings to Jewish hearers. Vice lists were a standard rhetorical form (e.g., Plato *Leges* 1.649D; Aristotle *Ethica Eudemia* 2.3.4, 1220b-21a: *On Virtues and Vices* 1249a-51b; Epictetus *Discourses* 2.8.23; Diogenes

Epistle 36 to Timomachus; Maximus of Tyre *Discourses* 36.4; 1QS 4.9-11 [*serek hayyahad* from Qumran Cave 1]; Wisdom 14:25-26; Philo *De Sacrificiis Abelis et Caini* 32; *De Posteritate Caini* 52; *Sibylline Oracles* 2.255-82; *Testament of Levi* 17:11; *Didache* 5).

[30]See, for example, C. G. Montefiore, "The Spirit of Judaism," in *The Beginnings of Christianity*, ed. F. J. Foakes Jackson and Kirsopp Lake (Grand Rapids, Mich.: Baker Book House, 1979), 1:35-81, p. 43. For Abraham as a model proselyte see *Mekilta Nezikin* 18:36ff.; *b. Sukka* 49b; *Genesis Rabbah* 39:8; *Numbers Rabbah* 8:9.

[31]Cf. Sirach 25:24; *1 Enoch* 98:4; *Life of Adam and Eve* 44.3-4; *Sifre Deuteronomy* 323.5.1; 339.1.2; and especially 4 Ezra 3:7, 20-22, 30; 7:118-26; *2 Apocalypse of Baruch* 17:2-3; 23:4; 48:42-45; 54:15, 19; 56:5-6.

[32]Aristotle *Politica* 1.2.13.1254b; Seneca *Dialogi* 2.16.1; *Epistle to Lucilius* 8.5; Epictetus *Discourses* 1.3.3; Plutarch *Isis* 78; *Moralia* 382F; Marcus Aurelius *Meditations* 2.2; *Epistle of Aristeas* 245, 277; 4 Maccabees 1:29; 2:18, 21-22; 3:2-5; Philo *De Gigantibus* 29; *Sentences of Sextus* 139.204-9.

[33]1QS 3.25—4.1 [*serek hayyahad* from Qumran Cave 1]; Cairo *Damascus Document* 2.15-16; *Jubilees* 35:9; 4 Ezra 7:92; *Testament of Judah* 20:1 2; *m. 'Abot* 2:11; *Sifra Shemini Mekilta deMiluim* 99.2.3; *Sifra Ahare Mot* pq. 13.194.2.11; *Sifre Numbers* 40.1.3; *Sifre Deuteronomy* 32.3.1; 45.1.3.

[34]Romans 10:6-10 borrows the language of Deuteronomy 30, comparing Jesus with Torah. Cf. discussions in M. Jack Suggs, " 'The Word Is Near You': Romans 10:6-8 Within the Purpose of the Letter," in *Christian History and Interpretation: Studies Presented to John Knox*, ed. W. R. Farmer, C. F. D Moule and R. R. Niebuhr (Cambridge: Cambridge University Press, 1967), pp. 289-312, especially pp. 299-308; Daniel P. Fuller, *Gospel and Law: Contrast or Continuum* (Grand Rapids, Mich.: Eerdmans, 1980), pp. 66-86; Archibald M. Hunter, *The Gospel According to St. Paul* (Philadelphia: Westminster Press, 1966), p. 68; W. D. Davies, *Torah in the Messianic Age and/or the Age to Come*, Journal of Biblical Literature Monograph 7 (Philadelphia: Society of Biblical Literature, 1952), p. 87; compare also relevant texts in *Pesiqta Rabbati* 47:4; *Ruth Rabbah* 2:3; Ephraim E. Urbach, *The Sages: Their Concepts and Beliefs*, trans. Israel Abrahams, 2nd ed., 2 vols. (Jerusalem: Magnes, 1979), 1:329. For possible polemical imagery compare *Sifre Deuteronomy* 49.2.1. But the language may simply reflect a common hyperbolic image of the day (cf. Chariton *Chaereas and Callirhoe* 3.2.5, 7).

[35]This is one of the most controversial passages in Romans, but it seems unlikely that by "Israel" Paul means something different here from what he meant in the preceding context. Cf. Johannes Munck, *Christ and Israel: An Interpretation of Romans 9-11* (Philadelphia: Fortress, 1967), p. 136; George E. Ladd, "Israel and the Church," *Evangelical Quarterly* 36 (1964): 206-13.

[36]On the Gentile mission in Luke-Acts see Jacques Dupont, *The Salvation of the Gentiles: Essays on the Acts of the Apostles*, trans. John R. Keating (New York: Paulist, 1979). On Luke's geographical schema see especially James M. Scott, "Luke's Geographical Horizon," in *The Book of Acts in Its Greco-Roman Setting*, ed. David W. J. Gill and Conrad Gempf, vol. 2 in *The Book of Acts in Its First-Century Setting* (Grand Rapids, Mich.: Eerdmans; Carlisle, U.K.: Paternoster, 1994), pp.

483-544.

[37]See more fully my *Matthew,* IVP New Testament Commentary Series (Downers Grove, Ill.: InterVarsity Press, 1997).

[38]*M. 'Abot* 1:5; *b. Berakot* 43b; *'Erubin* 53b; *y. Soṭa* 1:1, §7; *'Aboda Zara* 2:3, §1; in some later traditions even God avoids talking with women *(Genesis Rabbah* 48:20; 63:7).

[39]Asking for water would not be considered promiscuous (cf. *b. Qiddušin* 9a) but could have conjugal connotations (e.g., the girl who acts like Rebekah and wishes Rabbi Joshua to act like Eliezer in *Lamentations Rabbah* 1.1.19). Also recall that Jacob, whose well this reportedly was, had met Rachel at a well (Gen 29:9-10); for echoes of conjugal tradition in Genesis 24 compare Norman R. Bomneau, "The Woman at the Well—John 4 and Genesis 24," *Bible Translator* 67 (October 1973): 1252-59; for Jacob traditions in the passage, see J. H. Neyrey, "Jacob Traditions and the Interpretation of John 4:10-26," *Catholic Biblical Quarterly* 41, no. 3 (July 1979): 419-37. The woman's assertion of singleness (Jn 4:17) could have been construed as a sexual invitation (cf. *b. Soṭa* 10a).

[40]For Samaritan religious strictness, see S. Dar, "Three *Menorot* from Western Samaria," *Israel Exploration Quarterly* 34, no. 2-3 (1984): 177-79 and plate 20BC.

[41]See *m. Ṭoharot* 5:8; *Niddah* 4:1; *t. Niddah* 5:1; *b. Šabbat* 17a; cf. *Yebamot* 86a.

[42]Jewish people also often used "our father Jacob" (e.g., the later *Pesiqta de Rab Kahana* 23:2) and sometimes complained that Samaritans identified themselves with the Jewish people only when it was convenient (Josephus *Antiquities of the Jews* 11.340-41).

[43]See Josephus *Jewish Wars* 1.63-66; R. J. Bull, "Field Report Xll," *Bulletin of the American Schools of Oriental Research* 180 (December 1965): 37-41, p. 41; R. J. Bull, "An Archaeological Context for Understanding John 4:20," *Biblical Archaeology* 38, no. 1 (March 1975): 54-59; Jack Finegan, *The Archaeology of the New Testament: The Life of Jesus and the Beginning of the Early Church* (Princeton, N.J.: Princeton University Press, 1969), p. 35.

[44]I have borrowed these examples from my research for *Black Man's Religion,* although they appear at various locations in that book.

[45]Compare Ida Rousseau Mukenge, *The Black Church in Urban America: A Case Study in Political Economy* (Lanham, Md.: University Press of America, 1983), p. 27.

[46]Mark A. Noll, *A History of Christianity in the United States and Canada* (Grand Rapids, Mich.: Eerdmans, 1992), p. 138. On Liele and David George, see also James Melvin Washington, *Frustrated Fellowship: The Black Baptist Quest for Social Power* (Macon, Ga.: Mercer University Press, 1986), pp. 8-9: Owen D. Pelt and Ralph Lee Smith, *The Story of the National Baptists* (New York: Vantage, 1960), pp. 29-41; on Bryan see Pelt and Smith, *National Baptists,* pp. 41-45; Milton C. Semett, ed., *Afro-American History: A Documentary Witness* (Durham, N.C.: Duke University Press, 1985), pp. 48-50.

[47]Noll, *History of Christianity,* pp. 138-39.

[48]Washington, *Frustrated Fellowship,* p. 11.

[49]See Lamin Sanneh, *West African Christianity: The Religious Impact* (Maryknoll, N.Y.: Orbis, 1983), p. 76: Noll, *History of Christianity,* p. 136. On George, see more

fully Grant Gordon, *From Slavery to Freedom: The Life of David George, Pioneer Black Baptist Minister* (Hantsport, Novia Scotia: Lancelot, 1993).

[50] Albert J. Raboteau, *Slave Religion: The "Invisible Institution" in the Antebellum South* (New York: Oxford University Press, 1978), p. 132, cf. p. 148; John Brown Childs, *The Political Black Minister: A Study in Afro-American Politics and Religion* (Boston: G. K. Hall, 1980), pp. 29-30.

[51] Raboteau, *Slave Religion*, pp. 133-41.

[52] Noll, *History of Christianity*, p. 109, emphasizing that the Great Awakening bridged "the chasm between white and black cultures."

[53] Lerone Bennett Jr., *Before the Mayflower: A History of the Negro in America, 1619-1964*, rev. ed. (Baltimore: Penguin, 1966), p. 63.

[54] Monroe Fordham, *Major Themes in Northern Black Religious Thought, 1800-1860* (Hicksville, N.Y.: Exposition, 1975), p. 111.

[55] See Herbert S. Klein, "Anglicanism, Catholicism and the Negro Slave," in *The Debate over Slavery*, ed. Ann Lane (Urbana, Ill.: University of Illinois Press, 1971), pp. 137-90, especially pp. 172-73.

[56] John Woolman, *Some Considerations on the Keeping of Negroes, 1754; Considerations on Keeping Negroes, 1762* (Philadelphia: James Chattin, 1754; reprint New York: Viking, 1976).

[57] Raboteau, *Slave Religion*, p. 143; Childs, *Political Black Minister*, pp. 27-28.

[58] Wilmore, *Black Religion and Black Radicalism*, p. 34.

[59] Alice Dana Adams, *The Neglected Period of Anti-slavery in America (1808-1831)* (Gloucester, Mass.: Peter Smith, 1964), p. 97.

[60] Friends (Quakers) were strongly antislavery (Adams, *Negelcted Period of Anti-Slavery*, pp. 101-3; Daniel P. Mannix with Malcolm Cowley, *Black Cargoes: A History of the Atlantic Slave Trade, 1518-1865* [New York: Viking, 1962], pp. 171-90).

[61] Although Baptists by their polity had no central organization from which to make pronouncements, some ministers even in the South and as early as 1808 were working against slavery (Adams, *Neglected Period of Anti-slavery*, pp. 100-101; Leonard L. Haynes Jr. *The Negro Community Within American Protestantism, 1619-1844* [Boston: Christopher, 1953], pp. 111-12). For Baptist antislavery work, see further Washington, *Frustrated Fellowship*, pp. 27-38.

[62] Adams, *Neglected Period of Anti-slavery*, pp. 98-100.

[63] Episcopalians and Catholics apparently remained largely neutral (ibid., p. 101). On the Unitarians (lamenting their slow response to abolitionism), see Samuel J. May, *Some Recollections of Our Antislavery Conflict* (Boston: Fields, Osgood, 1869); for Congregationalist antislavery, Calvin Montague Clark, *American Slavery and Maine Congregationalists* (Bangor, Maine: C. M. Clark, 1940).

[64] Pelt and Smith, *National Baptists*, p. 27.

[65] Wilmore, *Black Religion and Black Radicalism*, p. 56.

[66] See documents in *Witness for Freedom*, pp. 201-10.

[67] See Wilmore, *Black Religion and Black Radicalism*, p. 31.

[68] Ibid., p. 32.

[69] Bennett, *Before the Mayflower*, p. 196.

[70] Sara Bullard, *Free at Last: A History of the Civil Rights Movement and Those Who Died*

in the Struggle (New York: Oxford University Press; Southern Poverty Law Center, 1993), pp. 66-67. For some other whites who served the black community, see Cornel West, Race Matters (Boston: Beacon, 1993), p. 85.

[71]See Lester B. Scherer, Slavery and the Churches in Early America, 1619-1819 (Grand Rapids, Mich.: Eerdmans, 1975).

[72]Dorothy Sterling, We Are Your Sisters: Black Women in the Nineteenth Century (New York: Norton, 1984), p. 115.

[73]On the dichotomy see Ronald J. Sider, One-Sided Christianity? Uniting the Church to Heal a Lost and Broken World (Grand Rapids, Mich.: Zondervan; San Francisco: HarperSanFrancisco, 1993).

[74]We survey this more fully in Usry and Keener, Black Man's Religion, pp. 98-109.

[75]For the social activism of nineteenth-century evangelicals see, for example, Timothy L. Smith, Revivalism and Social Reform: American Protestantism on the Eve of the Civil War (Baltimore: Johns Hopkins University Press, 1980; Norris Magnuson, Salvation in the Slums: Evangelical Social Work, 1865-1920, American Theological Library Association Monograph 190 (Metuchen, N.J.: Scarecrow, 1977; Grand Rapids: Baker Book House, 1990).

[76]Even in the social gospel movement of the early twentieth century, when the polarization that would lead to the modernist-fundamentalist controversy of the 1920s was beginning, "More often in the black church one encounters a figure like Francis J. Grimke, who was a theological conservative making liberal social pronouncements" than the reverse (Ronald C. White Jr., Liberty and Justice for All: Racial Reform and the Social Gospel (1877-1925), Rauschenbusch Lectures, n.s. 2 [San Francisco: Harper & Row, 1990], p. 120).

Chapter 8: Acts 10:34, a Text for Racial and Cultural Reconciliation Among Christians/Scott

[1]Ephesians 4:1; Philippians 1:27; Colossians 1:10; 1 Thessalonians 2:12. Scripture quotations in this essay, unless otherwise noted, follow the Revised Standard Version.

[2]The word is prosōpolēmptēs. It occurs only here in the New Testament. It means "one who shows partiality"; here, with the negative, it speaks of God as "he who is not one to show partiality" (Walter Bauer, William F. Arndt and F. Wilbur Gingrich, A Greek-English Lexicon of the New Testament and Other Early Christian Literature, 2nd ed. [Chicago: University of Chicago Press, 1979], p. 720). The concept of impartiality is also conveyed with other words in the Greek New Testament; ou lambaneis prosōpon (= "not receive the face," as in the Septuagint, Lk 20:21); prosōpolēmpsia (= show partiality, Rom 2:11; Eph 6:9; Col 3:25; Jas 2:1); diastolē (= distinction or difference, Rom 10:12); and prosklisis (= inclination [with kata = in the spirit of partiality], 1 Tim 5:21).

[3]This interplay between foods and people may reflect the same kind of thinking implicit in some of the Jewish interpretive methods, such as the seven middoth of Hillel; cf. Moses Mielziner, Introduction to the Talmud (1894; reprint New York: Bloch, 1968), pp. 117-19; H. L. Strack and G. Stemberger, Introduction to the Talmud and Midrash, trans. Markus Bockmuehl (Edinburgh: T & T Clark, 1991); and

J. Julius Scott Jr., *Customs and Controversies: Intertestamental Jewish Background of the New Testament* (Grand Rapids, Mich.: Baker Book House, 1995), pp. 127-33. Two of these rules may be especially significant. *Qal Wahomer* (from the light [less important] to the heavy [more important]) asserts that what applies to less significant persons, things or actions applies equally to the more significant. This principle seems to be behind Jesus' reference to birds and people in Matthew 6:25-27 and Luke 12:22-25. If God provides for birds (the lighter or less significant), how much more will he do so for people [the heavier or more significant]? *Kelal u-ferat u-ferat u-Relal* (the general and particular, the particular and the general) asserts that truths, principles or procedures relating to a particular thing or incidents also relate to general classes and groups; what can be said of the general applies as well to the particular. Thus what could be said about foods or eating companions (the lesser) should apply as well to the greater, to all parts of the system and to all persons, even Gentiles. If God pronounced foods clean (a particular part of the general structure that maintained Jewish distinctiveness) then the whole structure might also be involved.

[4]See E. Lohse, "προσωπολημπσία," *Theological Dictionary of the New Testament*, ed. Gerhard Kittel and Geoffrey W. Bromiley, 10 vols. (Grand Rapids, Mich.: Eerdmans, 1964-1976), 6:779-80; Jouette M. Bassler, "Luke and Paul on Impartiality," *Biblica* 66, no. 4 (1985): 546-52.

[5]Literally the Hebrew *lo' wissa' panim* means that God "does not lift up his face." The Septuagint Greek, *ou thaumazei prosōpon,* means that God "regards not persons."

[6]Note also the intertestamental Jewish writing *Psalms of Solomon* 2:19.

[7]Job 12:8, 10; Proverbs 18:5; 28:21; Isaiah 3:9; Malachi 2:9.

[8]Exodus 23:3; Leviticus 19:15; Deuteronomy 1:17; 16:19; Psalm 82:2; Proverbs 24:23.

[9]For a more detailed discussion see J. Julius Scott Jr., "The Cornelius Incident in the Light of Its Jewish Setting," *Journal of the Evangelical Theological Society* 34, no. 4 (December 1991): 475-84.

[10]The apostolic fathers: *1 Clement* 1.3; *Epistle of Pseudo-Barnabas* 4.12; and *Epistle of Polycarp* 6.1.

[11]Jeremiah Wright, "The Black Church Since World War II: The Invisible Giant," a lecture given at Wheaton College on February 26, 1996, in celebration of African-American History Week (a tape recording is available from the Media Resources Department, Wheaton College, Wheaton, IL 60187). Wright frequently insisted, "Difference is not deficiency."

[12]F. F. Bruce sees the joint principles of "Christian liberty and Christian charity" behind Paul's statements in Romans 14:1—15:6 (F. F. Bruce, *The Letter of Paul the Apostle to the Romans,* rev. ed., Tyndale New Testament Commentaries [Grand Rapids, Mich.: Eerdmans, 1985], pp. 230-41). I have suggested that the injunction to abstain from "things strangled" in the decrees of the Jerusalem Council (Acts 15:20, 29; cf. Acts 21:25) involves the request that Gentiles show sensitivity and consideration toward those Jewish practices that do not involve theological or moral issues; see J. Julius Scott Jr., *The Church of Jerusalem,* A.D. *30-100: An*

Investigation of the Growth of Internal Factions and the Extension of the Influence in the Larger Church, unpublished Ph.D. dissertation presented to the University of Manchester, England (1969), pp. 183-91. See also J. Julius Scott Jr., "Parties in the Church of Jerusalem as Seen in the Book of Acts," *Journal of the Evangelical Theological Society* 18, no. 4 (Fall 1975): 217-27; J. Julius Scott Jr., "Textual Variants of the Apostolic Decrees and Their Setting in the Early Church," in *The Living and Active Word of God: Studies in Honor of Samuel J. Schultz,* ed. Morris Inch and Ronald Youngblood (Winona Lake, Ind.: Eisenbrauns, 1983), pp. 174-75.

[13]Justin Martyr *Dialogue with Trypho* 47 (written about A.D. 135) speaks of some Gentile Christians who do not believe certain Jews will be saved, although they recognize that Jesus is the Messiah, believe in and obey him but wish to observe Jewish institutions and customs. Justin himself believes that these Jewish Christians will be saved.

[14]See J. Julius Scott Jr., "Race Relations, Social Change and the Church," *Presbuteron: Covenant Seminary Review* 3, no. 1 (Spring 1977): 20-29. The journal article is a slightly altered form of material from a pamphlet by the same title that was printed by Belhaven College in Jackson, Mississippi (1966).

[15]I gratefully acknowledge the suggestions and assistance of friends John and Annette McRay and Robert D. Carlson, and my wife, Florence.

Chapter 9: How We Do Church/Sanders

[1]Cheryl Townsend Gilkes, "We Have a Beautiful Mother," in *Living the Intersection,* ed. Cheryl Sanders (Minneapolis: Fortress, 1995).

[2]C. Eric Lincoln, *The Black Church Since Frazier* (New York: Schocken, 1974), p. 116.

[3]Ephraim Radner, "From 'Liberation' to 'Exile': A New Image for Church Mission," *The Christian Century* 106, no. 30 (October 18, 1989): 931.

[4]Ibid.

[5]Ibid., p. 932.

[6]For further discussion of the concept of exile and exilic ecclesiology see Cheryl J. Sanders, *Saints in Exile: The Holiness-Pentecostal Experience in African American Religion and Culture* (New York: Oxford University Press, 1996).

[7]Radner, "From 'Liberation' to 'Exile,' " p. 933.

[8]Ibid.

[9]Ibid., p. 934.

Chapter 10: Meeting Messiah/Powell

[1]Ruby K. Payne, *A Framework: Understanding and Working with Students and Adults from Poverty* (Baytown, Tex.: RFT Publications, 1995).

Contributors

Vincent Bacote is a doctoral student in theology at Drew University.

Michael Cartwright is assistant professor and chair of the philosophy and religion department at the University of Indianapolis. He has edited and authored a number of publications, including *The Royal Priesthood* by John Howard Yoder.

Gary Deddo is associate director of Graduate Student Ministry with InterVarsity Christian Fellowship in New York and New Jersey. He also serves as adjunct assistant professor at Fuller Theological Seminary. He has published articles on Karl Barth's theology in journals such as *The Scottish Journal of Theology.*

Willie Jennings is associate dean and assistant professor of systematic theology and black church studies at the Divinity School, Duke University.

Craig Keener is visiting professor at Eastern Baptist Theological Seminary and an ordained minister in the National Baptist Convention. Besides many articles in New Testament studies, he has coauthored two books on African-Americans and religion—*Black Man's Religion* and *Defending Black Faith.*

Dennis Okholm is associate professor of theology at Wheaton College. He is coauthor of an introduction to evangelical Christianity *(Welcome to the Family)* and coeditor of several books, including *The Nature of Confession* and *Christian Apologetics in the Postmodern World.*

Ronald Potter is theologian in residence at Antioch Christian Community (Jackson, Mississippi) and adjunct professor at Belhaven College. His essays appear in such books as *Christian Apologetics in the Postmodern World,* and he is at work on a forthcoming book to be published by InterVarsity Press. In addition, he has served in the leadership of the National Black Evangelical Association.

Pamela Powell is an ordained minister in the Presbyterian Church (USA), currently pastoring Messiah Presbyterian Church in Lubbock, Texas. She has recently published several articles in *ReNews.*

Eugene Rivers serves as pastor at the Azusa Christian Community in Boston and pioneered the Ten Point Coalition, a growing network of religious entities in Boston, which he now coleads. In addition to several journal articles and magazine publications, he serves as a fellow at the Center for the Study of Values and Public Life at Harvard Divinity School.

Cheryl Sanders is associate professor of Christian ethics at Howard University School of Divinity and senior pastor at the Third Street Church of God (Washington, D.C.). Her books include *Ministry at the Margins* and *Saints in Exile.*

Julius Scott is professor of New Testament at Wheaton Graduate School. He has recently published a book on hermeneutics as well as *Customs and Controversies of Old Testament Times: Intertestamental Jewish Backgrounds of the New Testament.*